PIMLICO

613

WHITE EAGLE, RED STAR

Norman Davies C.M.G., F.B.A. is Professor
Emeritus of the University of London, and
Supernumerary Fellow of Wolfson College,
Oxford. He speaks Russian and Polish and is
the author of several books on Polish and
European history, including *God's Playground*,
Europe and *Microcosm*. He wrote *White Eagle,
Red Star* when he was Alistair Horne
Research Fellow at St. Antony's College,
Oxford.

WHITE EAGLE, RED STAR

The Polish–Soviet War 1919-20
and 'the miracle on the Vistula'

———

NORMAN DAVIES

PIMLICO

Published by Pimlico 2003

6 8 10 9 7 5

Copyright © Norman Davies 1972

Norman Davies has asserted his right under the Copyright,
Designs and Patents Act 1988 to be identified as the author of this work

First published in Great Britain in 1972 by Macdonald & Co
Reprinted 1983 by Orbis Books

Pimlico edition 2003
Pimlico
Random House, 20 Vauxhall Bridge Road,
London SW1V 2SA

Random House Australia (Pty) Limited
20 Alfred Street, Milsons Point, Sydney,
New South Wales 2061, Australia

Random House New Zealand Limited
18 Poland Road, Glenfield,
Auckland 10, New Zealand

Random House (Pty) Limited
Isle of Houghton, Corner of Boundary Road & Carse O'Gowrie,
Houghton 2198, South Africa

Random House UK Limited Reg. No. 954009

A CIP catalogue record for this book
is available from the British Library

ISBN 9780712606943 (from January 2007)
ISBN 0712606947

Papers used by Random House UK Limited are natural,
recycled products made from wood grown in sustainable forests.
The manufacturing processes conform to the environmental
regulations of the country of origin

Printed and bound in Great Britain by Mackays of Chatham plc, Chatham, Kent

To my
FATHER-IN-LAW
Whom Fate cast into the midst
of this absurdity, and, who,
Thank God, survived.

CONTENTS

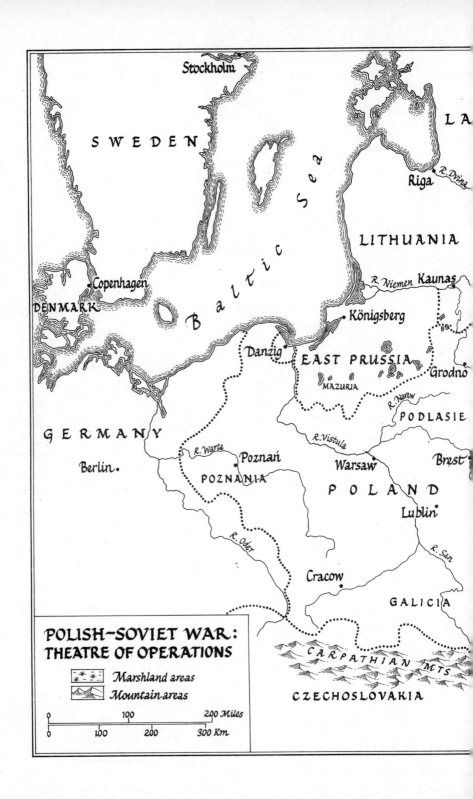

POLISH–SOVIET WAR:
THEATRE OF OPERATIONS

⁎⁎⁎ Marshland areas
🗻 Mountain areas

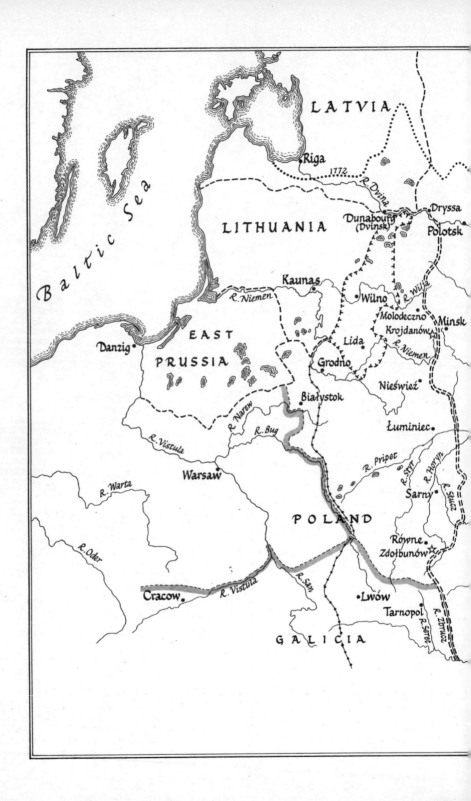

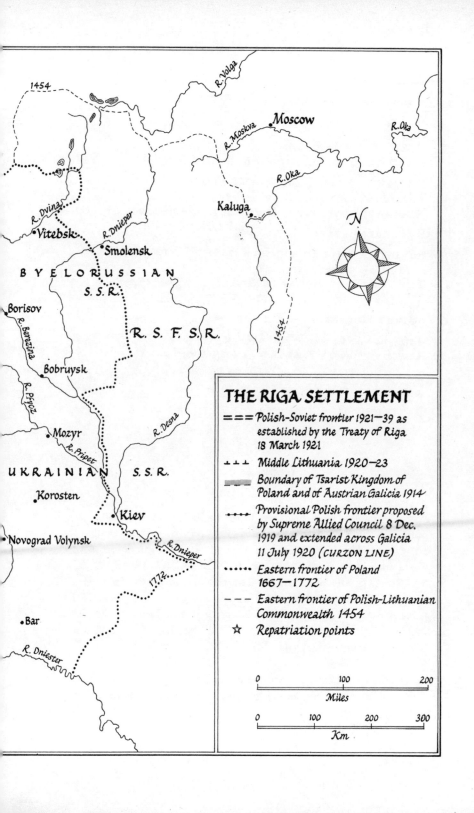

1454

R. Volga

Moscow

R. Moskva

R. Oka

R. Oka

Kaluga

N

R. Dvina

Vitebsk

R. Dnieper

Smolensk

B Y E L O R U S S I A N
S. S. R.

Borisov

R. Berezina

R. S. F. S. R.

1454

Bobruysk

R. Piyoz

R. Desna

Mozyr

R. Pripet

U K R A I N I A N   S. S. R.

Korosten

Kiev

Novograd Volynsk

R. Dnieper

1772

Bar

R. Dniester

THE RIGA SETTLEMENT

=== Polish-Soviet frontier 1921–39 as
    established by the Treaty of Riga
    18 March 1921

⊥⊥⊥ Middle Lithuania 1920–23

    Boundary of Tsarist Kingdom of
    Poland and of Austrian Galicia 1914

···· Provisional Polish frontier proposed
    by Supreme Allied Council 8 Dec.
    1919 and extended across Galicia
    11 July 1920 (CURZON LINE)

····· Eastern frontier of Poland
    1667–1772

– – – Eastern frontier of Polish-Lithuanian
    Commonwealth 1454

 ☆   Repatriation points

0   100   200

Miles

0   100   200   300

Km

LIST OF MAPS

ILLUSTRATIONS

For permission to reproduce illustrations the author and the publishers wish to thank the following: akg-images (6, 7, 10, 11, 13, 14, 16–18, 46); Collection Viollet (19); L'Illustration (48); Karta Institute, Warsaw (20, 21, 23, 26, 30–32, 37, 38, 45, 49, 57, 59, 62, 63); Musée d'histoire contemporaine, Paris (35); Paul Popper Ltd (5); Pilsudski Institute, London (2, 3, 4, 42); Lt.-Col. J. Sienkiewicz (1, 24, 29, 61); Sikorski Institute, London (25, 27, 28, 33, 36, 39, 40, 43, 44, 47, 50, 51, 52, 53, 54, 55, 56, 58, 60); University Library, Uppsala (34).

This is a very remarkable book. Its subject, though of great importance and interest, has hitherto been neglected or, where studied, misunderstood. The Polish–Soviet War was not the final episode in the wars of intervention. It was an independent enterprise on the Polish side, and the Entente Powers, far from aiding Poland, regarded her activities with irritation. Poland won her independence for twenty years by her own efforts under the leadership of Piłsudski.

The war was nevertheless far more than an episode in East European affairs. It largely determined the course of European history for the next twenty years or more. After the treaty of Riga, Soviet Russia retreated behind the cordon sanitaire. Unavowedly and almost unconsciously, the Soviet leaders abandoned the cause of international revolution. "Socialism in one country" and the Stalinist dictatorship which accompanied it were implicit in the outcome of the Polish–Soviet war. Soviet Russia was forced on the path of intensive industrialisation which was to make her in time the second greatest industrial Power in the world.

The outcome was equally fateful for Poland. Placed as she was between Germany and Soviet Russia, it seemed that she must choose friendship with one of them. Victory over Soviet Russia led the leaders of Poland to believe that they need choose neither. For twenty years they stood proudly alone, convinced that they could maintain their independence against both their mighty neighbours. In 1939 the Poles were still confident that they could defeat Germany without Soviet aid, just as they had defeated Soviet Russia without the aid of either Germany or the Entente. Their confidence brought disaster for Poland. What is more, the conquest of Poland opened the way for Germany into Russia. Hitler was lured into a war which brought destruction for both himself and Germany. Ironically, the Soviet defeat before Warsaw in 1920 ultimately led the Soviet armies to Berlin and Vienna in 1945.

The subject is not regarded with favour now in either Poland

or Soviet Russia. This is not surprising. Present day Poland
does not wish to revive hopeless memories of her past independence. Soviet Russia does not wish to dwell on past failures.
The success of an English scholar is all the more remarkable.
Norman Davies has mastered the abundant Polish sources and
has not been thwarted by the relative scarcity of Soviet sources.
He understands the principal characters—Piłsudski, Lenin
and even Lloyd George. Military and political history are skilfully combined. It is rare to be able to commend a book without reserve. I do so now. Norman Davies's book is a permanent
contribution to historical knowledge and international understanding.

A. J. P. TAYLOR

INTRODUCTION

A history of the Polish-Soviet War of 1919–20 needs no apology. An episode which embraced the first advance of the Red Army into Europe and the first attempt to export Red Revolution by force, which revealed a major political miscalculation by Lenin and the rumblings of Stalin's feud with Trotsky, obviously provides ample scope for scholarly controversy. The dramatis personae reads like the index to a dictionary of 20th-century political biography. The personalities intimately involved, apart from the Bolshevik pantheon, include Piłsudski and Budyonny, Tukhachevsky and Voroshilov, Sikorski and Winston Churchill, Weygand and de Gaulle, Lloyd George, Pius XI, and Feliks Dzierżyński. It is not difficult to see the irony of a drama uniting these particular players.

It may seem strange that the Polish-Soviet War has never been the subject of a major historical study. English historians have largely ignored it. Soviet historians skip over it, dismissing it as a fragment of the Civil War and the Intervention. Polish historians of the inter-war generation, whilst realizing the significance of the events of 1919–21, were still too close for a balanced appreciation. Post-war conditions in Eastern Europe have not encouraged scholarly advance in this field. The reticence of Soviet commentators and the bitterness of Polish *émigré* historians reflect political sensitivities which persist to the present day. Papers on particular aspects of the Polish-Soviet War can, of course, be found in specialist journals especially in Poland. Detailed and authoritative studies have been made of the political and diplomatic aspect, most recently by Professor Wandycz. Polish regimental histories are the fervent concern of many soldier exiles in Britain and America. Passing comment on the Soviet side can be found in studies of the Red Army, of the Intervention, and of the Civil War. But no attempt has been made to fuse these multifarious and frequently contradictory aspects and opinions into any general synthesis.

Nor is it likely that a definitive study can be written at present. So long as the Soviet archives remain closed for the examination of topics which may reflect adversely on the Soviet record, several aspects of the Polish-Soviet War will remain unillumined. Access to the Polish archives, whose management follows a more confident policy, only accentuates the one-sided nature of present research. There is small point in documenting the plans of Piłsudski's army, if one cannot match them with a full documentation of the plans and intentions of his opponents.

The collections of published documents are far from satisfactory. The voluminous series, *Dokumenty i Materiały do Historii Stosunków Polsko-Radzieckich* ('Documents and Materials for the History of Polish-Soviet Relations'), published simultaneously in Warsaw and Moscow since 1962, is very disappointing.[1] Volumes II and III cover the entire period of the Polish-Soviet War, and one could have hoped for a full exposition. Yet the series contains only a partial selection. The Soviet documents in particular have been very feebly edited, containing nothing but known diplomatic correspondence, public speeches, and regular propaganda. Even the Polish documents are not always reliable, especially on Poland's relations with the Entente.

This is not to say that information about the Polish-Soviet War is hard to find. Both Polish and Soviet governments put out collections of documents soon after the conclusion of peace. The *Dokumenty Materiały . . .* for all their faults, are a mine of detail. Recent Soviet collections including the work of Lithuanian and Byelorussian scholars and the invaluable *Direktivy Glavnogo Komandovaniya Krasnoy Armii* ('Directives of the Supreme Command of the Red Army, 1917–20'), have done much to compensate for previous shortcomings. Tukhachevsky, the Soviet commander, published his account *Pokhod za Vislu* ('Advance beyond the Vistula') in 1923, provoking Piłsudski's polemical reply *Rok 1920* ('The Year 1920') which appeared two years later. Volume III of Trotsky's military writings, *Kak vooruzhalas' Revoluyutsiya* ('How the Revolution was armed') contains important analyses. Generals Sikorski, Kutrzeba, Kukiel, and Szeptycki on the Polish side, and Kakurin and Melikov on the Soviet side composed detailed

chronicles. There are many relevant memoirs and reminiscences, among them those of Budyonny, D'Abernon, Dąbski,
Ghai, Putna, Radek, Sergeyev, Witos, and Weygand. Officially
sponsored versions in the Polish Academy of Sciences' *Historia
Polski* Volume IV Part 1 (1966) and the Soviet *Istoriya Grazhdanskoy Voyny* ('History of the Civil War') (1957–60) require
careful consideration. Izaak Babel's stories *Konarmiya* ('Red
Cavalry') provide unsurpassable human and psychological
comment. The Smolensk Archives at Harvard contain unique
material relating to the Soviet Western Regions. The thaw
at the Public Record Office in 1968 made British files fully
available. Source material, therefore, though partial and
problematical, is not lacking in quantity.[2]

The immediate need is for a work of summary and discussion.
A précis of the military campaigns is indispensable to clarify
points which have long remained confused. The outbreak of
war, the aims of Piłsudski's attack on the Ukraine and of
Tukhachevsky's attack on Poland, the exploits of the First
Cavalry Army, the role of General Weygand, the state of the
Red Army after the Battle of Warsaw, and so on, can now be
described with some confidence. Equally interesting are the
political implications of the war. Although in this field it is
not possible to give definitive answers, an integrated survey is
long overdue. The Polish-Soviet War occupied a central place
in the early development of Soviet ideology and foreign policy,
in the formation of Polish society between the wars, in the
Europe-wide fears of the 'Bolshevik Bogey', and in the rise of
Fascism. In short, the implications of the Polish-Soviet War are
to be encountered throughout the Eastern European crises
which led in unbroken line from the First World War to the
Second.

It is the aim of this volume to combine a summary of the
military, political, and diplomatic events of the Polish-Soviet
War with a short review of the implications. Space is found
for the experiences of the civil population, including the Jews
of the former Pale. Documents have been quoted as extensively
as possible. The narrative chapters lead from the outbreak in
February 1919, when the Polish-Soviet War was a relatively
parochial affair, through August 1920, when it was the leading
international sensation of the day, to March 1921, when peace

was signed. The last chapter deals with the repercussions of the Polish-Soviet War on subsequent events.

ORTHOGRAPHY presents a complex puzzle for any East European study in English. Where accepted English versions exist, as *Warsaw*, *Kiev*, *Brest-Litovsk*, *Cracow*, these have been used. Where different names have been accepted locally at different times, the version relevant to the period after 1921 has been preferred—*Lwów* not Lemberg or Lvov or Lviv, *Wilno* not Vilna or Vilnius, *Mozyr* not Możyrz, *Zhitomir* not Żytomierz, etc. Russian cyrillic forms have been transliterated into the accepted English style, except where the people or places concerned were actually Polish, as was the case with the several Bolsheviks such as Feliks Dzierżyński or Karol Radek.

It will both surprise and help the English reader to know that Polish spelling is phonetic and regular. The stress invariably falls on the penultimate syllable. The following rough notes may make for easier reading of frequently recurring names:

w resembles English v in the middle of a word, and f at the end. *Lwów* is pronounced 'Lvoof'.

ł resembles English w. It is equivalent to the Cockney pronunciation of l in peel, as 'peewit' without the '-it'.
Piłsudski is pronounced peew-soot-ski.
Łómża is pronounced Woom-zha.

sz and *si* resemble the English 'sh' in ship and sheep.
Szeptycki is pronounced Shep-tyt-ski.
Sikorski is pronounced Shee-core-ski.
ś is similar.
Śmigły-Rydz is pronounced Shmikwy-Ridz.

c resembles ts.
cz resembles ch in church.
Mickiewicz is pronounced Meetski-áyvich.

ą and ę are nasal vowels roughly equivalent to French -on and
-ein

Dąbski is pronounced Dompski.

Ostrołeka is pronounced Ostro-w(ein)ka.

rz and *ż(Ƶ)* resemble the French j in joli.

dż and *dzi* resemble the English j in jam.

Włodzimierz is pronounced Vwo-jee-myerzh.

Ƶeligowski is pronounced Zhely-gof-ski.

ó and *u* are both pronounced as 'oo'.

ń is soft, like Spanish ñ in mañana.

AAN	Archiwum Akt Nowych, Warsaw.
AIJP	Paderewski Papers.
AOK	Armee Ober Kommando.
ARA	American Relief Administration.
BBWR	Non-Party Block for Co-operation with the Government.
Cab	Cabinet Papers.
Cheka	Soviet Extraordinary (Security) Commission.
DBFP	Documents on British Foreign Policy
D.I.	Division of Infantry.
D.L.	Division of Legionaries.
FO	Foreign Office, London
Glavkom	Soviet Supreme Commander
H.M.(G)	His Majesty's (Government)
Kavkor	Soviet Cavalry Corps
KNP	Polish National Committee (Paris) 1917–19.
Konarmiya	Soviet Cavalry Army
KOK	Committee for the Defence of the Borders, Warsaw
KPP	Polish Communist Party (1926–39)
KPRP	Polish Communist Workers' Party (1918–26)
Lit-Byel	S.S.R. of Lithuania-Byelorussia, 1919
MSZ	Ministry of Foreign Affairs, Warsaw
Narkomindel	Soviet Commissariat of Foreign Affairs
ND. (Endecja)	National Democratic Party
NEP	New Economic Policy
NKN	Supreme National Committee (Poland) (1914–18)
Ober-Ost	Ober Kommando Ostfront
Ozon	Camp of National Unity
Pol'biuro	Polish Bureau, Bolshevik Party
Politbiuro	Political Bureau, Bolshevik Party Central Committee
POW	Polish Military Organisation
PPS	Polish Socialist Party
PRM	Presidium of the Council of Ministers, Warsaw
PRO	Public Record Office, London
PSL	Polskie Stronnictwo Ludowe. (Populist Party)
ROP	Council of State Defence, Warsaw (1920)

ROS	Council for the Defence of the Capital, Warsaw (1920)
ROSTA	Russian Telegraphic Agency
RSDRP(b)	Russian Social Democratic Workers' Party (Bolsheviks)
RSFSR	Russian Soviet Federative Socialist Republic
Samoobrona	Government of Self-Defence
SDKPiL	Social Democratic Party of the Kingdom of Poland and Lithuania 1895–1918.
TKRP	Provisional Revolutionary Committee of Poland (Polrevkom)
Ts.G.A.O.R.	Central state Archives of the October Revolution, Moscow
Ts.G.A.S.A.	Central State Archives of the Soviet Army, Moscow
Ts.P.A.I.M.L.	Central Party Archives of the Marx-Lenin Institute, Moscow
Uk.S.S.R.	Ukrainian Soviet Socialist Republic
U.N.R.	Ukrainian People's Republic (Petlurist)
WO	War Office, London
WP	Wojsko Polskie—Polish Army
Zapfront	Soviet Western Front
ZCZW	Civil Office for the Eastern Territories, (Poland)

CHAPTER ONE

ONE CONFLAGRATION AMONG MANY

In the latter stages of the First World War, Eastern Europe fell to pieces. The old empires were atomized by war and revolution. Russia, in particular, was in an advanced state of decomposition, its heart in Moscow and Petrograd controlled by the 'power of the Soviets', its far-flung regions in the hands of assorted anti-Soviet provinciocrats. Of the former Tsarist provinces, Finland, Estonia, Latvia, Lithuania, and Poland had declared their independence; the Ukraine was ruled by a German-sponsored 'Directory'; the Don and Kuban Cossacks had their own assemblies; Georgia, Armenia, and Azerbaijan were Menshevik; Siberia and Archangel had 'White' governments. The Austro-Hungarian Empire had disintegrated in like manner, its territory taken over by new or reconstituted states—the republics of Austria and Czechoslovakia, the kingdoms of Hungary, Yugoslavia, and greater Rumania. The German Empire, though almost intact territorially, had collapsed politically. The Tsar had been assassinated; the Emperor-King and the Kaiser had abdicated and fled.

In the centre of this kaleidoscope, the reborn Republic of Poland inherited lands not just from Russia, but from all three dismembered empires. Its capital, Warsaw, had been the main city of the former Tsarist 'Congress Kingdom of Poland'; Lwów and Cracow had been the main cities of Austrian Galicia; Poznań, until it rebelled in December 1918, was German. When, on 11 November 1918, the German army of occupation was disarmed in the streets of Warsaw, a new sovereign republic came into being. Its leader, newly released from German internment was Józef Piłsudski—Russian revolutionary, Austrian general, and Polish patriot.

Piłsudski's triumph came at the end of a year in which

Polish independence had often seemed as distant and un-attainable as at any time during the previous century. Poland was occupied by the apparently invincible armies of the Central Powers, victorious in the East and until July still holding the initiative in the West. The manifestos and declarations of intent concerning Polish independence, issued by the Tsarist Grand Duke Nicholas on 14 August 1914, by President Wilson of the United States on 22 January 1917, by the Provisional Government of Russia on 30 March 1917, and by the Allied governments in unison on 3 June 1918, could not alter the fact that Poland was ruled from Berlin. The Polish National Committee in Paris had no direct contact with the country it claimed to represent. The Polish Liquidation Commission in Petrograd was turned into an office for maintaining communication between the Soviet authorities in Russia and the German authorities in Warsaw. The Germans envisaged a monarchical Polish state dependent on the Central Powers and confined to the territories conquered from Russia. To this end they appointed a Regency Council, whose competence extended no further than the realms of Education and Justice. On 22 July 1917 they had arrested Piłsudski whose Polish Legions fought on their side for the first two years of the war but who had since refused to swear the required oath of fraternity with the armies of Germany and Austria-Hungary. On 3 March 1918, they signed the Treaty of Brest-Litovsk with the Bolshevik leaders to whom they awarded wide areas of Polish territory, including the district of Chełm to the west of the Bug. Few people realized that the 123 years of Poland's bondage were nearing completion. Few people, whether in Germany, Russia, or the Allied countries, seriously believed that Poland could sustain an independent existence, even if the opportunity occurred. No one foresaw that Piłsudski could cast aside the despair of the preceding years and could defeat the ambitions of his more influential and better respected rivals. But the improbable happened. On 11 November 1918, the day of the armistice on the Western Front, Piłsudski, newly released from Magdeburg Castle, arrived in Warsaw. Three days later he was invited by the Regency Council to assume power as Chief-of-State and Commander-in-Chief of the Republic, the first independent ruler of Poland since the partitions of the 18th century.

The Western Armistice had little immediate effect on the military situation in Eastern Europe. The Eastern Front had been quiet since March 1918, when Soviet Russia made a separate peace with Germany and Austria by the Treaty of Brest-Litovsk. The German army of the east stayed in position, patrolling its vast area of remaining occupation, the Oberkommando-Ostfront, or Ober-Ost, which stretched 1,500 miles from the Gulf of Bothnia to the Sea of Azov. In every quarter local wars were in progress. Soviet Russia was fighting for its life against all the other successor provinces simultaneously, on fifteen fronts. Russian 'White' armies sprang up on all sides — Yudenich before Petrograd, Kolchak in Siberia, Denikin on the Volga. Allied armies of intervention were sent to guard the interests of the Entente, the British in Archangel, Murmansk, and the Caucasus, the French in Odessa, the Americans and Japanese in Vladivostok. In many parts of Russia, in the Baltic provinces and in the Ukraine, multi-sided wars were in progress, between the Reds, the Whites, the local guerrillas or 'Greens', the nationalists, and the Germans. Then the succession states began fighting among themselves—the Rumanians with the Hungarians in Transylvania, the Yugoslavs with the Italians at Rijeka, the Czechs with the Poles in Teschen, the Poles with the Ukrainians in Galicia, the Poles with the Germans in Poznania. Post-war social unrest in many European cities produced communist revolutions on the Soviet model, each involving still more fighting—in Munich in November 1918, in Berlin in December, in Budapest in March 1919, in Košice in Slovakia in June. While Western Europe rested, and prepared for the Peace Conference at Versailles, Eastern Europe burned out of control with a score of conflagrations. As Churchill commented to Lloyd George on the night of the Armistice, 'the War of the Giants has ended; the quarrels of the pygmies have begun.'

To pay special attention to just one of these conflagrations may seem superfluous. Yet the Polish-Soviet War was different. Whereas all the other disputes in which Poland was involved were simple border disputes, the conflict with Soviet Russia was something more; whereas all the other fronts on which the

Red Army was fighting were integral parts of the Russian Civil War, the Polish front had further implications. Unlike all the other post-war squabbles with which it is frequently equated, the Polish-Soviet War raised wider issues—the clash of ideologies, the export of revolution, the future of Europe itself. For this reason, it aroused greater passions among contemporaries, and deserves the deeper curiosity of historians.

Historians who believe that grand events are launched by grand beginnings will find little satisfaction, however. Here was a war whose momentous climax in 1920 stands in strict contrast to its obscure beginnings. Indeed, many historians have ignored the first year of the war altogether. In official Soviet histories, as in works by E. H. Carr and A. J. P. Taylor, the 'outbreak' of the Polish-Soviet War occurs in April 1920. The early fighting is frequently overlooked or dismissed as mere frontier skirmishing.

The error cannot be passed over lightly. It is not possible to explain why two exhausted nations should have committed themselves to massive military action in 1920, unless one takes into consideration the hostilities which had persisted throughout the previous year. The dramatic action of 1920 is part of an unbroken sequence of events which began in obscurity at Bereza Kartuska in Byelorussia on 14 February 1919.

It may seem absurd to suggest that a war could begin without two armies to fight it. But wars can be traced to a scuffle between a man and a boy, both of whom summon aid to their respective sides. In that case, the armies can be said to form after the commencement of hostilities. The Polish-Soviet War was exactly such a scuffle. It was quite unplanned. There was no declaration of war. The armies, in the sense of organized and co-ordinated soldiery, were summoned weeks after the first shots were fired. It was more than a year before the combatants realized that they had launched themselves into a major military contest.

In this situation, the procedure followed by chroniclers of other wars, of describing the armies before the conflict, must be reversed. Classical accounts of the Franco-Prussian War or of the Spanish Civil War, open with descriptions of the traditions, numbers, dispositions, equipment, and leadership of the respective armies. But in Byelorussia in February 1919, there was no such clear-cut confrontation of forces. The Soviet Western Army was separated from Poland by the German Ober-Ost. The Polish Army had not yet been formally organized. Only local irregulars guarded the eastern marches of the new republic. The Poles and the Soviets would have been incapable of fighting each other but for a complicated political situation in which the German army still held the balance. It was a German decision, the decision to evacuate the Ober-Ost, which in the first instance set the Poles and the Soviets at each others' throats.

In the chaos prevailing in the first weeks of 1919, it is hard to believe that anyone in Soviet Russia or in the new Republic of Poland should have deliberately courted a major, foreign war. Soviet Russia had barely survived its second winter of blockade and mass starvation. Lenin's writ ran only in a restricted area of Central Russia, walled in on all sides by powerful enemies who denied all access to the outside world. Even if the Bolshevik leaders had wanted to attack their western neighbours, they would have been physically incapable of doing so.

Poland's plight was little better. For four years the Eastern Front of the World War had ebbed and flowed across Polish territory. Forced requisitions of goods, conscriptions of men, and, in the case of the eastern provinces, transportation of entire communities, had drained the country's physical and human resources. Piłsudski's government in Warsaw possessed only nominal control over the land it purported to rule. Three wars were already in progress. Six worthless currencies and the bureaucrats of three defunct powers were still in circulation, spreading confusion. Industry was at a standstill. The proletariat was starving. The deserters and refugees of wartime were still at large, spreading crime and typhus. The first elections to the Polish national assembly, the Sejm, in January, were followed by an attempted *coup d'état*. The conciliatory ministry of Ignacy Paderewski, the pianist, postponed the crisis but could not conceal the conflicts between multifarious political factions. Poland waited on the Western Allies for a clear delimitation of her frontiers. The American Relief Administration led by Herbert Hoover battled to keep starvation and disease at bay. The political problems remained unsolved.

Caught between the twin miseries of Soviet Russia and Poland, the German army of the Ober-Ost occupied a difficult position of diminishing strategic value. In March 1918, when the German occupation was established, the Ober-Ost had formed the eastern bastion of German-controlled Europe, guarded in the rear by the German and Austrian zones of occupation in Poland and on its wings by the pro-German regimes in Lithuania and the Ukraine. But the collapse of the Austrians in October followed by the expulsion of German forces from central Poland in November left the Ober-Ost dangling in space, severed from all support except in the north. There remained only a grotesquely elongated rump, over 1,000 miles long and in places only fifty miles wide. Its headquarters, and its Chief of Staff, General Max Hoffman, were in Königsberg in East Prussia. Its two main sectors were the region controlled by General von Falkenhayn's Tenth Army based at Grodno in the north, and the *Heeresgruppe Kiew* in the south. Its main artery was the railway line Białystok–Brest-Litovsk–Kowel–Równe. Its only links with Germany were the single-track lines running into East Prussia from Grodno and Białystok. Its entire length was open to simultaneous attack from west and east. Sooner or later the Ober-Ost would have to be evacuated. (See map, p. 28)

The timing of the evacuation, however, presented a difficult problem. The German army in the east was still undefeated. It was the only disciplined force of any consequence in the area. For the time being, there was no one able to dislodge it. The Western Allies could not decide what to do. The relevant article of the Armistice stated that German troops on former Russian soil must return home 'as soon as the Allies shall think the moment suitable'. The French wanted them to withdraw immediately as a preliminary step to the disbandment of all German forces; the British and Americans thought that they should stay where they were to prevent a Bolshevik advance into Europe.

As it happened, Germany in chaos was quite unable to conduct an adventurous eastern policy. The abdication of the

Kaiser and the terms of the Western Armistice put an end to political enterprise. The mutiny in Kiel, the communist risings in Munich and Berlin, the formation of Soldiers' councils in the German army, all made law and order at home the first priority. Hoffman, the Chief of Staff of the Ober-Ost, bowed to the wider requirements of his country. Discussions about the evacuation began in November and the main withdrawal proceeded from December onwards.

The nature and details of German policy during the evacuation of the Ober-Ost have only recently been clarified[1]. Unwilling to follow an independent line of his own, Hoffman referred decisions to Berlin whence they were forwarded to the Allied powers in Paris. He regarded Poles and Bolsheviks with equal contempt. As the man who had dictated the terms of the Treaty of Brest-Litovsk and as undefeated Governor of the East, he was convinced that after his own departure the deluge was inevitable. His only concern was for the safety of his men. His relations with the Poles were particularly poor. He had been humiliated by the disarming of his troops in Warsaw and embarrassed by their murderous reprisals on the civilian population following an attempt to disarm them in the province of Podlasie. Although a local agreement was signed on 24 November for the evacuation of German positions on the River Bug, the more important negotiations, for transporting the *Heeresgruppe Kiew* through Poland to Silesia failed. Agreement was not reached until February, when developments on the Soviet side of the Ober-Ost, particularly in Wilno, forced both Germans and Poles to settle their differences.

In the first week of 1919, Wilno underwent two revolutions. On New Year's Day a group of local Polish officers led by Generals Wejtko and Mokrzycki staged a coup, establishing the 'Samoobrona' or Government of Self-Defence. Their aim was to forestall the communist 'Workers' Council' which was planning to seize power when the Germans withdrew and which had already issued a manifesto describing itself as the provisional government.[2] They attacked the Communist Party House in the city during the night. Some four people were killed, five committed suicide, and seventy-six were arrested. Four days later, the Samoobrona itself was overturned when the Soviet Western Army marched in from Smolensk to protect the

Workers' Council. This turn of events was equally unbearable for Piłsudski, who was a native of Wilno, and for Hoffman, whose troops had been stampeded into premature retreat. Polish and German representatives, enjoying the full authority of their respective governments, met at Białystok on 5 February and signed an evacuation agreement. Article 5 stated that ten battalions of Polish troops, some 10,000 men, were to pass through the German lines in the area of Wołkowysk and occupy the Bolshevik front. Article 4 stated that the Germans were to enjoy temporary control of the Suwałki region until their evacuation was complete.[3]

Some commentators have charged Hoffman with playing a double game, with leading the Bolsheviks into the Ober-Ost from the east and the Poles from the west in the hope of exploiting the ensuing conflict.[4] This view is too subtle. By this time, Hoffman had little choice. German sergeants were taking leave to instruct the local Red Guards. German officers had long been in contact with the anti-Bolshevik elements. Once the decision to evacuate was known, the Ober-Ost was bound to crumble.

Polish and Soviet apologists offer diametrically opposed explanations of the evacuation of the Ober-Ost. Polish historians have talked of the Soviet 'invasion' of the Borderlands, as if the Borders formed an established part of Poland. Soviet historians talk of 'Polish aggression', as if the Borders were an established part of Soviet Russia. Neither view is valid. The Borders 'belonged' to nobody in 1919, unless it was to the local population whom neither Poles nor Soviets had any way of consulting. It is true that the Soviet advance into the Ober-Ost began first, with the creation on 16 November 1918 of the Soviet Western Army, which had occupied Minsk and Wilno before the Polish army made any move at all.[5] On 12 January 1919 the Soviet Supreme Command ordered a 'reconnaissance in depth' as far as the rivers Niemen and Szczara and on 12 February as far as the Bug.[6] It is problematical whether this operation, which bore the code name 'Target Vistula' was intended to bring the Red Army as conquering heroes into Warsaw. Its name suggests so. Yet the extremely tentative phrasing of its directives and the extremely parlous state of the Western Army suggest otherwise.[7] 'Target Vistula' was probably no more than a phrase inspired by revolutionary bravado. Although the Soviets might well have continued their march into Poland if unchecked, they were obviously feeling their way rather than following any grand plan. The Warsaw government regarded the code name as proof of intent, however, and it was in this vein that Piłsudski wired Clemenceau on 28 December.[8] Yet the Poles had little grounds for self-righteousness. As Piłsudski would have been the first to admit, he too would have sent his army into the Ober-Ost in November or December had circumstances permitted.

As it was, the retirement of the German troops created a vacuum into which Polish and Soviet units moved spontaneously. Neither side needed encouragement. The Poles set off on 9 February. A Northern Group moved up the main railway line towards Baranowicze; a Southern Group pushed towards Pińsk. The Soviet Western Army was already advancing from its new bases in Minsk and Wilno. The collision occurred at seven o'clock on the morning of 14 February, when a Captain Mienicki of the Polish Wilno Detachment led fifty-seven men and five officers into the township of Bereza Kartuska.[9] He found it occupied by the Bolsheviks. There was a short engagement in which eighty Red Army soldiers were taken prisoner. The Polish-Soviet War had begun.

Although the evacuation of the Ober-Ost provided the immediate cause of the fighting, deeper causes for conflict did indeed exist. Some sort of conflict between Poland and Soviet Russia, though not necessarily military conflict, had been very likely from the moment the new Poland was created.

It is almost impossible nowadays to conceive how dear the Eastern Borders were to Poles of an earlier generation. When Adam Mickiewicz, the greatest poet in Polish literature and Pushkin's only rival for the laurels of Slavonic lyricism, spoke of his homeland, he spoke not of Warsaw or of Cracow, but of Lithuania:

Litwo, ojczyzna moja, ty jesteś jak zdrowie;
Ile cię cenić trzeba, ten tylko się dowie
Kto cię stracił.
(Lithuania, my fatherland, you are like health; only he who has lost you can know how much you must be valued).[10]

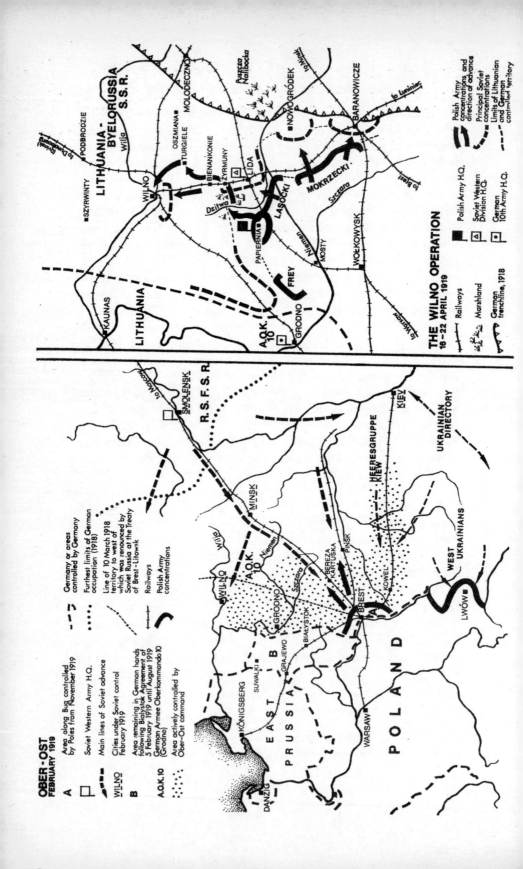

OBER-OST
FEBRUARY 1919

A

△   Area along Bug controlled by Poles from November 1919

☐   Soviet Western Army H.Q.

━ ━ ━   Main lines of Soviet advance

WILNO   Cities under Soviet control February 1919

B

Area remaining in German hands following Bialystok Agreement of 5 February 1919 until August 1919 (Grodno)

A.O.K. 10   German Armee Oberkommando 10

⋰⋰   Area actively controlled by Ober-Ost command

━ ━   Germany or areas controlled by Germany

⋯⋯   Furthest limits of German occupation (1918)

Line of 10 March 1918 territory to west of which was renounced by Soviet Russia at the Treaty of Brest-Litowsk

⊦⊦⊦   Railways

◢   Polish Army concentrations

THE WILNO OPERATION
16–22 APRIL 1919

◢   Polish Army concentrations and direction of advance

━ ━   Principal Soviet concentrations

━ ━ ━   Limits of Lithuanian and German controlled territory

■   Polish Army H.Q.

△   Soviet Western Division H.Q.

☐   German 10th Army H.Q.

⊦⊦⊦   Railways

🌿   Marshland

᚛᚛᚛   German trenchline, 1918

LITHUANIA–BYELORUSSIA S.S.R.

PODBRODZIE SZYRWINTY PODBRODZIE OSZMIANA TURGIELE MOLODECZNO Puszcza Nalibocka NOWOGRÓDEK BARANOWICZE to Luniniec

Wilja WILNO BIENAKONIE ŻYRMUNY LIDA LASOCKI MOKRZECKI Szczara to Brest

Dzitwa PAPIERNIA FREY Niemen MOSTY WOŁKOWYSK

KAUNAS **LITHUANIA** GRODNO A.O.K. 10 to Wołpa

R.S.F.S.R.

to Moscow SMOLENSK

MINSK KIEV **UKRAINIAN DIRECTORY**

WILNO Wilja A.O.K. 10 Niemen BEREZA KARTUSKA PINSK **HEERESGRUPPE KIEV** KOWEL

GRODNO Szczara BIALYSTOK BREST **WEST UKRAINIANS** LWÓW

KÖNIGSBERG SUWALKI GRAJEWO **EAST PRUSSIA**

DANZIG WARSAW **POLAND**

When he sang the glories of nature, he was thinking of the
great beauty of the Borders. When he made his famous *cri de
coeur*, 'Let us love one another', it was a cry for harmony
amongst the many races and classes of the Borders. When
Henryk Sienkiewicz set Poland alight with his tales of chivalry,
it was Cossack life in 17th-century Poland that stirred his
readers. Just as many great 'Englishmen' turn out to be
Irishmen or Scots, so many great 'Poles', like Mickiewicz,
Słowacki, or Kościuszko, turn out to be Lithuanians.

Historic Poland, from 1386 until it was dismantled in 1795,
was a united commonwealth, in which the Kingdom of
Poland and the Grand-Duchy of Lithuania were ruled by one
king and later by one parliament, as was the case with England
and Scotland after 1603. It stretched from the Baltic to the
Black Sea, from the Oder to the Dnieper, inhabited by a
dozen nations enjoying greater liberty than any of their
neighbours. It was the outpost of Christendom, warring with
the Turks and Tartars in defence of the Faith, and with the
Muscovites for the sway of the steppes. In 1918, when the
Poles regained their independence, it was Mickiewicz and
Sienkiewicz whom they read; the only Poland they knew was
the historic one, with its heart in the Borders.

The Bolsheviks, too, had their reasons for caring. Their
love for the Borders was born not of nationalism or romanticism, which were attitudes they despised, but of Marxist
dogma. The Borders constituted their land-link with Europe,
the bridge over which the Revolution would have to march if
it was to spread and survive. According to the prevailing
theory, the Revolution in Russia would perish unless it could
be joined by revolution in Lithuania, Poland, and, most essentially, in Germany. Many Bolsheviks knew the Borders
intimately. Trotsky, Commissar for War, was born in Yanovka,
near Kherson, Feliks Dzierżyński, founder of the Cheka near
Wilno, Karol Radek in Lwów.

Polish plans for the Borders came in two variants—'incorporation' and 'federation'. 'Incorporation' was advocated
by Roman Dmowski, leader of the National Democratic
Party, founder of the Polish National Committee in Paris and
chief Polish delegate to the Peace Conference. It sought to
include in Poland all lands within the historical frontiers of

1772, and envisaged no special treatment for those areas where Poles were only a minority of the population. 'Federation', as advocated by Piłsudski, recognized that the non-Polish nationalities of the Borders required institutions of their own. Piłsudski argued that Poland, as the strongest state, had a duty to guarantee the conditions of self-determination for all the nations in the area. He was sure that, given a free choice, all the Border states from Finland to the Caucasus would willingly join a democratic federation. Needless to say, they took no account of the plans and aspirations existing in Moscow.

The Bolsheviks regarded the Western Borderlands as an ideal territory for political experiment, in spite of the fact that Soviet power was highly precarious there. They acted on a conviction that the historical process would very soon lead to the rule of the proletariat in all nations, and that the withering of national states would eventually lead to a world-wide communist union. They were able to preach the principles both of national self-determination and of international communism, in the belief that the one would inevitably lead to the other. Their problem in a backward area was to decide whether to try and accelerate the historical process or whether to let it run its course. The problem for their opponents—assuming they understood Bolshevik reasoning—was to guess how permanent any particular statement by the Bolsheviks was likely to be. The Bolshevik leaders repeatedly professed their respect for Polish independence for instance. At the same time they openly supported Polish internationalist communists who were working for the downfall of the Polish Republic. Most observers regarded this as hypocritical double-talk. It was suspected that in practice Bolshevik 'independence' meant nothing more than autonomy within a leonine federation, where a centralized ruling party would limit national freedom to matters of schools and street signs. The suspicion was confirmed by the nature of the Ukrainian Soviet Socialist Republic as declared in January 1919, and of the Lit-Byel, established in February 1919. The Bolshevik leaders identified the frontiers of Poland with those of the Tsarist 'Congress Kingdom'. To the west of the River Bug, they were ready to tolerate for the time being some sort of Polish national state; to the east of the Bug, they assumed they would inherit the realm of the Tsars. Needless to say, they took no account of the plans and aspirations that might exist in Warsaw.

Diametrically opposed plans were constructed on opposite sides of a yawning ideological gulf. Soviet Russia was created by Marxist idealists, who rejected the principles on which established European society was based. Poland was created by a generation of politicians whose sole purpose was to give full expression to those principles in an independent Polish state. From November 1917 Soviet Russia was ruled by a dictatorship, consciously committed to the abolition of religion, of private enterprises, of social class, and of 'bourgeois' sovereignty. The Polish Republic was a parliamentary democracy, intensely religious, and vying with Spain for the title of Most Catholic Nation; it was run by men for whom the Church, private property, class interests, and patriotism were the pillars of society. The Bolshevik Party was inspired by pride in the world's first socialist state. Piłsudski, was inspired by romantic dreams of the past. These two ideologies could not easily live in harmony.

Ideological tensions were heightened by historical tradition. Russia and Poland were traditional enemies. The Russians saw Piłsudski as the heir to the Polish lords who had conquered Moscow in 1611, who had ruled in Kiev until 1662, and whose only accomplishments were rent-collecting and rebellion. The Poles saw Lenin as a new Tsar, whose only thought was to renew their bondage. Both Russia and Poland in February 1919 were states in their infancy, the one sixteen months old the other only four months old. Both were chronically insecure, gasping for life and given to screaming. In the opinion of senior members of the European family neither infant was expected to live long. Soviet Russia was regarded in conservative circles as an abortion, whose continuing survival was an inexplicable misfortune; Poland was regarded as an unhealthy foundling, incapable of a vigorous, independent life. Soviet and Polish leaders, resenting these opinions, compensated for them by grandiose schemes of expansion, the one by plans of imminent world revolution, the other by schemes of territorial aggrandizement. It was impossible to keep their schemes apart. Conflicting ideas are more inflammatory among near neighbours than between distant relations. There were some 800,000 Poles on

Soviet territory—soldiers, prisoners, deportees. There were many Polish citizens receptive to Bolshevik ideas, especially the restive proletariat of Warsaw and Łódź. The two ideologies were locked in competition for the minds of neighbour nations not yet possessing formal frontiers.

Tensions were further increased by diplomatic isolation. At that time Soviet Russia was treated by the world at large as a case of political rabies with whom all contact was dangerous. The Polish government was unsure whether contact with the Soviets was good form or not. The German Ober-Ost obstructed direct communication. There was no trade, no telegraph, and no trains. Warsaw could only talk with Moscow on a primitive radio relay, whose waves were far from confidential and whose performance was erratic. In the four months which preceded the outbreak of hostilities, no real dialogue was established, even though a number of tentative approaches were made. In October 1918—before Polish independence was actually established—the Soviet Commissar for Foreign Affairs, Chicherin, offered to send an ambassador to Warsaw.[11] His choice was Julian Marchlewski. The exchanges which followed with Wasilewski, the first Polish Foreign Minister, were bedevilled by a complete absence of trust. Wasilewski refused to discuss diplomacy until the leader of the Regency Council mission in Moscow, Alexander Lednicki, was released from prison.[12] Then he objected to the presence of Polish units in the Red Army, especially when they were used against the Samoobrona in Wilno.[13] Chicherin pointed in turn to the presence of Polish units in the Russian 'White' armies, and protested against the cold-blooded murder in Poland of a Soviet Red Cross mission.[14] This mission, led by a Polish communist, Bronisław Wesołowski, had arrived in Warsaw on 20 December to discuss the repatriation of Russian prisoners left over from the World War. Its members were promptly arrested on suspicion of spreading subversive propaganda, and formally expelled. On the last stage of their journey to the demarcation line, they were dragged by Polish gendarmes from the cart in which they were travelling, taken to a wood, and shot. Wesołowski and three assistants died; but one man escaped by feigning death and reported the details to Chicherin. This incident, which occurred on 2 January 1919, soured the chances of two other

missions—a Soviet trade delegation headed by a former
member of the Polish Socialist Party, Wincenty Jastrzębski,
and a Polish political mission headed by Aleksander
Więckowski, which did not reach Moscow until the fighting
had already begun. Więckowski handed Chicherin a letter
from the Polish Socialist Party proposing free elections throughout the Borders.[15] When Chicherin assented, the proposal was
sharply dropped. It does not seem to have had Piłsudski's
assent. Five months of fitful diplomacy had established nothing,
not even diplomatic relations. Więckowski eventually returned
home on 25 April, empty-handed.

The arena in which the Polish-Soviet War was to be fought is
something of a generals' paradise. The eastern part of the
North European Plain presents plenty of features to try a
soldier's fieldcraft, but no major obstacles to the movement of
armies. On the lateral axis there is no natural barrier west of
the Urals. In reality it is a fools' paradise, and has humbled the
greatest generals who ever risked their fortunes there, among
them Charles XII of Sweden and Napoleon Bonaparte.

Certain parts of the terrain, of course, are less favourable than
others. The northern reaches form part of a glacial lakeland,
600-miles long, stretching from the province of Mazuria near
Warsaw to the Valday Region near Moscow. The ground here
is spangled with myriads of small lakes, separated by pine-
covered moraines. Large armies are forced to break formation,
and, once split up, find communication between their different
sections hard to maintain. (See front endpaper map.)

In the centre lie the 60,000 square miles of Polesie, popularly
known as the Pripet Marshes. Contrary to popular belief,
these are not impenetrable swamps, but extensive riverlands,
where innumerable streams, ponds, and canals intersect in a
countryside of lush meadows, birch groves, and willow glades.
Sandy heaths covered with scrub-pine, oak forests, salt flats, and
peat bogs make for constant variety. It is fine duckshooting
country, but not the place for an army on the move. Settle-
ments were few, supplies sparse, and metalled roads non-
existent.

On either side of Polesie run two long upland zones. At no
point does the altitude exceed a thousand feet; but it is sufficient

to alter the terrain distinctively. The long, flat downs are broken at intervals by broad rivers. The soldier, marching for hours between one low ridge and the next, each with its views of boundless horizons, passes only occasional groups of wooden huts, huddled above the strips of farmland. There are huge swathes of wood and heath, some of them, like the Białowieża Forest, pristine and primeval, 'a kingdom of beasts', where wolves and bison roam unhindered. The northerly zone, between the Lakes and Polesie, carries the railway and high-road from Warsaw to Moscow, through Brest–Litovsk, Minsk, Borisov and Smolensk. The more southerly zone, between Polesie and the Carpathian Alps, stretches from the Vistula to the Dnieper, joining Cracow and Lwów with Kiev. Any army moving into Russia from Poland will invariably prefer to march through one of these upland zones. It must march for 400 miles to reach Smolensk or Kiev. A Russian army moving into Europe has the same foot-weary journey before reaching the first towns of Poland.

The configuration of these natural zones has an odd strategic effect. The vast wedge of Polesie has its point at the western end, its broad side in the east. Whereas the army advancing out of Russia must be split into two separate columns, one on either side of the wedge, an army defending Poland, with its nerve centre in Warsaw or Brest, can operate as one body. When the Russian army reaches Poland, the core of the defending army continues to keep the columns apart, thus inhibiting co-ordinated attack. The Polish Command was well aware of the advantage and in 1920 exploited it with maximum effect.

Climate adds a fickle element to soldiering on the Borders. It is a climate of extremes—a winter with forty degrees of frost and a summer with forty degrees of baking heat. In the winter, a soldier without boots and furs can lose his toes and fingers in a single night. Frost, however, is not the worst enemy. Men can fight well enough in the lowest temperatures, providing they are suitably clad and the ground is hard. What they cannot easily endure are the rapid changes, the sudden east wind which can paralyse a mild autumn day with Siberian finality, the sudden storm from the west which can transform a settled snowbound scene into a morass of mud and freezing slush. It was just such a

storm, which in December 1812 melted the Berezina in a
matter of minutes and drowned the remnants of Napoleon's
Grande Armée. Melt-water and floods are a more serious
military hazard than snow or ice, and for this reason, spring is
the only time of year when campaigning has to stop. In March
and early April, the mud always gives a second chance to
diplomacy.

The population of this vast territory, disputed for centuries
by Russians and Poles, was neither Russian nor Polish. In the
north the peasantry was Lithuanian, in the centre Byelorussian,
in the south Ukrainian. The towns were predominantly
Jewish, since this had been the Pale of Jewish Settlement of
the Tsarist Empire. The Poles of the Borders were weak
numerically, but strong socially and culturally. They formed
the backbone of a landed aristocracy dating from Poland's
medieval conquests and the most prosperous element of the
city bourgeoisie. Wilno and Lwów were Polish cities set in an
alien sea. There were almost no native Great Russians.

Nationality, it must be stressed, had little meaning in the
Borders. The people were distinguished as much by their
religion as by their language. An investigator who in 1920
asked a Byelorussian peasant what was his nationality, received
the reply, 'I am a Catholic of these parts.' They had all been
subjects of the Tsar; none, with the exception of the Poles,
had any recent traditions of separate national existence with
which to construct a new order. The national movements in
Lithuania, Byelorussia, and the Western Ukraine, were
directed by a handful of intellectuals, 'who', in the words of
Namier, 'could all have sat together on one small sofa'.
Polish nationalism and Great Russian nationalism were equally
foreign.

Warfare in the Borders had a quality all of its own. The
immensity of the theatre of operations, the impossibility of
garrisoning it efficiently, turned the attention of armies to
specific, limited objectives—rivers, railways, and small towns.
Rivers formed the only lines of natural defence. The Berezina
served as the Soviets' moat throughout the winter of 1919,
the Vistula as Poland's last ditch in 1920. Railways formed the
only network of reliable communications, the only means of
supplying the armies. Obscure junctions, like Baranowicze or

Mozyr gave cause for stubborn battles. Isolated townships often formed the only military targets, in the absence of industrial centres or power installations. They alone offered the promise of loot and shelter, the only measure of success where armies were like pebbles cast on an ocean.

Fighting, for psychological as well as for logistical reasons, proceeded by fits and starts, jerking from one township to the next perhaps fifty miles on, like sparks building up energy in a terminal before jumping the gap. Action followed the lines of communication in a game of generals' leap-frog, back and forward between one station and another. It was dictated by the terrain. It called for the skills of the scout and the skirmisher, but only on rare occasions for the brute strength of massed battalions. Piłsudski talked of 'the strategy of the wolf and the blackcock.' The line was too thin to be held for long. The flank was always exposed. To attack was easy; to retreat was always possible. Offensives, once successfully launched, would keep rolling by their own inertia for hundreds of miles. When the historian writes of 'a general offensive' or 'an advance on a wide front', he is rationalizing a thousand individual engagements. Border warfare was essentially local and fragmentary, spasmodic and infinitely confused. To capture the very special atmosphere, one is obliged to turn to eye-witness accounts and to the pages of literature. Fortunately, the stories of Isaak Babel, himself a Red Cavalryman in the Polish campaigns, provide both:

We stormed Czesniki on the 31st. The troops were massed in the forest near the village and we attacked at about five in the evening. The enemy held a height a couple of miles off; he was waiting for us. We galloped those two miles on already exhausted horses and rushed the slope. We were faced by a deadly wall of black uniforms and pale faces. They were Cossacks who had defected...and had been formed into a brigade by Cossack Captain Yakovlev. With his horsemen formed up into a square, Yakovlev awaited us with un-sheathed sabre. A gold tooth gleamed in his mouth, and his pitch-black beard lay on his chest like an icon on a corpse. The enemy machine-guns were rattling at twenty paces, mowing down our men. We crashed into the enemy, trampling over our wounded. But the square didn't budge. Then we fled. This was how the turncoat Cossacks won an ephemeral victory over the 6th Division.[16]

Babel's adversaries shared his privations and his sentiments:

A Forest near Brody.

My Dear Parents,

I'm so tired I don't know how to start—so many sleepless nights, such ceaseless noise. We all look like prophets—lean, unshaven, exhausted. A couple of days ago near Mikołajów the Bolsheviks shattered a squadron of the 11th Uhlans and Leszek Garbiński got hacked to pieces. He was caught on the temple with a sabre. My immediate superior, Cadet Bogusławski, lost a leg from a grenade and died two days later from the gangrene...People die like flies, but it's worse for the wounded. We've no lorries or waggons, and it's sixty miles to the nearest railway...We captured Łopatyn at eleven o'clock at night. The horses were unsaddled and we were just going to sleep when ten machine guns opened up on all sides. We somehow retired without loss, but had to stand all night in line, ready to charge. In the afternoon we retook Łopatyn, and went on to the River Styr whose bridge was only taken at the fourth attempt. And so, day after day...

I kiss your hands. Please don't forget me, and embrace my brothers.

Your loving son,
Kazik.' 17

General descriptions stifle the rich human interest. On the Polish side one could point to the teenage volunteers, still in students' caps and unable to lift their heavy English rifles, to the colonel, 'oozing honour from his ears and his nostrils', who fell on his sword rather than surrender to a communist, or to the prisoners stripping to their underpants in the snow so that their Bolshevik captors could not recognize and shoot the officers. On the Soviet side one may turn to Babel's portraits: of Pavlichenko, his divisional commander, a herdsman from the Kuban, who travelled home for the express purpose of kicking his master to death; of Sidorov the wounded anarchist, dreaming of the Italian sunshine and planning to desert for the fifth time; of Prishchepa the Cossack, 'an inveterate bully expelled from the Party, a future dope-peddler, a light-hearted syphilitic, an unhurried liar', who hanged dogs, burned cattle, and shot old women when he was annoyed. The civilians are no less colourful—old Gedali of Zhitomir, in silk hat and curls, who said 'Yes' to the Revolution and 'Yes' to the Sabbath; Romuald, the priest's assistant, a castrato, 'who would certainly have made a bishop if he hadn't been a spy', Romuald, 'who called us "Comrade"', and whom, in Babel's words, 'we casually shot'.

The fighting in the Polish-Soviet War was undoubtedly vicious. The Poles frequently shot captured commissars outright. The Soviets shot captured officers and cut the throats of priests and landlords. On occasion, both sides murdered Jews. The atmosphere was somehow ripe for atrocity. The soldier was surrounded by confusion and insecurity. He rarely found himself in a comfortable trench, or in the reassuring company of his regiment. More often he was on his own out in the forest, or standing guard on the edge of a village, never knowing whether the surprise attack would come from in front or behind, never knowing whether the frontline had moved forward or back. Ambushes and raids bred panic, and invited vengeance. Meetings with the enemy were infrequent but bloodthirsty.

In February 1919, the new Soviet Socialist Republic of Lithuania-Byelorussia, the Lit-Byel, was ill-prepared for war, both politically and militarily. Its leading figure was a remarkable Armenian, Alexander Myasnikov, who dominated the communist movement in the area from the first appearance of the 'frontline soviets' in March 1917 to the fall of the Lit-Byel in April 1919. In 1917, in co-operation with Mikhail Frunze, Myasnikov organized the 'Frontline Committee of Minsk', which won local Tsarist military units over to the revolutionary cause and in July prevented General Kornilov from marching on Petrograd and carrying out a right-wing *coup d'état*. After the October Revolution, he was chairman of the 'Soviet of National Commissars of the Western Regions' and commander of the Soviet Western Army. In the first months of 1918, he organized resistance to the anti-Bolshevik corps of General Dowbór-Muśnicki in a campaign which was terminated by the German occupation. Dowbór-Muśnicki, in control of Minsk when the Germans arrived, was interned; Myasnikov retired to Smolensk. Soviet authority in the Western Regions was extremely precarious. It was only with difficulty that the Bolsheviks held their own, even amongst their fellow revolutionaries. The Minsk Soviet still maintained a Menshevik and Socialist Revolutionary majority long after the Bolshevik

Revolution in Petrograd. Myasnikov survived in November 1917 only because his friends to the east sent an armoured train to protect him. The Bolsheviks prevailed because they were the one faction which could command an army.

The Soviet Western Army, the XVI Army, based on Smolensk, consisted of four elements—the Pskov (Lithuanian) Infantry Division, the 17th (Vitebsk) Rifle Division, the 'Western Division of Riflemen', and the men of the 2nd Region of Frontier Defence. At the end of 1918 it totalled only 19,000 men. Artillery and cavalry were lacking. There were eight guns and 261 horses in the whole army. In the following months it was enlarged by conscription and by the mobilization of able-bodied Party members, bringing it up to 46,000 by the end of February.[18] Even so, it was an inadequate force both in numbers and quality, to hold an area as big as England and Wales. The recruits retained the character of Red Guards, useful enough for picketing their locality, but not easily adaptable to large-scale or offensive action. The Western Army received the lowest priority in the eyes of Trotsky's central Commissariat of War. For the time being the threat of conflict with Poland was of secondary importance.

On 12 February 1919, the Soviet Supreme Commander, Vatsetis, created a Western Command from the preceding Northern Front. He kept the Estonian and Latvian operations, which he still considered to be the most important, under the same command as the Western Army. In his first directive describing the tasks of the new front, he included 'reconnaisance in depth' as far as Tilsit, Brest-Litovsk, Kowel, and Równe. He ordered special attention to be given to the defence of the main railway junctions, including Wilno, Lida, Baranowicze, and Łuniniec.[19]

Within the Western Army, the Western Division of Polish Riflemen (Zachodnia Dywizja Strzelców Polskich) occupied a special position. By Decree No. 115 of 21 October 1918, the Soviet Revolutionary War Council had ordered all Poles serving in the Red Army to be collected into one unit. After a training period in the Moscow region followed by service on the Don, the Western Division was despatched to Minsk to join in the advance into the territory of the Ober-Ost. On 5 January 1919 it went into action against the Samoobrona at Wilno. The original commander and the historian of the Western Division, Stanisław Żbikowski was replaced by General Łągwa, a member of the Polish Socialist Party. His political commissar was Adam Sławinski. The 8,000 men in the division belonged to several regiments all with Polish names—the 1st Revolutionary Regiment of Red Warsaw, the 2nd Lublin Regiment, the 3rd Siedlecki Regiment, the 4th Red Regiment of Warsaw Hussars, the 5th Lithuanian-Wilno Regiment, the 6th Regiment of Mazurian Uhlans—and were distributed into three infantry brigades, with artillery and cavalry brigades in support. The Western Division gradually lost its exclusively Polish character, but continued to be the spearhead of the Soviet political campaign in the west, supplying the storm troops of the Revolution.

Political control of the Red Army was strict. Every commander was shadowed by a political officer, commonly referred to as commissar, supervising his orders. Every unit had its war council over which the commander and political officer presided with dual authority. Every division had its revolutionary tribunal, which hunted down cases of political deviation. Trotsky's Commissariat of War exercised close watch over the commanders, and the Bolshevik Party over the commissars. Even in 1919, when the Civil War fronts were still occupying his main attention, Trotsky might always be expected to pay a flying visit to the Western Army, leaping from his armoured train and spreading fear, confidence, and efficiency on all sides. Revolutionary politics made the Red Army a strange new world, where even the enthusiasts could be bewildered by bureaucratic proliferation and by the jargon which attended it. Abbreviation of names was considered a revolutionary habit and gave the erroneous impression that bureaucracy itself was being abbreviated. A newcomer to the *Zapfront* was ruled by his *voyenruk* and his *politruk*, quoting orders from the *komdiv* or from the *politotdel*, from the *R.V.S.*, the *Nashtarevvoyensov*, the *Glavkom*, the *Narkom*, the *predrevvoyensovrep* or even the *predsovnarkom* himself.*

*Abbreviations for, respectively: Western Front, military instructor, political instructor, divisional commander, political section, Revolutionary War Council, Chief of Staff of the Revolutionary War Council, Supreme Commander, People's Commissar, Chairman of the Revolutionary War Council of the Republic (Trotsky), Chairman of the Council of People's Commissars (Lenin).

The Polish army was even less prepared for war. The Soviets did at least possess a central command and a year's experience in co-ordinating operations. The Poles had neither. The law which formalized the structure of the armed forces was not passed in the Sejm (parliament) until 26 February 1919, two weeks after the fighting with Soviet Russia had already begun. Up to that time the country was defended by a rag-bag of units left over in Poland from the World War and having nothing in common except their allegiance to the Republic and to Piłsudski as Commander-in-Chief.

At the moment of the Army Law, Poland possessed 110,000 serving soldiers. These were increased to 170,000 in April of whom 80,000 were combatants. A nucleus had been formed from the Polnische Wehrmacht, 9,000 strong, the remnant of a force raised by the Germans in 1917–18. Some 75,000 volunteers were added in the first weeks of independence, mainly from members of Piłsudski's Legions, who had fought for Austria until disbanded in 1917. In December 1918, the Poznanian regiments of the German army declared for Poland. Conscription, introduced on 7 March 1919, doubled the men available, but in practice very few of the draftees saw service in 1919. Polish military expenditure in 1919 absorbed forty-nine per cent of the national income and was proportionately greater than that of any country in the world, with the sole exception of Soviet Russia.

In the course of the following months, various Polish units arrived from abroad. In April, the Polish army in France commanded by General Józef Haller arrived, 50,000 well-armed veterans who had been instructed by French officers. They included elements of the Bayonne Legion, a Polish company attached to the Légion Etrangère. In June, the Polish division of General Lucjan Żeligowski tramped into Lwów after a historic three-month march round the Balkans from Odessa, where it had been campaigning with the Russian Whites. A Polish detachment from Murmansk reached Poland at the end of 1919, and one from Vladivostok, consisting of 10,000 survivors of the Polish Siberian Brigade of Colonel Rumsza, sailed into Danzig in July 1920. These last three formations had been raised among Polish conscripts in the Tsarist army stranded in Russia by the outbreak of Revolution.

A number of independent units were formed by the Poles of the Borders. The Samoobrona of Wilno had had its counterparts in Minsk and Grodno. Most of their recruits, surprised by the pace of the Soviet advance into the Ober-Ost, found their own way to the Polish lines. In the first week of Polish independence a Committee for the Defence of the Borders (Komitet Obrony Kresów) was formed in Warsaw. Its first president, Prince Eustachy Sapieha was representative of the other members, mainly aristocrats, whose main aim was to recover their occupied marcher properties. It organized and financed the so-called Lithuanian-Byelorussian Division under General Iwaszkiewicz which began recruiting in Szczucyn, Zambrów and Łapy; in the event it attracted fewer volunteers from the Borders than from the cities of central Poland.

The process of amalgamating these different units and their commands was long and difficult. Most of the ranking officers had seen service in the Austrian army. General Szeptycki had been Governor of the Austrian zone of occupation of southern Poland, Tadeusz Rozwadowski a full General in 1913, Inspector of Sappers in the Royal and Imperial Army, Commander of the Polnische Wehrmacht in 1918, and Minister of Military Affairs under the German-sponsored Regency Council. Piłsudski obviously preferred the men who had served with him in the Legions—Lieutenant-Colonel Edward Śmigły-Rydz, commander of the secret 'POW', (Polish Military Organization), Colonel Władysław Sikorski, General Kazimierz Sosnkowski. A number of officers had seen Tsarist service, notably General Wacław Iwaszkiewicz, General Dowbór-Muśnicki, leader of the anti-Bolshevik cause in Byelorussia and one-time commander of the I Polish Corps, General Aleksander Ośinski, commander of the III Polish Corps. No Poles rose to the highest levels of the Tsarist Staff, owing to a clause excluding Roman Catholics, nor to the upper echelons of the Prussian Staff owing to sheer prejudice. The Poznanians provided the best NCOs but few officers. Some Poles succeeded in serving in several armies. General Józef Haller changed sides three times. In March 1918, he took his Austrian Legionary Regiment over to the Russians in protest against the Treaty of Brest-Litovsk; he fought with a Polish corps in Russia against the Bolsheviks, before escaping via Murmansk to take command of the Polish army in France.

All these men were forced in 1919 to forget their old military habits and adapt to the new order. In February a Ministry of Military Affairs under General Leśniewski was created; also a General Staff under General Szeptycki, later under General Stanisław Haller, which took charge of operations. General Rozwadowski was sent to Paris to liaise with the Allied governments. Drill books, weapon training, language of command, rules of seniority, all the details which make an army move, had to be re-organized. Friction was inevitable. Units with French rifles were issued with German ammunition; Austrian officers resented serving under Tsarist colleagues whom they had 'defeated'; Poznanian units disliked serving in the east when Poznań was still threatened by the Germans in the west. Only in July 1919 was it decided to rely exclusively on French army manuals and procedures, and to submit to the instruction of General Henrys and his military mission. Somehow, despite the obstacles, patriotism triumphed, and the Polish army, defunct since 1831, was reborn.

The 1st Polish Cavalry Division serves as an admirable illustration of the motley origins of the army as a whole. It consisted of six regiments. The 8th Uhlans were entirely 'Royal and Imperial' and were raised from the sons of the Galician gentry. The 9th Uhlans were also Galicians, although they boasted a more democratic tradition. Many of their officers had served in the Austrian *Landwehr* or in the Legions. They were fitted out with English uniforms. The 14th Uhlans were still more exotic. They were Russian by training and in large measure Russian by blood. They had been in the saddle for five years already, having fought in the World War on the Eastern Front and in the Russian Civil War in the Kuban. They came to Poland with General Żeligowski. They intensely disliked the Austrian equipment with which they were issued. The officers retained their high Caucasian saddles, long reins, short stirrups, and steeplechase style. The 1st (Krechowiecki) Uhlans had seen Russian service in the Pulavy Legion. The 2nd Hussars were former Austrian legionaries. The 16th Uhlans were Poznanians. They wore antique uniforms, including high *rogatywka* hats surmounted by a red rosette. Their

horses were unusually large and their Prussian equipment
unusually heavy. Every man carried lance, sabre, bayonet,
mask, entrenching tool, and canteen. On the move they clanked
and rattled like a company of medieval knights. In all these
regiments local traditions were strong, and national patriotism
relatively weak. They were like six prodigal sons, born of the
one Polish mother from three different fathers. They were
first sent into battle in April 1920.[20]

The central figure in the organization of the Polish army
was Kazimierz Sosnkowski. He was the Deputy Minister for
Military Affairs. Although not yet thirty-four years of age,
he had already the creation of several armies to his credit.
In 1908, whilst still a student in Lwów, he founded on his own
initiative the Związek Walki Czynnej (Union of Active
Struggle), the predecessor of many similar, para-military,
nationalist organizations. In 1914, he was the Chief of Staff
of Piłsudski's Legions. In 1917, he succeeded Piłsudski at the
War Department of the Regency Council, and founded the
Polnische Wehrmacht. In 1918, after a spell in Spandau
prison, he joined Piłsudski in Magdeburg Castle. Piłsudski
called him his 'conscience' and his 'guardian angel'. He
possessed the political tact and personal ease which Piłsudski
lacked. In 1919, he was given the task of reconciling Piłsudski's
consuming military interests with the democratic institutions
of the new Republic. His speeches to the Sejm, his detailed
supervision of the Army Bills, provided the confidence, will,
and expertise which overcame the politicians' reluctance. This
young man, whose tall frame and commanding presence were
complemented by a modest disposition and precise habits,
performed a feat, comparable to that of Trotsky or Carnot,
which has rarely been recognized outside Polish circles.

At first, only a small proportion of the Polish army could
be spared for the Soviet front. At no time in 1919 was the Red
Army capable of mounting a major offensive, and the largest
part of the Polish army was used for more urgent tasks on the
Ukrainian, Czechoslovak, or German fronts. In February
1919, the 'Ten Thousand' who moved into the Ober-Ost were
organized in two groups. The Northern Group under General
Iwaszkiewicz was at Wołkowysk, and the Southern Group
under General Listowski at Brest-Litovsk. The commander

of this Byelorussian Front, General Wejtko, was replaced by General Szeptycki, whose twelve battalions of infantry, twelve squadrons of cavalry, and three artillery companies fairly matched the quality but not the numbers of the Soviet Western Army across the line.

The military equipment available in Eastern Europe in 1919 was extremely limited. The Polish-Soviet War was fought on First World War surplus. Both sides had to depend on what they could beg or capture. The Soviet Western Army benefited from its share of Civil War trophies—Japanese rifles from Siberia, English guns from Archangel and the Caucasus. In the later stages, the Poles gained an advantage in that they received direct supplies from the Allied powers, especially from France. Distribution of the armaments was uneven. Infantry divisions, which varied in strength between 2,000 and 8,000 men, might possess anything from forty to 250 machine-guns, and from twelve to seventy howitzers. Only Józef Haller's army, fully equipped in France, was up to First World War standards. Cavalry divisions trailed three or four heavy machine-guns mounted on horse-drawn *tachanki*. Transport was effected mainly by horse-wagons, of which the Polish *furmanka*, a long, V-shaped contraption, amazed Western observers by its speed and efficiency. Motor cars were only used by the most fortunate staff officers. Signalling was rudimentary; radios only existed at the chief command posts. It was not unknown for units to have one rifle between three men. For want of anything better, both sides often resorted to cold steel. Uniforms were as multifarious as the weapons. In theory, the Red Army wore blanket capes and Tartar caps with a star, the officers not distinguished from the men. In practice they wore whatever was at hand. Babel mentions Cossacks wearing bast bandages on their feet and captured bowler hats on their heads. Tsarist uniforms stripped of their insignia were very common. The Poles looked no better. The Poznanians wore Prussian outfits; Haller's 'Blue Army' was entirely French. A small white eagle pinned onto Austrian or Tsarist uniforms, or German helmets painted red and white, caused confusion to friend and foe alike. When facing the enemy, one had to see not just the whites of their eyes but the shape of the eagle on their caps before knowing whether to shoot. Only the Polish officer corps, resplendent in their gold braid and distinctively shaped hats were obviously dressed for the part.

Artillery fell far short of World War standards. The Polish 1st Light Artillery (Legionary) Regiment, for instance, was originally equipped with Austrian recoilless 9-cm. guns dating from 1875, found in the fortress at Cracow and pulled by horses from the Animal Shelter. In May 1919, it received an assignment of Russian three-inchers, captured from the Ukrainians, followed by an assortment of Austrian, Italian, and French howitzers. Consistent training and efficient performance were not possible.

Armoured trains soon became a speciality. The early models were armoured with concrete or with sandbags, the 'advanced' types with steel plating. They were propelled by an armoured locomotive placed between personnel cars, which were surmounted by revolving machine gun turrets. At front and back were heavy gun platforms and wagons carrying track-laying equipment. The trains could carry a strike force of two or three hundred men, and represented the only arm disposing of mobile and concentrated fire-power. In campaigns where control of the railways was vital, they provided a morale and surprise element of the first importance. Their operations were restricted however to the railway network and to track of their own gauge. Although in the first half of 1919 the Polish sappers converted the main routes to standard European gauge, most of the lines in the eastern areas kept the wide Russian gauge.[21]

Cavalry remained the principal offensive arm. In this respect, the war which started in 1919 was no different from those of previous centuries. The Poles preferred heavy lancers, the Soviets sabre-swinging horsemen of the Cossack variety. Even so, cavalry was not immediately available. The Red Army could not concentrate a large cavalry force on the Polish front until May 1920. The Polish army did not match them till August of the same year.

Sophisticated equipment did not make its appearance until the end of the war, and then only in small quantities. Aeroplanes, tanks, and motor lorries were new-fangled devices which suffered more from mechanical breakdown than from enemy attacks.

The first months of hostilities saw little more than manoeuvrings for position. Gradually a front was established, from the Niemen at Mosty, down the Szczara River, the Ogiński Canal, and the Jasiołda River to the Pripet east of Pińsk. Its 300-mile length straddled the northern upland zone, and was bounded in the north-west by the rump of the Ober-Ost in Grodno and in the south-east by the lands of the Ukrainian Directory. On average, each side could only field one soldier for every fifty yards of front, which meant that huge stretches, especially in the south, could be patrolled but not defended. Attention was concentrated on the northern sector, where the Soviets had the advantage of a lateral railway. Wilno, the only city in the area, and Baranowicze, a six-point railway junction, were both under Soviet control. The Soviets held the superior position, and a Polish offensive would be needed to wrest it from them. In the spring floods, this was out of the question. The only event of any strategic importance was the establishment of a Polish bridgehead across the Niemen. And so for six weeks the front rested.

The Soviet authorities were distracted by a counter-revolutionary rising in Byelorussia. Two regiments of the Red Army holding the line against the Ukrainians in the area of Ovruch mutinied, crossed the Pripet, and marched on Gomel' which they occupied from 24 to 29 March in the name of a 'free republic'. The suppression of the rising absorbed the attention of the Soviet Western Command for several weeks at the end of March and the beginning of April, and took their minds off the activities of the Poles.[22]

The Poles, too, had their troubles. An ugly incident occurred at Pińsk, held by the company of a Major Łuzyński. In Pińsk, as in other towns held by the Poles, all public meetings had been banned for fear of civil disturbance. A guard of only thirty men was posted. On 5 April, the soldiers were called to a meeting taking place behind closed doors. They assumed it to be a Bolshevik meeting. When resistance was offered and a crowd formed, they feared a trap. They seized thirty-five people as hostages, whom Łuzyński then ordered to be summarily shot to make an example. The town was pacified. But the incident was to have international repercussions. Pińsk was a Jewish town. 20,000 of its 24,000 inhabitants were Jews.

Most of the victims were Jews. Almost instantaneously, reports appeared in the European press of a 'Polish pogrom at Pińsk'. The phrase was nicely alliterative and well suited for sensational headlines. Although the first Allied investigators on the spot denied that the executions were motivated by anti-semitism— the United States representative on the investigation, Lieutenant Foster, actually stated that Major Łuzyński's action was fully justified in the circumstances—and although the nature of the illegal meeting, variously described as a Bolshevik cell, an assembly of the local co-operative society and a meeting of the Committee for American Relief, was never clarified, the publicity reflected badly on the Polish army. Coming as it did on the heels of similar reports from Lwów, the Pińsk incident confirmed the popular idea throughout the world that all Polish soldiers were anti-semites and all Bolsheviks Jews.[23]

Soon after the events in Pińsk were reported, news arrived of the fall of Wilno which Piłsudski had decided to liberate in person. Wilno was at once the only major city on the Soviet front, the only significant concentration of Poles in the northern Borders and the essential centre for Piłsudski's intended 'Federation'. It was the city where Piłsudski had been educated, where he had learned that quaint, nostalgic, and romantic brand of patriotism which inspired all his actions. It was desperately in need of firm government. Eight different régimes had succeeded each other in the space of two years— the Tsarist regime, the Russian Provisional Government, the German military occupation, the Lithuanian national government, the Workers' Council, the Samoobrona, the Lithuanian SSR, and now the Lit-Byel. The Lithuanian SSR and the Lit-Byel had been a particularly thorough and painful political experiment. They turned Wilno into a laboratory of social pharmacology where the full range of communist panaceas were tested out on the luckless inhabitants. In the space of three months, they issued a whole codex of decrees for the limitation of property, for the mobilization of communists, for forced requisitioning, for the shooting of 'criminal and counter-revolutionary elements', for the nationalization of factories, for a state art museum, for workers' social security, for the abolition of ranks and titles, for a seven-hour day in tobacco factories, for equality of nationalities, for military conscription, for a state symphony orchestra, for the dis-establishment of the Church, for introducing universal labour service, for making the house of Adam Mickiewicz at Nowogródek a state monument...[24]

Piłsudski arrived at the front on 15 April. He supervised the secret deployment of reinforcements sent from Warsaw, two infantry divisions and a cavalry brigade, which he had con-cealed in the neighbourhood of Papiernia, only sixteen miles from the headquarters of the Soviet Western Division in Lida. His plan was simple but risky. The main thrust was to exploit the gap between the Soviet concentrations in Wilno and Lida, and to advance boldly along the road and railway route towards the city. The risk was that the Soviets controlled the railway and could therefore rush reserves to the scene of an engagement. To keep them guessing about the objective of his main attack, Piłsudski ordered a series of diversionary attacks, against Lida by General Lasocki and against Nowogródek and Baranowicze by General Mokrzecki. A smaller group under Colonel Frey was to engage the Soviets to the west of Wilno at the junction with the German lines, to prevent any inter-vention from that quarter. (see map p. 28)

At dawn, on 16 April, the Polish storm-column debouched from Papiernia. In the van went the cavalry group of Colonel Belina-Prażmowski, nine squadrons with a light battery of horse artillery. Behind them marched the infantry of General Śmigły-Rydz, three battalions of the 1st Infantry Division with two batteries of heavy artillery. Crossing the Soviet line in the marshy land of the Dzitwa stream, they moved onto the Wilno road in the vicinity of Żyrmuny. At the end of the first day, with seventy miles still to go, they had met no significant resistance.

The storm-column's early success was due to the diversionary actions. Before dawn on the 16th, the Polish artillery had opened up on Lida, apparently heralding an attack in that direction. When General Mokrzecki moved in strength on Nowogródek and Baranowicze with nine battalions, the impression was given that these two towns were the main objective. Certainly they were important. Nowogródek's hill

fortress commanded the middle Niemen, and Baranowicze
the railway network. Moreover, the Soviet Western Division
was holding this central sector, and it was known that the
Polish Command was spoiling to teach the 'traitors' a lesson.
The fighting was brisk, the defence stubborn. Lida held firm
for two days, Nowogródek for three, and Baranowicze for four.
By the time the Western Division withdrew behind the Niemen
on the evening of the 19th, half of Wilno was already in Polish
hands.

Belina's cavalry made good time. On the 17th they camped
at Turgiele, having left the road to avoid any force sent out
to meet them, and to approach the city by surprise from the
south-east. The infantry was at Bienankonie, thirty-six hours'
march behind, having covered forty miles in two days. Soviet
communication between Wilno and the Western Division had
been broken. On the 18th, Belina bivouacked in the woods
before Wilno, poised for the attack. There were two courses
of action open to him: to wait perhaps two days for the
infantry and lose the element of surprise, or to send the
cavalry into the city streets unsupported. He chose the second
course. He knew that he could count on the citizens to rise in
support, and that the defenders would have difficulty in
organizing barricades and machine-gun traps. At six o'clock
on the 19th, the Polish cavalry charged into the startled suburbs
and made for the station. Some reports say they had changed
into Red Army uniforms. They seized a train and sent it off
down the line to collect the infantry. They then fanned out
into the streets. All day they galloped to and fro, spreading
panic in the garrison, which was never presented with a single
target worth attacking. By the evening the captured trains
began ferrying in the Polish infantry. The Soviets withdrew
across the bridges into the northern suburbs. Two days of
street fighting followed, in which the Soviet Pskov Division,
deprived of all support, was gradually levered out of the city
to the north-west. A last, vain stand was made behind the
walls of the Jewish cemetery. On the 21st, Piłsudski himself
reached Wilno. A victory parade celebrated his return.

As soon as the fighting was over, Piłsudski issued a statement
of his political intentions. His 'Proclamation to the inhabitants

of the former Grand-Duchy of Lithuania' contained the blueprint for his Federation of the Borders:

For more than a century your country has known no freedom. It has been oppressed by the hostile force of Germans, Russians, and Bolsheviks, who, whilst never consulting the population, imposed alien codes of conduct which frustrated your wants and interrupted your way of life.

I, who was born in this unhappy land, am well acquainted with its state of perpetual subjection, a state which must be removed once and for all. Now at last, in this land which God seemed to have forsaken, liberty must reign, with the right of full and unrestricted expression of aspirations and needs.

The Polish Army brings Liberty and Freedom to you all. It is an army which I led here in person to expel the rule of force and violence, and to abolish governments which are contrary to the will of the people.

I wish to create an opportunity for settling your nationality problems and religious affairs in a manner that you yourselves will determine, without any sort of force or pressure from Poland.

For this reason, even though martial action still thunders in the land and blood is still being shed, I am introducing a civil administration and not a military one, to which in due course I shall call local people, sons of this land.

The aims of this Civil Administration will be as follows:

1. to enable the population, through freely elected representatives, to determine their own fate and needs. The elections will take place on the basis of secret, universal, and direct voting, without distinction between the sexes;

2. to provide assistance for those who need it, to provide essential supplies, constructive employment, an assurance of calm and harmony;

3. to care for all without reference to race or creed.

At the head of this Administration I have set Jerzy Osmolowski, to whom directly or to whose appointees you may turn openly and sincerely in any matter which pains or concerns you.

Wilno, 22 April 1919.   J. Piłsudski[25]

The style and ideas, the dramatic turn of phrase, are indubitably Piłsudski's own. He returned to Warsaw on 27 April.

The loss of Wilno sparked off a series of recriminations in the Soviet camp. Myasnikov made light of the whole affair, putting it down to 'a White Guard rising', the treachery of the railwaymen, and the absence of the Cheka—to everything in fact except the shortcomings of his own army. This so enraged the Prime Minister of the Lit-Byel, Mickiewicz-Kapsukas, that he published an article in the Moscow *Izvestiya*, entitled, 'The causes of the fall of Wilno':

We strained every nerve. All communists were mobilized and political workers were despatched to the front. But our units were completely exhausted after four months of camp life and three months at the front in very nasty conditions. The breakdown in railway communication, and the insufficiency of provisions and of horses to bring provisions, made the situation in several frontline towns quite unbearable. Disorderly requisitioning and endless demands provoked mistrust, and embittered even those sections of the population who had formerly welcomed the Red Army as their liberators from the hated German occupation and from landlord oppression. Desertion from the army occurred on a considerable scale, further depleting its already inadequate numbers. It was impossible to fill the ranks of the Red Army with local men owing to their hostility towards it. A mass influx of volunteers only occurred at the very beginning of the Red Army's advance into Lithuania, and then it was impossible to accept them because of a total lack of uniforms, boots, and weapons.
Taking account of this situation, we repeatedly turned to the central authorities for reinforcements. We pointed to the catastrophic situation on our front and to our impotence in coping with a growing crisis. We pointed to the complete estrangement of the government of the Lithuanian-Byelorussian SSR from the Command of the Western Army in Smolensk, pressing for various changes, which, however, brought no result.
Wilno was *not* taken by a rising of White Guards, but by regular Polish forces. Comrade Unschlicht, the Commissar for War [in the Lit-Byel] and Comrade Rasikas, the district commissar, had to act on their own initiative. By their efforts a reconnaissance party was sent out, but it had to retreat before overwhelming numbers. A scratch formation was then improvised, but it too had to retreat on the morning of 19 April. That same day it was decided to mobilize members of the industrial unions, members of the communist and socialist parties, and the communist youth movement, but all that was far too late.
Indeed, it was the lack of a powerful Soviet authority resting on the support of a broad mass of workers, which enabled the Legionaries to seize Wilno so quickly. To put it down to the absence of the Cheka is naive...The so-called 'Special Department', the organ

which is supposed to fight the counter-revolution and speculation, *was* in Wilno, but, needless to say, it did nothing.

The main cause of these shortcomings is the absence of a firm base for political action. There are very few industrial workers and those there are represent a motley collection of nationalities. Agricultural workers are widely dispersed.

Our predicament was further aggravated by poor food supplies, which brought the poorest people in Wilno to starvation. Never having experienced the charms of Polish or Lithuanian 'independence', they began to dream of it, as of their salvation.[26]

Although Mickiewicz-Kapsukas had cause to exaggerate his difficulties, his frank testimony hardly requires comment. It shows how badly the Soviets had blundered in Wilno, how weak was their appeal, how divided their counsels, how demoralized at this stage the Red Army had become. Myasnikov was dismissed. Mickiewicz-Kapsukas and his government withdrew to Minsk.

Lenin was incensed. He had been very interested in the developments in Wilno. As early as December 1918, he telegraphed the Western Army headquarters 'to liberate Wilno more quickly'.[27] Now he ordered that it be reconquered immediately: 'The loss of Vilna has strengthened the Entente still further. It is essential to ensure the maximum speed for the recovery of Vilna in the shortest possible time...Hasten the movement of reinforcements already on the way, and act more energetically...'[28] This order remained a dead letter for fifteen months.

If Piłsudski's Proclamation provided the theory and the long-term ideals of the Polish occupation, the army provided the immediate practice. Anyone suspected of having connexions with the Lit-Byel was arrested. The more important Bolshevik prisoners like Stanisław Berson, a Pole who had been People's Commissar for Nationalities in the Western Regions and a Minister of the Lit-Byel, were shot.

The Polish citizens of Wilno on the whole were delighted. They set up their city corporation, and, after a century's demise, the Polish university. Their politicians envisaged a separate Lithuanian state closely allied with Poland, on the lines of the medieval Polish-Lithuanian commonwealth. The representative assembly, the Polish Councils of Lithuania and

Byelorussia hastily despatched delegates to the Peace Conference in Paris, confident of their case.

Even the Jewish population, which was the only other sizable community in Wilno, welcomed the Polish occupation. Isaac Cohen, a British Zionist who was no friend of Poland, and whose articles in *The Times* first started the scare about 'Polish pogroms', later admitted that Wilno Jewry was glad to see the Bolsheviks go. The Jewish community was intensely religious and conservative. Although a considerable number of young Jews did join the Bolsheviks, they did so at the cost of renouncing their family and people entirely. The mass of the ghetto was appalled by Bolshevik atheism, by the doctrine of class-struggle, and by the russification programme, whereby the Russian language had been forced on a city without a single Russian resident.[29]

The military effects of the capture of Wilno were not dramatic. The Soviets lost their first line of defence, and were forced to fall back on Minsk. Soviet counter-attacks from Podbrodzie, Oszmiana, and Szyrwinty were all repulsed by General Śmigły-Rydz's Wilno Group, which in mid-May reached Lake Narocz. In the centre, the Polish positions were protected by the former German trench lines and by the Puszcza Nalibocka, a marshy depression in the upper Niemen valley. In the south, General Listowski was held for months before Łuniniec, and only advanced in the strategically useless territory south of the Pripet, to the line of the Styr. The Poles inherited the railway network, but not the rolling-stock and proper organization, which could have made it a valuable asset. There was no point in advancing further until the new gains had been digested.

Life in Byelorussia in the early summer of 1919 droned on without much incident. The sun was warm and the midges troublesome; the enemy, it seemed, far away. The politicians were busier than the soldiers.

The small town of Nieśwież, for instance, was occupied by the 1st Brigade of the Soviet Western Division, mainly men of the Lublin Regiment. It clustered round the abandoned castle of the Radziwiłł family. The castle's interior had been plundered by Russians and Germans; its art treasures were stored in Warsaw; its doors were affixed by the official seal of the local party committee; its park and landscaped lakes alone attested to the tranquil, princely life of its past. On 4 June the commissar of the 1st Brigade in Nieśwież composing his weekly report to the Polish Communist Party Central Committee, spoke optimistically of the progress being made:

The men are in warlike mood. All are burning with the desire for an early victory. The Command Staff, with the exception of several old [Tsarist] officers, is working well. Weapons are sufficient, although we are short of lubricating oil. There is enough to drink, but a shortage of meat. Uniforms are lacking, especially boots.

Party work among the soldiers is progressing favourably, thanks to the communists from Minsk. Party cells have been set up in all units. Communist literature is being distributed among our Polish soldiers. The Nieśwież Soviet does feel the need, however, for more experienced workers to work with the town population.

In the frontier zone, the Polish legionaries have been burning villages whose inhabitants sympathize with and help the Soviet authorities and look after our soldiers. They have burned some of the houses at Kamenka, for instance. When the peasants of this village rushed forward to save their property enemy machine-gunners opened fire on them.

The general morale of the Brigade is better, and as the holding of the enemy in our sector shows, the Brigade will be ready to do its duty.[30]

A less sanguine view was expressed by Julian Marchlewski who spent three days in the same area in the middle of July:

Although the mood of the soldiers could be worse, their command is very deficient. An incident occurred when I was there when fifty legionaries came upon 400 of our men, caught them sleeping, attacked, and captured three machine-guns and a mass of prisoners. My impression is that such an army will not be able to keep the Poles in check. Unless they are reinforced, they will have to retire from Minsk and where they will stop is impossible to say. Speeches about the need for 'revolutionary warfare' are simply laughable. It is a regrettable thing, but desertions do occur. Recently two battalion commanders fled to the other side. One stole the battalion's safe containing several tens of thousands of roubles; the other took two troopers with him. These betrayals are unavoidable in a situation where Poles are fighting against Poles.[31]

The Western Army was making a serious attempt to improve both recruitment to the ranks and the standard of the officer corps. The Western Division had official recruiting bureaux as far afield as Orenburg, Samara, and Astrakhan, as well as clandestine recruiting officers in Poland itself.

In July, the first batch of cadets passed out from the Western Division's new military academy in Minsk. Finding officers for the proletarian army, or 'commanders' as they were called, was no easy task. Eighty per cent of them were former Tsarist officers and NCOs, retrained and re-indoctrinated. Their oath, as taken at the passing out parade, ran as follows:

I, a son of the working people, a citizen of the Republic of Soviets, accept the position of soldier in the Workers' Army.

With regard to the working classes of Russia and of the whole world, I undertake to carry my position with dignity, to perfect myself in the art of war, and, as the apple of my own eye, to protect the property of the people and of the army from theft and decay.

I undertake, strictly and unconditionally, to observe revolutionary discipline, and to execute without word of protest all the orders of commanders issued by the Government of Workers and Peasants.

I undertake to restrain myself and my comrades from any conduct which could lower the dignity of a Soviet citizen, and to direct all my thoughts and acts towards one goal—the liberation of all proletarians.

I undertake, at the first call, to defend the Republic of Soviets from all dangers and encroachments, and to fight for the cause of socialism and the brotherhood of peoples, sparing neither life nor strength.

If by ill-will, I break this my solemn undertaking, may I meet with universal contempt and be punished by the terrible hand of revolutionary justice.[32]

Most of the dignitaries of the Lit-Byel were present. Speeches were made by General Łagwa, by his new commissar, Nikitin, by Szeryński, the Commissar for Education, by Leński on behalf of the Polish Bureau of the Bolshevik Party, and by Bobiński, who was the Polish member on the All-Russian Central Executive Committee of the Soviets. Leński talked about the formation of 'the leading cadre of the Red Army of the Polish proletariat.' 'This cadre,' he said, 'will fight and lead wherever the International Revolution calls it. Every one of our Red commanders must be aware that only through the victory of the International Revolution can Workers' Poland be born.' Bobiński was equally explicit. He greeted the commanders as 'the steel guard of the dictatorship of the Polish proletariat, children of revolutionary Warsaw, which today is battling with a rampaging counter-revolution. You, Poland's Red commanders,' he said, 'must assist Workers' Poland and march to meet your battling brothers.' Whatever the intentions of the Bolshevik leadership at this stage, there was no doubt about the Western Division's future role in the minds of the Polish communist leaders.[33]

The Polish army acquiesced in the spontaneous lull. A Whitsun recess suited their purposes. They, too, were organizing their rear, not by founding party cells and revolutionary cadres but by consolidating the Civil Administration of the Eastern Lands (Z.C.Z.W). It had three districts, Wilno, Brest, and Volhynia. Its programme was inspired by a voluntary organization, the Straż Kresowa (Border Watch), but in practice, it was closely controlled by the landowners who saw it as little more than an export agency for their timber and linen. Trade and peaceful work were beginning to revive.

The military calm was prolonged by complicated events on other fronts. At the time of the capture of Wilno, Soviet Russia was bracing itself for the crisis of the Civil War. The Soviet II Army expelled from Estonia in February, was now entrenched in the suburbs of Petrograd awaiting the onslaught of General Yudenich. The VII Army, which had established a Soviet regime in Latvia in January, had been expelled from Riga and was fighting for its life. The XII Army, which conquered Kiev in February from the Directory, was now hard-pressed by the growing confidence of Denikin. Kolchak was poised to cross the Urals. The Soviets were clenched in an iron fist, of which the Western Front was no more than a knuckle of the smallest finger.

The Poles, too, were preoccupied. Their capture of Wilno had thwarted the ambitions of the Lithuanian nationalist government in Kaunas. Although very few Lithuanians lived in the city at that time, Wilno, or Vilnius as they called it, was the historic capital of Lithuania; the nationalists could not resign themselves to its loss. Fighting broke out which defied all efforts at mediation. The 'Foch Line' of 27 July left Wilno on the Polish side. In August a Polish uprising in Sejny and an attempt by Piłsudski to organize a *putsch* in Kaunas destroyed any inclination the Lithuanians might have had to negotiate.

Having lost their German patrons who withdrew their last forces to East Prussia in July, the Lithuanians sought comfort from the Soviets. The Lithuanian-Soviet combination was a constant threat.

In the south, the Poles were engaged with the Ukrainians, in Volhynia and in East Galicia. The Volhynian campaign was a minor matter involving some 5,000 Polish troops advancing from Chetm into the territory held by the Directory. It lasted from December 1918 to May 1919. The East Galician campaign, in contrast, was a major affair. While it lasted, it was the major preoccupation of the Polish army. The dispute there was with the so-called 'West Ukrainian Republic' over the city of Lwów, and over the rich province of which it was the capital. The Ukrainians, having a majority of the population in the province, though not in the city, had seized Lwów for their own. It took nine months to remove them. The crucial period was in April, contemporary with the Wilno operation, when General Haller's army arrived from France. It was not until July that the Poles reached the River Zbrucz and could rest content.

The eclipse of the Ukrainians, first the Directory and then the 'West Ukrainians', had an important effect on the Polish-Soviet War. As independent Ukrainian states were relentlessly squeezed out of existence from the west and from the east, the Poles and the Soviets automatically came into contact. This new contact was made near Kowel in Volhynia in May, and in East Galicia on the Zbrucz in July. The Polish-Soviet front, which had initially covered some 300 miles in Byelorussia, was progressively extended till it reached over 500 miles right across the Ukraine to the Rumanian frontier. The doubling of the front raised entirely new strategic and logistical problems, which could not be solved in a day. From July onwards it was clear that the first round of the Polish-Soviet conflict was nearing its end. It was also clear that if a second round was to be fought the war would lose its parochial character and would involve massive operations in which the survival of Soviet Russia and the Polish Republic would be thrown into the balance. In face of such a prospect, both sides hesitated.

Before a halt was called, however, the Polish High Command was intent on striking one more blow. If the Poles could break the Soviet Western Division, it would prevent the Red Army from re-forming effectively during the period of a ceasefire. In Polish eyes, the Western Division was a nest of vipers, whose poisonous influence should not be granted the chance to multiply. And so the blow fell on Minsk. (See map, p. 60)

There was a good strategic argument for capturing Minsk, as it was the centre of the next complex of lateral railway lines. Control of the Polotsk—Molodeczno—Minsk—Łuniniec network would deny the Soviets the essential means of uniting their scattered forces. A move in this direction had been made at the beginning of July when Molodeczno was taken.

During July reinforcements were sent to General Szeptycki, still commanding the Northern Group. Its main element was the Poznanian Army released from service in the west by the German signature of the Treaty of Versailles. It included the renowned 15th (Poznanian) Lancers commanded by Lieutenant-Colonel Władysław Anders. In all General Szeptycki could dispose of 12,000 infantry, 2,000 cavalry, and 40 guns, not counting the support he might summon from the Southern Group.

The heaviest engagement was certain to occur on the Minsk heights to the north-west of the city. For this Szeptycki concentrated the 1st Infantry Division and the Poznanian Army in Molodeczno. To ease their task, a wide pincer movement was prepared on both extremities of the Soviet positions. One arm consisting of the cavalry brigade was to race over the heights to the north. The other arm, consisting of General Mokrzecki's Group was to turn the flank of the Western Division in Nieśwież in the south. In the centre, General Lasocki was to spring from the Puszcza Nalibocka.

The battle raged throughout the first week of August. The issue was rarely in doubt, once the Polish cavalry cutting the railway behind Minsk, denied the defenders all significant reinforcements. Anders rode fifty miles round the back of the city, and ambushed the last train out. The Red Army made its stand at Radoszkowicze, with their backs to the ridge of the Minsk Heights. They lost many men. At the end of the week, on 8 August, Minsk fell, and the Red Army was stumbling eastwards in full retreat. The lesson was clear. Concerted attack

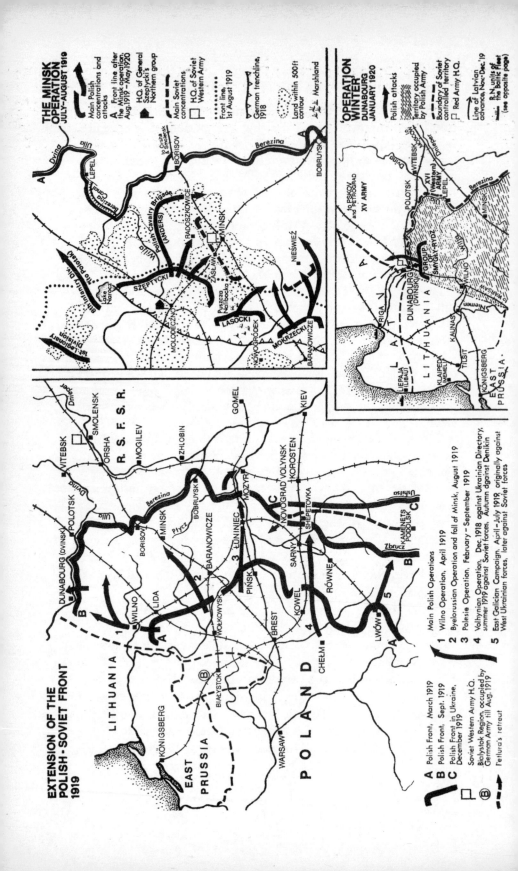

THE MINSK OPERATION
JULY–AUGUST 1919

⤷ Main Polish concentrations and attacks

▲ Front line after the Minsk operation, Aug.1919 – May1920

▲ H.Q. of General Szeptycki's Northern group

◆ Main Soviet concentrations

▭ H.Q. of Soviet Western Army

╍╍ Front line, 1st August 1919

⊣⊣⊣ German trenchline, 1918

Land within 500ft contour

⬳⬳ Marshland

'OPERATION WINTER'
DUNABOURG
JANUARY 1920

➤ Polish attacks

Territory occupied by Polish Army

Boundary of Soviet controlled territory

▭ Red Army H.Q.

╍╍ Line of Latvian advance, Nov.-Dec.'19

⋯⋯ R.N. in the Baltic Fleet (see opposite page)

EXTENSION OF THE POLISH · SOVIET FRONT
1919

A Polish Front, March 1919

B Polish Front, Sept. 1919

C Polish Front in Ukraine, December 1919

▭ Soviet Western Army H.Q.

Ⓑ Bialystok Region, occupied by German Army till Aug.1919

⤷ Petlura's retreat

Main Polish Operations

1 Wilno Operation, April 1919

2 Byelorussian Operation and fall of Minsk, August 1919

3 Polesie Operation, February – September 1919

4 Volhynian Operation, Dec.1918 against Ukrainian Directory, summer 1919 against Soviet forces, Autumn against Denikin

5 East Galician Campaign, April–July 1919, originally against West Ukrainian forces, later against Soviet forces

in the Borders paid dividends; defence, no matter how heroic, could always be outflanked.

The Soviet Western Army pulled right out of the area, to the River Dvina in the north and to the Berezina in the east. This was to be their station for nearly nine months. The Polish 1st Division raced to the Dvina, gazing across the river on Dunaburg; the 8th Division was before Polotsk; the 2nd Legionary Division reached Borisov; the Poznanians occupied the old fortress at Bobruysk; Generals Lasocki and Mokrzecki joined forces and they too moved to the Berezina.

The success of the Northern Group was transmitted like an electric shock right down the front. The Southern Group, now commanded by General Władysław Sikorski, broke the obstinate defence of Łuniniec. General Listowski, who had taken over the Volhynian Front, took Krzemieniec and Równe. General Iwaszkiewicz in East Galicia, already holding the right bank of the Zbrucz, tidied up his northern wing to stream-line his junction with Listowski.

By the end of August, the Polish army had reached a line which Piłsudski forbade it to cross. All three cities of the Borders—Wilno, Minsk, and Lwów—were secure, as were the areas of Polish settlement. Piłsudski, for all his romantic dreams, was not rash enough to imitate Napoleon and make for Moscow in the autumn. (See map, p. 60)

In any case, the Polish-Soviet War had run out of political steam. Neither side was interested in the conquest of more Border territory for its own sake. The Soviets were still pre-occupied with the Civil War, especially now with Denikin, who, unlike Piłsudski, *did* intend to imitate Napoleon. On 19 September, Denikin captured Kiev and kept marching. Piłsudski, having put 150 miles between the Soviets and his beloved Wilno, was ready to talk. Diplomacy, of the conspiratorial sort which Piłsudski preferred, was now to have its season.

CHAPTER TWO

A WINTER OF DISILLUSIONMENT

Józef Kiemens Ginet-Piłsudski was undoubtedly the central personality of the Polish-Soviet War. His critics would say that the war was his private adventure. As Polish Head of State and Commander-in-Chief of the Polish army, he directly controlled the war's political and military management. No leader on the Soviet side could give the same individual attention to the war or enjoyed the same degree of undelegated control.

In the early months of the war, Piłsudski could sometimes be seen in a small restaurant in Warsaw, eating a frugal supper late in the evening after the day's work at Belweder palace. He sat at the corner table, in the shadows and alone. He wore a threadbare military uniform with high, buttoned collar and no insignia of rank. His steel grey hair was cropped and razored in the Prussian style; his face was long and cadaverous; his skin disconcertingly pallid. His drooping, oriental moustache added to the inscrutable appearance. But most remarkable were his eyes. No one who met Piłsudski failed to comment on his grey-blue eyes. Deep-set, narrow, intense, piercing, they were the one unmistakable sign of the inward fire which consumed him.

Piłsudski's personality was the product of a lifetime spent in revolt and danger. He was a Lithuanian of Polish culture, born in 1867, the son of a landed family which boasted Scottish Jacobite blood. Educated in the Tsarist gymnasium at Wilno, he was drenched from his student days in Polish romanticism and Polish nationalism. Surrounded by the apathy and despair which had descended after the Polish Rising of 1863, his inner powers were devoted from an early age to resisting the mood of his contemporaries—hence the self-discipline, the long silences, the essential loneliness. His physical energies were devoted to fighting the absolute power and oppression of Russia—hence the conspiratorial habits, the devious mind, the military training, the ingrained banditry. For twenty years he was a member of the Polish Socialist Party. In 1905–7, during the revolutionary strikes, he was perhaps their most active leader. But after 1907, when revolutionary action was no longer possible, his enthusiasm for socialism waned. He turned increasingly to para-military organizations, like Sosnkowski's Union of Active Struggle in Austrian Poland. His own Riflemen's Associations concealed their true political intentions behind the thin veil of sporting exercises. By 1912, his Polish Legions were officially recognized by the Royal and Imperial Army and held full-scale manoeuvres in the Tatra Mountains. His leadership of the Legions put him at the head of the movement for Polish independence, threw him into the maelstrom of politics and campaigns on the Eastern Front in the First World War, landed him in a German jail at Magdeburg in 1917, and finally raised him at the age of fifty-two to be the unchallenged and unchallengeable leader of the reborn Poland. When at the end of 1918, his former socialist colleagues approached him with the request for political support he is reported to have said: 'Comrades, I rode on the red-painted tramcar of socialism as far as the stop called Independence, but there I alighted. You are free to drive on to the terminus if you can, but please address me as Sir!' Not even his close colleagues knew what Piłsudski was really thinking. All they knew was that he expected to be obeyed.

It was a nice irony that Piłsudski had a revolutionary past as impeccable as that of any of the Bolsheviks. His adult life started at the age of twenty with five years of exile in north-east Siberia. His brother Bronisław was implicated in the attempted assassination of Tsar Alexander III, for which the elder Ulyanov paid with his life. He himself became the first editor-in-chief of *Robotnik*, the Polish socialist daily. He served a term of exile in London, between 1896 and 1905, and a year in a Russian lunatic asylum in 1906–7, through feigning madness to avoid a harsher sentence for conspiracy. After his escape from the asylum, he organized a mail train robbery at Bezdany near Wilno on 20 September 1908, which netted 200,000 roubles in silver for the revolutionary cause. The frustrations of revolutionary conspiracy matured a ruthless streak. As he told a veteran socialist associate:

Let others play at throwing bouquets, to socialism or to Polonism or to anything they like. I can't, not in this present atmosphere of a latrine,... *I* want to conquer. My latest idea is to create...an organization of physical force, of brute force, to use an expression which is insupportable to the humanitarians. I have promised to realize it or perish.[1]

As a journalist turned army leader he was in the class of Trotsky; as professional gangster he rivalled Stalin; as gentleman turned party organizer he had something in common with Lenin. Although he lacked the intellectual development of the Bolsheviks, he owed them nothing in dedication or success.

It is impossible to say that Piłsudski was liked. He was idolized by his legionaries, and by many common patriots with whom he had no contact. He was respected and feared by the politicians, who could not but admire his constancy of purpose. The diplomats resented his imperviousness to the wishes of their governments. The Allied representatives thought him arrogant. The French officers in Poland were shocked to find themselves treated like mercenaries. The British Minister, Sir Horace Rumbold described him as 'the biggest man in this part of Europe...the undisputed boss of this country...a gambler, a conspirator, an interesting study, an anachronism, not a great man but a remarkable man who will control for some time the destinies of this nation.'[2] He likened both his appearance and his character to that of Lord Kitchener. Piłsudski enjoyed no high reputation abroad. In the west he was seen to present that worst of combinations—a radical turned jingoist; in Russia, he was seen as a renegade from the revolutionary camp. His strong personality inspired either adoration or hate, but fondness never.

In judging the developments of the second phase of the Polish-Soviet War, the historian's estimate of Piłsudski's personality is of paramount importance. In the first phase, personal judgement and grand strategy had played little part.

But the next moves were to be determined, not in response to events at the front, but by the instincts of the Polish leader.

The key to Piłsudski's reading of the situation lay in his belief that the Bolsheviks intended sooner or later to conquer the Borders by force. For him the scale of the 'Target Vistula' operation and the thoroughness of the Lit-Byel experiment were proof enough of their ambitions. Hard experience of this sort weighed more than the wordy protestations of Soviet propaganda. There seemed every likelihood that the Red Army would attempt to reverse the Polish victories of 1919, as soon as it freed itself from preoccupations elsewhere.

So long as he held the tactical advantage, Piłsudski must have been sorely tempted to press his luck and deliver a pre-emptive blow. It was certainly in his nature to do so. The *fait accompli* was a manoeuvre for which he was already notorious. He had used it to good effect on 2 August 1914 when his Legions marched on Kielce without advising the Austrian High Command. He used it twice in 1919, when he faced the Peace Conference in Paris, first with the unauthorized capture of Wilno in April, secondly with the forbidden occupation of East Galicia in May. Now, a number of considerations held his hand. Firstly, a knock-out blow was almost impossible to execute in the Borders. The Red Army could always retire to the depths of Russia where no Polish soldier could follow. A Polish advance into Russia proper would be sure to rally patriotic support for the Soviet regime. Secondly, the mere defeat of the Soviets would not necessarily benefit Poland. If the Soviet regime were to be replaced by Denikin, Polish independence would be less secure than before. The Russian Civil War must first be decided before Russia's relations with Poland could be firmly settled. Thirdly, Poland was too weak to gather the fruits of victory in Russia. The Polish economy could hardly support a war of defence. The Polish administration could hardly organize its home territory. The Polish army could hardly protect its own frontiers. There was no hope whatsoever that Poland unaided could manage, organize, administer, and police even part of Russia. There were also a large number of imponderables. No one could tell how well Denikin's campaign would fare, how far the Allied governments would pursue intervention, how long the other Border states from Finland to Georgia could refuse to treat with the Soviets.

It would be wrong perhaps to imagine Piłsudski weighing these considerations like a chess player planning his moves. He worked less by logic than by animal cunning. One is tempted to liken him to a rhinoceros—indestructible, myopic, unpredictable. Having won a clearing for himself, he watched all possible intruders through small mistrustful eyes. Having once been provoked, there was always the possibility that he would charge again.

The situation within the Soviet leadership was entirely different. After the collapse of the Lit-Byel, no-one cared to take special responsibility for the Polish front. Throughout 1919, the preoccupations of the Civil War in Russia proper compelled the Soviet leaders to forgo any immediate plans for recovering the western borders. Theoretical arguments figured more prominently than practical action.

The belief that Soviet Russia could not easily survive without a favourable end to the confrontation with Poland was universally accepted. Poland was the 'Red Bridge' to the west, Russia's natural link with the advanced societies of Europe, with technical progress, with proletarian solidarity, with future revolution. Although the quiet on the Polish front in the autumn of 1919 was welcome, it was generally recognized that a solution of the Polish problem could not be postponed indefinitely. The debate in Russia was not *whether* the Polish bridge should be crossed, but *how* and *when*.

The debate centred on three propositions, each of which gained ascendancy at different times. The first held that the war with Poland should be renewed at the earliest opportunity. The failure of the 'Target Vistula' operation gave special urgency to increased military efforts in the west. This course of action tended to appeal to those who put a literal interpretation on their Marxist guidebooks or who had learned their politics abroad in Europe. For them, the continuing isolation of Soviet Russia presented an intolerable prospect to be avoided at all costs. The second proposition held that expansion to the west should await the consolidation of Soviet power in Russia. There was no point in involving the new Soviet state in a foreign war until it possessed a firm political and economic base. This counsel was supported by the 'homespun' communists, the Bolsheviks who, caring little for international Marxism, were brought into the party by the Civil War. For them, it was unthinkable that the success of the revolution in Russia should be jeopardized by an 'adventure' abroad. The third proposition held that the revolution should spread eastwards. The best way to undermine the capitalist states of Europe was to destroy their empires in Asia and Africa. Trotsky once said in this connexion that 'the road to London and Paris lies through Calcutta'. This reasoning was preferred by those who combined an ideological commitment to the permanent revolution with a realistic assessment of the might of the capitalist world. For them, a frontal assault on Poland was a futile gesture which would provoke the Allied powers into full-scale intervention.

It is not a simple matter to match these propositions to the people who supported them. It was common at the time to talk in terms of a Bolshevik 'Peace Party' led by Lenin, and a 'War Party' led by Trotsky. This is not only a simplification; it is fundamentally false. It is derived from the facile assumption that Lenin, as signatory of the Soviet Peace Notes, was *ipso facto* in favour of peace, and that Trotsky, as Commissar for War, was necessarily in favour of war. The situation was far more fluid and confused. If one were to judge exclusively from the peaceable tone of Lenin's official speeches, it would be impossible to explain why he ever allowed 'Target Vistula' to proceed in the first place. One must distinguish between statements intended for home consumption and those directed abroad. It is clear that in front of foreign journalists Trotsky in particular played the part of the bloodcurdling Bolshevik in a way that would be pointless in front of the Politburo.

In the last analysis, the decision for or against the Polish war rested with Lenin. Yet Lenin knew little about Poland, and in 1919 could lend scant attention to it. His approach to the Polish war was a matter of daily improvisation. He lived from hand to mouth, tasting the morsels of advice served up to him by rival aides in turn. Trotsky, as Commissar for War, had the right to press the military viewpoint. In spite of his reputation, Trotsky was cautious. As creator of the Red Army, he knew its limitations and its state of exhaustion. Its success in the Civil

War was not to be put at risk lightly. Chicherin, the Commissar for Foreign Affairs, was also cautious, both by nature and by interest. His influence depended on his ability to conduct relations with the outside world, and he could hardly advocate a policy which might provoke the Allied powers into subjecting Russia to redoubled blockade and renewed isolation. Dzierżyński, head of the Cheka, like his deputy, Mężyński, was a Pole. He had serious reservations about the war on account of the resistance expected from the civilian population, whose pacification would become his responsibility. Stalin, the Commissar for Nationalities, though willing enough to see the nationalities of the Borders subjected to his control, rarely showed enthusiasm for the war except when it was already running in the Soviets' favour. None of these leading advisers can have pushed Lenin towards war. There remained only the Polish Bureau of the Bolshevik Party, a lowly body in the hierarchy but very relevant to Soviet relations with Poland. Its leaders, like Leński and Bobiński, were political émigrés. They were already training officers and creating military cadres for the service of the revolution in Poland. Their advice must inevitably have been coloured by their overwhelming desire to return to Poland. They favoured a Soviet invasion. But their advice was far from unanimous. Their most influential member, Karol Radek, who had worked with Róża Luksemburg in Germany, consistently warned that an armed advance into Poland would meet with failure. Over all, the weight of opinion in Moscow was against a Polish war. Yet Lenin allowed it to start, and at certain stages prosecuted it with great vigour. One can only assume that Lenin was not the 'dove' he would like to have appeared; when occasion merited, he disregarded the advice of his subordinates in the hope of reaping the fruits of military victory.

Lenin's willingness to wage war with Poland was clearest at the beginning of 1919. He was not prepared to accept Piłsudski's occupation of Wilno, and gave immediate orders for its recapture. Thereafter he hesitated. Once the initial phase was over, Soviet policy on the war was characterized by manifold contradictions, by preparations for war and propaganda for peace conducted simultaneously, by threats of subversion and promises of negotiation. These contradictions were interpreted by the Poles as proof of treachery; they can equally be seen as the product of divided counsels and of Lenin's indecision.

At the end of 1919, Lenin passed once more into a period of bouyant optimism, inspired by victories in the Civil War. Now at last he felt confident that the Revolution would survive and would sweep triumphant over Europe. It was also a period when his sources of information and direct contacts with the outside world were particularly sparse. He became overconfident, messianic even. In April 1920, he completed *The Infantile Disease of 'Leftism' in Communism*—a work which was intended to guide the Revolution through the few remaining months before its consummation. As his mood gathered momentum, he was less and less likely to resist the drift towards more serious war with Poland.

Trotsky's attitude to the war was also contradictory. In the week that Minsk fell, he suggested a moratorium on efforts for a European revolution. He envisaged the formation of a cavalry army which would advance, not to Warsaw, but across the Pamirs to Kabul and Delhi. In later years, he claimed that he had opposed the Polish war:

> Of course I never had any occasion to express my sympathy with the Poland of Piłsudski, that is a Poland of oppression and repression under a cloak of patriotic phraseology and heroic braggadacio. But to draw from this the conclusion that we wanted a war with Poland, or were even preparing it is to lie in the face of facts and common sense. We strained every effort to avoid that war... We were trying with all our might to secure peace even at the price of the greatest concessions. Even more than anyone else I did not want this war because I realized only too clearly how difficult it would be to prosecute it after three years of civil war.[3]

It is hard to reconcile these statements with the fact that Trotsky *did* prosecute the Polish war for two full seasons; it was Trotsky who made that most bellicose of declarations about Soviet intentions, which appeared in the French Communist Party's *L'Internationale Communiste* on 15 December 1919: 'The Polish lords and gentry will snatch a temporary, marauders' victory,' he said, 'but when we have finished with Denikin, we shall throw the full weight of our reserves onto the Polish front.' Trotsky was torn between the ideological propriety of the Polish war and its practical dangers. He acquiesced in the Polish war sullenly and without enthusiasm. When the war was going well, he did little to restrain it; when negotiations were possible, he was ready, like Lenin, to explore them.

In the autumn of 1919, a basis for renewing negotiations gradually became apparent. The Poles had lost their anxieties about Wilno and about an imminent Soviet invasion; their poor relations with the Entente gave them new anxieties about fighting alone. The Soviets, hard pressed by Denikin's advance in the south, needed a respite in the west. Most importantly, both Poles and Soviets experienced the unbending hostility of the Russian Whites. In June 1919 Kolchak had deeply offended Polish sensitivities by affirming that Poland's eastern frontier must be referred to a Russian Constituent Assembly. Denikin, now in the flush of success, was no more conciliatory.

The credit for re-opening the contacts, broken off in April, must be given to Julian Marchlewski, the man once proposed as the first Soviet ambassador to Poland. Marchlewski was another of those Polish communists who like Karol Radek and Róża Luksemburg commuted between the Bolshevik Party in Russia, the Social Democratic Party of Poland and Lithuania (SDKPiL) and the Spartakists in Germany. In January 1919 he travelled illegally to Berlin, having been refused official entry at the German frontier as leader of a Soviet delegation. From Berlin he went to the Ruhr where, having been trailed by the police, he avoided arrest by concealing himself among a group of seasonal agricultural workers returning to Galicia. In March, he found himself in Poland, unannounced and un-detected. He used his time trying to dissuade Polish socialist opinion against war with the Soviets in the columns of *Robotnik*. In June, he seized the occasion presented by Kolchak's statement on the Polish frontier question to contact Piłsudski, and through the medium of Józef Beck (Senior), Vice-Minister of Internal Affairs, to offer his services as an intermediary for secret negotiations with Lenin. Piłsudski consented. Marchlew-ski left for Moscow on 18 June.

Back in Russia, Marchlewski's adventures gave rise to a serious difference of opinion. Lenin welcomed Marchlewski's initiative; but the Central Committee of the Polish Communist Party (KPRP) meeting in Minsk on 2 July condemned it:

The conversations of Comrade Marchlewski with representatives of the Polish government and his journey to Russia with their propositions have been undertaken without the consent and knowledge of the Central Committee and are inadmissible, bearing in mind that Marchlewski as a member of the Party is subject to the decisions and directives of its leading organs.[4]

Leński and his followers saw no point in negotiations which could only result in the weakening of Soviet Russia's vigilance on their Western Front. A week later Marchlewski faced his critics and explained Lenin's viewpoint. He argued that peace with the Poles was necessary in the interest of Soviet victory on the more crucial civil war fronts. He assured them that territorial concessions could be made in the knowledge that 'all frontier lines will soon lose their meaning since the revolutionary upheaval throughout Europe is only a few years away;' Finally, he tried to cajole them into believing that an unsuccessful Soviet invasion of Poland would spell the end for the Polish communist movement. Leński did not repent, and maintained his conviction for a revolutionary war. Not that Leński's protests mattered. Marchlewski was even then on his way, armed with Lenin's formal authority, to cross the Polish lines.

Marchlewski's mission of July 1919 has been called the 'Białowieża Meeting'. He drove out of Minsk on the 10th. At the frontline post at Radoszkowice, he announced himself by the prearranged pseudonym of 'Pan Kujawski' and awaited the arrival of Olszamowski, Piłsudski's personal adjutant.

The Polish army treated him roughly. He was frisked, blindfolded, and induced to sign a paper, undertaking not to distribute funds for subversion nor, oddly enough, to converse with anyone in Poland. On the 21st, he was taken to the station at Baranowicze, where he met the Polish negotiator, Więckowski, and thence to a woodman's cottage in the depths of the Białowieża Forest. Most of his time was spent waiting, while Więckowski travelled to Warsaw for confirmation of his brief. At the end of the week nothing was agreed beyond arrangements for the exchange of hostages and an expressed desire for a future meeting of representatives of the Soviet and Polish Red Cross. Marchlewski's wider proposals, for territorial concessions, for a plebiscite, for the preliminaries of peace, did not impress the Poles at all at this stage. He was plainly disappointed. He recrossed the lines on 30 July.

The next meeting took ten weeks to materialize. The Presidium of the Council of Ministers in Warsaw discussed the matter on 26 August, but it was the last week of September before Piłsudski agreed. A Polish 'Red Cross' Mission was entrusted to Count Michał Kossakowski, who was an official of the Foreign Ministry, a member of the Committee for the Defence of the Borders, and, for the benefit of all historians of the period, a compulsive diarist. The Soviet Red Cross Mission was led by Marchlewski, complete this time with bowler hat, wing-collar, and Gladstone bag. The rendezvous was at Mikaszewice, a remote halt on the single-track railway line, sixty miles east of Pińsk. It was on the Polish side of the front at a point where the Polish forces to the west, the Bolsheviks to the north, the Denikinists to the east, and the Ukrainians to the south all came in contact. On 11 October, the day of the meeting, Denikin had just taken Oryol. Only Tula stood between Oryol and Moscow. In this situation it was not difficult for Kossakowski to extract a couple of very advantageous treaties. The one signed on 2 November provided for the unilateral return of Polish hostages held by the Bolsheviks;[5] the other, signed on 9 November, provided for the mutual exchange of civilian prisoners.[6]

Marchlewski was encouraged to make concessions to Kossakowski by the fact that he was simultaneously conducting highly confidential negotiations with Piłsudski's personal emissaries, Captain Ignacy Boerner and Lieutenant Birnbaum. He was probably correct in assuming that a direct approach to the Chief of State had more chance of success than an approach through official channels. Even Kossakowski was unaware what Boerner and Birnbaum were authorized to discuss.

On 3 November, Boerner confided Piłsudski's conditions for a ceasefire:

The Chief-of-State—
1) will not order the Polish army beyond the line Novograd Volynsk—Oleysk—River Ptich—Bobruysk—River Berezina— Berezina Canal—River Dvina
2) to avoid misunderstandings, suggests that a belt 10 kilometres wide shall divide the two armies

3) declares that he will support the Latvians' claim to Dunaburg
4) demands an end to communist agitation in the Polish army
5) demands that the Soviets shall not attack Petlura
6) not believing in the Soviets' powers of discretion, warns that any indiscretion will engender serious consequences
7) affirms that, if the Soviet government agrees to points 2, 4, and 5, a duly authorized representative will be sent to discuss all the conditions directly with Mr Lenin in person.[7]

Boerner was instructed to tell Marchlewski that assistance for Denikin did not coincide with Poland's interests, and that a Polish attack on Mozyr, which in conjunction with Denikin's attack on Oryol could well have broken the Soviet Southern front once and for all, had not been attempted. Lenin was pleased. He assumed that the Polish war was drawing to its close. Speaking at Sverdlov University on 24 October, he declared that 'we have clear indications that the time is past when we might have expected further encroachments by the Polish army.'[8] Sources close to Trotsky report that on 14 November the Politburo accepted Piłsudski's terms unanimously. Lenin's reply, which Boerner conveyed to Piłsudski on 26 November, quibbled only on point 5. According to Lenin, Petlura, whose 'capital' was in the hands of the Poles and whose main forces had deserted to Denikin, was a laughing-stock who could not be the subject of serious discussion. As late as 28 November Marchlewski wrote to Trotsky confirming that a cessation of hostilities was imminent. He said that rumours of mutiny in the Polish army were unfounded and warned that the Poles were strengthening their position daily. He foresaw no trouble over Petlura. He was most concerned to forward an idea, apparently mooted by Boerner but immediately dismissed by Lenin, to put the secret Polish nationalist organizations in the Ukraine at the Red Army's disposal for the struggle against Denikin.[9] Meanwhile, Lenin's quibble about Petlura stuck in Piłsudski's throat. Piłsudski would not or could not swallow it. He rejected it sharply, and contrary to all expectations, broke off negotiations forthwith. On 14 December Marchlewski and Kossakowski went their different ways. As their trains pulled out of Mikaszewice, the prospects for Polish–Soviet accord were once again as bleak as the snow-swept and now deserted platform.[10]

The failure of the secret negotiations is usually attributed to the Poles. Chicherin blamed it on Paderewski whom he quite erroneously assumed to have been pressing for co-operation with Denikin.[11] Kossakowski suggests that Piłsudski never had any intention of reaching agreement. He reports the following outburst:

It's the same for the Bolsheviks as for Denikin; there's only one thing to tell them: "*We* are a force in the world, and *you* are destined for the mortuary. I despise you and hold you in contempt... There can be no question of relations or diplomatic negotiations, where the fundamental conditions are trust and discretion. You don't practise the former and don't recognize the latter..." No, no I have not been negotiating. I have just been telling them unpleasant facts... I have ordered them to understand that with us they ought to be humble beggars.[12]

These words have been used as proof of Piłsudski's obstinate refusal to consider a ceasefire. Such a conclusion, however, pays too much attention to his bad temper on one particular evening. He did after all make specific proposals. It *is* true, that in the autumn of 1919 Lenin wanted peace. The point is that in the earlier stages of the Polish war, certainly up to April 1919, Lenin had *not* wanted peace. Piłsudski can be forgiven for believing that Lenin's change of heart was due to Soviet Russia's dire straits. The irony is that the negotiations‘ which had taken six months to organize, broke up at the very moment when, with the Soviet recapture of Kiev on 16 December, the issue of the civil war was being rapidly clarified and the prospects for agreement were daily improving.

The war had reached its divide. This was the moment of disillusion, when the participants saw the scales tip almost imperceptibly away from peace and towards intensified conflict.

The military actions which provided the setting for the secret negotiations were somewhat desultory. They may be seen as attempts to maintain the *status quo*, whereby the Poles retained the initiative and warded off periodic disturbances caused by turbulent events nearby in the Ukraine and the Baltic States. Only one action, the drive on Dunaburg, might merit the title of a campaign. (See map, p. 60)

The first incident occurred in the south as a result of the advance of Denikin's Volunteer Army through the Ukraine. Denikin, moving northwards from Odessa, pushed the forces of Petlura's Ukrainian Directory northwards, out of their base at Kamenets Podolsk and into the Polish lines near Novograd Volynsk. For several days at the end of August, Petlura was assailed from three sides, by Poles, Denikinists, and Bolsheviks. On 1 September he was forced to accept the Polish terms for a ceasefire and then to retire behind the Polish front. A demarcation line between the Poles and Petlura's forces was fixed from the Zbrucz to Bazaliya, Shepetovka, and Novograd Volynsk. Thus began Petlura's five-year political asylum in Poland. His army, which had been largely recruited in the Western Ukraine for the purpose of fighting the Poles, now passed into Polish service. His presence in the Polish ranks provided not only the point on which negotiations with the Bolsheviks foundered, but an important factor in Piłsudski's future strategy.

In October, Denikin briefly met the Polish Volhynian Group face to face. But Denikin retreated as fast as he had advanced. The Red Army pushed him away from Moscow and the Poles brushed him out of Volhynia. At the end of November, the Volhynian Group reinstalled Petlura in Novograd Volynsk, and in December the East Galician Group took up positions on the Uszycz to parry the Soviet reoccupation of the Ukraine. By the end of the year, Denikin had vanished and the Polish-Soviet front stretched once more to the Rumanian frontier on the Dniester.

In the north the situation was even more complicated. The Baltic States were the area of operations for three national armies—the Lithuanian, Latvian, and Estonian; for three White armies—those of Bermondt-Avalov in Latvia, Lieven in Courland, and Yudenich in Estonia; for three Soviet armies; and for the German Baltikum Army of General von der Goltz. The advance of the Baltikum volunteers in September 1919, in the wake of the last units of Wehrmacht, had the same effect on the Baltic situation as Denikin's volunteers had in the Ukraine.

The Poles could not stand entirely aloof from the Baltic turmoil. They shared the nationalist aspirations of the national armies and the fears of Bolshevism of the White armies. They permitted both Lieven and Yudyonich to maintain private recruiting offices in Poland. They were in conflict with the Lithuanians over Wilno and viewed the German connexions of Bermondt and von der Goltz with intense suspicion. It was only with the Latvians that they had any common cause.

Polish-Latvian co-operation focused on the fate of the city of Dunaburg. Dunaburg or Dvinsk on the north bank of the Dvina commanded the natural routes of communication between the Russian interior and the Gulf of Riga. Its population was Latvian. In the autumn of 1919, it was held by the Reds, though threatened from various directions by the Baltikum, the Poles, and the Latvians. If the Soviets managed to hold onto the city they would be able to consolidate the junction of their XVth and XVIth armies. If the Baltikum Army succeeded in capturing it, unwanted German influence would return to the area. The Polish army, under General Śmigły-Rydz, had been occupying the left bank of the Dvina since the end of August. At the beginning óf October, the Latvian Foreign Minister met Piłsudski in Wilno to receive the *de facto* recognition of his government and to ask for military assistance at Dunaburg. (See map, p. 60)

The Polish army was anxious for its own reasons to strengthen the Dvina sector. Its western flank was constantly being disrupted by the Baltic troubles, and in the middle of October an unexpected Soviet offensive had forced the 8th Division to withdraw for a week from Polotsk. Its effectives had been stiffened by the transfer of the 3rd Legionary Division from East Galicia.

The Dunaburg operation, despite its reputation, was a masterpiece of uncoordination. The original order for 'Operation Winter', as it was coded, was issued by the Polish Staff on 2 December, to be executed by the 15th. At this time the Latvian government was paralysed by the fear that the Polish minority in Latvia was going to demand union with Poland, and had laid no plans. The Latvian army was paralysed by the fear that its men would not attack the Latvian communists who had been added to the Red garrison in Dunaburg. When the Polish Military Mission in Riga established that the attack should begin sometime between 4 and 10 January the most

essential details were still missing. Communication between
the Polish and the Latvian forces was virtually impossible.
Railway and telegraph links were not functioning along the
intervening Lithuanian sections. The Latvian command had
not yet been persuaded to submit to Polish orders. A final
agreement was reached on 30 December. The Latvians were
to provide 10,000 men to support the Polish strike-force of
30,000. When on 3 January 1920, despite a temperature of
−25°C, the divisions of General Śmigły-Rydz charged across
the ice of the frozen Dvina, they could hardly have expected
their Latvian allies to do more than watch. The 3rd Legionary
Division stormed the citadel whilst the 1st Infantry Division
pressed round to the north to cut the Soviets' line of retreat.
The Polish artillery cracked the ice under its weight, and
partially sank in mid-stream. The garrison was thrown out
to the west where it surrendered to the Latvians. On 5 January,
when the operation was complete, Piłsudski announced that
Dunaburg was to be handed to the Latvian Republic and thus
started the story of magnanimity and close co-operation.

The fall of Dunaburg marks the true end of the Polish-Soviet
campaign of 1919. It ended a year of immense confusion and
complexity. After Dunaburg, the Polish and Soviet armies in
the north as in the south faced each other in unbroken, uninterrupted line. Unless the politicians could prevent it, the coming
campaign of 1920 promised action on a far vaster scale and of
far greater moment.

Life in the Borders deteriorated fast as the winter approached.
The Polish army kept men at the front without basic winter
clothing, sleeping in the open. General Carton de Wiart of the
British Military Mission which visited the front in November
1919 saw infantrymen without boots and overcoats. The
temperature stood at −14°C. 'I don't know how they stick it,'
he reported.[13] The plight of the Red Army can have been
no better.

Morale inevitably suffered, especially on the Polish side.
Although Carton de Wiart remarked on the 'wonderful spirit'
of the Poles, there is evidence to show that discipline was
beginning to break down. One of Piłsudski's closest confidants,

Władysław Sławek, commander of Sector II of the Byelo-russian Front sent him the following warning:

Wilno, 2 November 1919. My dear friend! General Szeptycki has ordered me to write to you privately. The number of instances where men refuse to go on patrol because of lack of boots or clothing is increasing. Armed robbery is becoming quite frequent. In short, the soldier does not have the will to fight. General Szeptycki is of the opinion that we should end the war with the Bolsheviks at all costs. He has said that if the Sejm doesn't understand the situation, you should declare yourself dictator and settle it yourself. My personal impression is that all is not well. Everywhere among the officers and commanders one meets a general tiredness and pessimism which paralyses their ability to inspire enthusiasm and alertness. All for now. Kindest regards. Yours, W. Sławek.[14]

Whereas the soldier in the Red Army could still feel that he was saving his country from Denikin and from the return of the propertied classes, the ordinary Polish ranker, threatened by no one, had nothing to save but his own skin.

In Poland itself, word was circulating about conditions at the front and there were cases where men defied the draft or where, as at Zamość, having been conscripted, they took to the countryside in large bands and terrorized the authorities.

Soviet propaganda spared no pains to push Polish discontent into open mutiny and revolution. Communist pamphlets urged peace and brotherhood. Specific appeals were made to units known to be disaffected:

To the soldiers of the 33rd Lómża Regiment! News has reached us, comrades, that you have already disobeyed orders, and that you are unwilling to take up your positions or to shed your proletarian blood in the cause of your masters. You were forced to return to the front by the armed police who surrounded you. We know that you really wish to come over to us, for you feel that the Red Army is fighting for the liberation of working people.

But there are those among you who believe your officers' tales that prisoners here are shot. Don't believe such a lie!

All of you, both conscripts and volunteers, unite with us, come over to our side, bring your weapons.

Together we shall end this fratricidal struggle. With our help, you will rid yourselves of your petty-minded officers and generals, Your bourgeois and hereditary lords.

Trust us comrades! Forward to the revolutionary ranks!
[Signed] Polish Workers of the Red Army.[15]

Sometimes appeals were issued by prisoners of war:

Comrades, colleagues! We, Polish prisoners of the Bolsheviks, send
you fraternal greetings. We wish to describe for you without any
exaggeration what the Soviet system means. Soviet Russia is a
hundredfold a better fatherland for us than Poland. Under the
Tsarist regime, the Russian worker was a slave. In Poland, the
hungry worker was often driven to crime. But here everyone works.
The workers administer the whole state through their councils to
which delegates are sent from every factory and farm. The workers
here have their own schools, their universities, newspapers and
palaces of labour. The Soviet regime guarantees real freedom.
    Comrades! Turn your arms on your oppressors.
    Brothers! Join the Red Army and the international revolution!
Signed, in the name of us all, S. Klepacki (4th Legionary Regiment);
Markarczuk, Cisielski, Siekierski, Burhat (4th Regiment of
Uhlans).[16]

One should not underestimate the novelty in 1919, and the
seductiveness, of such appeals. But it is hard to judge the scale
of their success. Desertion reached such proportions, it is
claimed, that the military prisons in Wilno and Minsk were
full to overflowing. At Polotsk, in the 35th Legionary Regiment,
the Polish officers reverted to the old Tsarist discipline of the
knout. At Lepel, a Cracovian regiment was withdrawn and
interned for fraternizing with the enemy. There were cases,
especially in the Warsaw regiments, where soldiers' councils
were formed on the Soviet model and where the military police
were beaten up. But many of the disturbances were in no
sense political. The greatest indiscipline occurred among the
most fervently anti-Bolshevik units, such as those of General
Żeligowski. Most of the complaints about indiscipline concerned drunkenness, forced requisitions, and banditry—which
can be attributed more to boredom and discomfort than to
propaganda. A number of brigands openly operated in the
frontline zone, some still in Polish uniforms, some claiming to
be 'Reds'. The politics of such people were not very serious.
    Of course, what one side calls a bandit, the other will call a

partisan; and specific attention was paid to this aspect of the
scene, particularly on the Soviet side. On 3 September 1919,
in Smolensk, the Bureau of Illegal Activities was formed to
co-ordinate activities behind the Polish lines. It was run by
the now unemployed leaders of the Lit-Byel,—Mickiewicz-
Kapsukas, Dolecki, and Sławinski. Their communist underground strove to establish a network of party cells, to evangelize
the peasantry, and to prepare the way for the return of the
Red Army. It was dangerous work, and the activists took their
life in their hands. Marian Dżemba, co-ordinator of the Minsk
region, was one of many to die in a Polish jail.

Despite the dangers, the Polish communists in Russia
preferred to fight with the partisans rather than rely on the
Red Army. In the autumn of 1919, they were greatly dis-
couraged by the inactivity of the Soviet Western Army and by
the eagerness of the Bolsheviks in Moscow to make peace. One
of them, Edward Kowalski was sufficiently disillusioned to
resign his command of the 4th (Warsaw) Regiment of the
Western Army in favour of work with the partisans in Polesie.
In a letter to Feliks Kon he described his experiences:

24 November 1919, Mozyr. Because of the snow, we have lost
contact with the Polish army completely. Forces are small on both
sides, and they fight mainly by raiding. One only meets cavalry
patrols, often composed of recruits, so it is not difficult to talk to
them.

The peasants in the frontline zone are not badly organized, and
through them we send 'literature' to the Poles. They have proved
far better agents than the commissars sent out by various Soviet
institutions for political work at the front. We have so many troubles
and disputes with the 'revolutionary war departments', their
staffs, subcommissions, and supply offices that one hopes they'll be
struck by lightning!

I have succeeded in putting two detachments across the front
each of 150 men with six to eight machine guns. One group, the
'Communards', had to smash its way past the Poles, but reached
its designated refuge in the Pińsk marshes without any losses.

As a great favour, I have just received a so-called 'cheque-book
for the supply of detachments' along with 100 pairs of boots,
padded jackets, and trousers, and, God be praised, new rifles. Up to
now they only sent us inferior Berdan guns.

The Poles are shameless in their efforts to maintain order and to punish by example. They end up by killing children, women and old people and razing their villages to the ground.

There are continual disturbances in Poland, and I hope that around Easter next year we shall be masters in Warsaw...[17]

The refuge of Kowalski's detachment was the village of Dąbrowica on the River Horyn, whence they planned to emerge and capture the Polish artillery depot at Olewsk. Unfortunately for them, in February Dąbrowica was searched by the Polish army, the detachment dispersed, and Kowalski taken prisoner.

The ease with which people wandered unchecked across the frontline is proof of the Poles' inability to control the vast area they had occupied. The so-called 'sunshine road' was trodden not just by partisans, but by refugees, by speculators, and by the ubiquitous Jewish traders. Salt, saccharine, cocaine, and, oddly enough, pigs' bristles. were the profitable commodities. The situation was well described by Vladimir Korostovets, a former Tsarist diplomat, who smuggled his own family out of Russia in the vicinity of Minsk. Disguised as the buyer of a Soviet co-operative agency, he trekked from farm to farm, chatting with soldiers and commissars alike until he met the peasant who, for a consideration of some 3,000 Tsarist roubles, led his party across the marshes and into the Poznanian lines.

The Poles, too, had their underground. Piłsudski's underground army, the POW (Polish Military Organization), formed in 1914 to fight for Polish independence in areas occupied by the Central Powers, had never been disbanded in the Borders. It was strongest in the south, in the Ukraine, where two years earlier Piłsudski's Legions had fought and disintegrated. Although the POW was no longer active in Poland proper, its third section, KN3, commanding the eastern territories, survived as a branch of the Polish General Staff in Warsaw. It controlled cells as distant as Rostov-on-Don and Stavropol in the Kuban. Its main function was as a major source of intelligence.

The administration of the Borders in the autumn of 1919 presented almost insuperable problems. On the Soviet side of the front, the struggle with Denikin precluded all thoughts of administrative organization. On the Polish side, the occupation of vast additional territories, notably Minsk and Volhynia, well beyond the natural limits of Polish settlement, involved the civil authorities in a social and political problem of intractable complexity. The 'preparation' of the new areas was given to the Straż Kresowa, which, in accordance with an order of 3 October 1919, was to work in close conjunction with the army. The Straż Kresowa, was by no means an instrument of ignorant repression. Its politics were radical and its social philosophy markedly progressive. Its reports stressed that 'the Polish cause was most frequently compromised by the behaviour of the landowning class'.[18] It intended to consolidate Polish influence by enforcing the same far-reaching agrarian reform that had been legislated in Poland. Unfortunately, resistance to their enlightened ideas was general, and not only from the mistrustful Byelorussian and Ukranian peasantry. The army was not interested in social reform; the gendarmerie was violent and corrupt; the civilian commissioners of the Z.C.Z.W. were helpless or incompetent. Worst of all were the great Polish families who returned on the coat tails of the army in full expectation that their rights and privileges would be restored. At Równe, at a meeting of the local landowners on 6 February 1920, the attempts of the liberal Count Zygmunt Krasicki to make proposals for parcelling the land and for its colonization by Polish veterans were rudely shouted down. An officer who watched the proceedings observed that 'the landowners have learned nothing, in spite of the war and of changed social and political conditions. They still intend to exploit their social position and their temporary advantage, to make no sacrifices and to profit as much as they can, even at the cost of their country and of other social classes.'[19] In the district of Łuck, an instructor of the Straż Kresowa reported that the local commissioner would not publish any decree which displeased him, that he extracted illegal contributions in the name of absentee landowners, and that he used the public courts to settle private disputes in favour of people like Princess Maria Lubomirska. 'Poland is a law-abiding country,' he concluded. In the interest of the Republic the guilty must be removed and brought to trial. This alone might yet convince the population of the sincerity of the central government.'[20] Needless to say, an administration battling against typhus, food-shortages, enemy propaganda, and civil obstruction, rarely had the inclination to prosecute its own members.

In the remoter parts, there were villages which resisted all attempts to administer them. In the turbulent years following the collapse of the Tsarist government in 1917, the peasants had formed their own 'village republics', independent in turn from the authority of the Germans, the Directory, and the Bolsheviks. In the course of 1919, the Poles had suppressed these helotocracies, and punished any reversion, as occurred at Sady, Dubno, and Dąbrowica, with draconian severity.

Re-equipment and reorganization of the armies was accelerated by the prospect of continuing hostilities. The improvisations to which both Polish and Soviet commands had resorted in 1919, would no longer suffice in the event of a major confrontation.

The Polish military authorities began to review their effectives as soon as Minsk was captured. In September 1919, the Polish army had 540,000 men under arms, of whom 230,000 manned the Soviet front. The rest were in training or guarding the German frontier. They were due to be joined on 15 November by 101,500 conscripts of the 1900 class and on 15 March of the following year by a further 75,200 of the 1901 class. The stocks and existing cadres were unable to accommodate the increase. Poland's main source of military supply was France, and on 27 September the Ministry of Military Affairs addressed an urgent request to the French government. It estimated that in order to survive the winter some 1,200,000 complete uniforms and 378,000 sets of equipment were required. Shortages in basic armaments were estimated as follows:

Rifles	186,000
Machine guns	620
Ammunition	340,000,000
75 mm guns	400
Ammunition waggons (75 mm guns)	750
75 mm shell	1,200,000
105 mm shell	
155 mm gun (short)	240
155 mm shell	230,000

65 mm mountain gun	30
65 mm mortar bomb	30,000
120 mm shell (long)	4,000

Shortages in railway stock amounted to 2,500 locomotives and 70,000 waggons. In order to soften the impact of his request, General Sosnkowski emphasized that it was made 'le coeur plein de reconnaissance que le peuple polonais accepte d'offrir l'impôt du sang pour maintenir la paix mondiale fixée sur les bases du Congrès de Versailles'.[21] Polish blood was to redeem the Polish budget.

On 15 October, the Polish Prime Minister addressed a still more urgent demand to the British Secretary for War, Winston Churchill:

Sir, I have just received news from our Bolshevist front. The situation there is desperate.

The promises of Mr. Lloyd George made on 27 June to assist our army have not materialised...

We are determined to hold our own against the barbarian bolshevist forces provided that no association with Germany is forced upon us. We have so far, I think, obtained considerable results...

We need 300,000 complete uniforms (greatcoats, tunics, trousers, socks and boots) delivered in Warsaw a fortnight hence at the latest. From your supply of railway rolling-stock now in France we need at least 200 locomotives and 2,000 wagons at once.

If such an assistance is not granted immediately, the entire line of our bolshevist front may break down at any moment and the worst can be expected.

Sir, Your obedient, humble servant, I. J. Paderewski.[22]

The Polish government dangled the Bolshevik bogey before Allied eyes for all it was worth. Yet on 24 October, Churchill replied, with regret, that the British Cabinet had refused to accede to the Polish request.[23] The Cabinet had established the principles that 'help for the Polish Army rested with the Allies generally and only to a very minor degree with Great Britain',[24] and that 'the French ought to take the main responsibility for arming Poland in view of British help for Denikin'.[25] Churchill *was* personally very eager to arm any anti-Bolshevik forces, including the Poles; but his opinion was not generally shared in Whitehall. In November, he succeeded in making Poland a gift of fifty aeroplanes and in February

1920 he let the Poles buy some surplus German rifles. On both occasions the Foreign Secretary, Lord Curzon, protested to the Prime Minister about the flouting of Cabinet decisions.[26]

The French government was somewhat more amenable. It extended a credit of 375 million francs to Poland for military purposes. At first, the Polish Purchasing Agency, headed in Paris by General Pomiankowski, had to pay current prices for all material supplied, even for captured German Mausers. Later, a fifty per cent discount was allowed, as on the important artillery stores forwarded from the warehouses of the 'Armée d'Orient' in Salonika and Galatea. Some twenty million francs were used to buy 100,000 Austrian Mannlicher rifles in Italy, along with a consignment of Balilla aircraft.

The United States government provided credit of fifty-six million dollars to cover its release to Poland of stocks left in France by the American army.

Poland's main supply problem lay in transporting her purchases back home. Only three routes were available—the first by rail through Italy (Turin-Vienna-Cracow), the second through Germany (Koblenz-Cottbus-Leszno), the third by sea to Danzig. The first route was frequently interrupted by the Czechoslovaks; the second was closed from May 1920 by the Germans; the third was interrupted first by strikes of the Danzig workers and eventually cut in August 1920 by the Red Cavalry.

Soviet Russia, of course, could not rely directly on foreign aid. The Red Army was supplied with what the workers and peasants could forge for themselves or what they could capture from their enemies. Until the Donbass was conquered at the end of 1919, only two major armaments factories, at Tula and Simbirsk, were in operation. They were producing less than 50,000 rifles a month for an army which in July 1919 was two million strong. Virtually no sophisticated military equipment was being produced. Soviet Russia produced its first aero-engine in June 1920. The total number of aeroplanes built or restored by the end of 1920 was 462. Since the demands of the Soviet Western Front enjoyed lowest priority until the end of 1919, the state of provision and supply there must have been far inferior to that of the Poles. Against this, one must allow for the fact that a fair proportion of Denikin's £100 million British

trousseau found its way into the bottom drawer of the
Bolsheviks. Hence the Allies unwittingly supplied both sides
in the Polish-Soviet War.

The Polish-Soviet front was significantly replenished during
and after the period of the secret negotiations. The Poles, with
fewer distractions, made a better start. Whereas the total
number of men available was steadily increased, the actual
number of men on the frontline was greatly reduced. In this
way, tactical reserves were concentrated at Wilno, Grodno,
and Kamenets-Podolsk, and a strategic reserve in Poland
proper. The Polish occupation of Pomerania, completed in
February 1920, and the arrival in Upper Silesia and Teschen
of Allied Plebiscite garrisons released further units. In due
course, the structure of command was transformed in response
to the new dispositions. By an order of 19 March 1920 the
status of the central command was significantly raised.
Piłsudski, as Commander-in-Chief was given the rank of
Marshal. General Stanisław Haller was confirmed as Chief of
the General Staff. The four separate 'fronts' in the east were
replaced by Army commands. The Byelorussian Front was
renamed First Army, commanded by General Żygadłowicz;
the Polesie Front became the Fourth Army of General
Szeptycki, the Volhynian Front became the Second Army of
General Listowski, the East Galician Front became the Sixth
Army of General Iwaszkiewicz. The Minister of Military
Affairs, General Leśniewski was given responsibility for the
ten divisions still being equipped and trained in the interior.

The fundamental consideration behind the dispositions of
the Polish army was their respect for the disproportionate size
of Soviet Russia. In Polish eyes, the war was a fight between
David and Goliath. Poland's survival depended on the success
of an early blow, which would interrupt the proper mobilization of Russia's superior resources. An early blow meant a
campaign in the south, where the winter ended sooner. The
details of such an offensive were provided by a plan prepared
in February 1919 by General Tadeusz Kutrzeba of the army's
planning office.

The relevant order is contained in a letter dated 22 December
1919 from Section I of the General Staff. It instructed the
Ministry of Military Affairs to bring the army by the first

days of April to a state of readiness 'not merely to resist
Bolshevik attacks but to permit a definitive settlement of the
Russian question.'[27]

Soviet preparations were slow to start. The Western Front
had been long neglected. Although Stalinist writers habitually
claimed that the Western Front was strengthened by Trotsky
in his devious efforts to contrive Soviet defeat on the fronts
where Stalin was operating, there is little evidence for this.
Certainly after the fall of Wilno in April 1919 the Red Army
had nothing to spare. Despite Trotsky's supposed efforts, one
regiment of the 8th Division found itself with only forty men.
The Western Front did not benefit until the end of the year
from the decree of 1 July 1919 for a regular, integrated Red
Army. The special conscription in the spring of 1919 of workers,
railwaymen, Party members, and criminals, in addition to the
1900 class, produced an army of 2,300,000, swelled in February
1920 by the 550,000 men of the 1901 class. But very few, if
any, of these went west. The integration of the XV (Latvian)
and XVI (Western) and XII (Volhynian) Armies under the
War Council of a united Western Front Command at Smolensk
was offset by the loan of the Latvians to the war against Denikin
and by the formation of labour battalions. At the New Year,
however, the situation changed rapidly. Polish intelligence
summarized the growth of Soviet divisions on the Polish front
as follows:

1 Jan. 1920	4 Infantry Divisions	1 Cavalry Brigade
1 Feb. 1920	5 Infantry Divisions	5 Cavalry Brigades
1 Mar. 1920	8 Infantry Divisions	4 Cavalry Brigades
1 April 1920	14 Infantry Divisions	3 Cavalry Brigades
15 April 1920	16 Infantry Divisions	3 Cavalry Brigades
25 April 1920	20 Infantry Divisions	5 Cavalry Brigades[28]

The reinforcements were distributed mainly among the XV,
III, and XVI Armies, on the northern sector; the XII and
XIV Armies in the south were comparatively weak. The two
main areas of concentration were at Vitebsk and Orsha
opposite the Berezina sector, and at Gomel and Mozyr in
Polesie.

The details of the Red Army's deployment were agreed on
10 March at a meeting at Smolensk between General Gittis,
the commander of the Western Front and Sergey Kamenev,

the new Commander-in-Chief of the Red Army. They adopted
a plan prepared by Shaposhnikov, head of the Red Army's
operations department. They agreed that Poland was the
principal threat to Soviet Russia. They anticipated that
fifteen divisions (99,000 men) should be concentrated on the
Berezina, three in Polesie (27,000 men), and four in Volhynia
(39,300 men) by April, when a major offensive was to be
launched in the direction of Wilno and Lida. The South-
Western Front was to remain at present strength until the
First Cavalry Army could be transferred from the Caucasus.
The Polish forces were to be engaged in Polesie to prevent
them from interfering with the main Soviet thrust in the north
or from mounting a diversion in the south.[29]

At the beginning of March, the Poles decided to deny the
Bolsheviks the use of Mozyr. This junction controlled all traffic
through Polesie into Russia as well as the vital transverse line
joining Vitebsk with Zhitomir. On 5 March, the 9th Infantry
Division, under Sikorski, advanced eastwards in two columns.
Heavy bombardment by railway-borne artillery surprised the
garrison, which had no time to summon aid. Mozyr was
occupied late on the 5th, Kalinkovichi on the 6th and Shachilki
on the 7th. Considerable booty was captured, including several
Dnieper gunboats and guns as well as an armoured train.

Soviet annoyance can be gauged by the fury of an unsuccessful counterattack launched on 19 March from Zhlobin.
Aircraft and tanks were used. The latter were British, captured
from Yudyonich before Petrograd and specially transported
from the north.

The early months of 1920 saw both Poles and Soviets making
urgent preparations for war. The spectacle seriously disturbed
the politicians. Both sides assumed that the other's preparations
gave proof of aggressive designs. Historians have repeated the
assumptions. Anti-communist historians argue that Soviet
Russia's deployment of its vastly superior forces justified Poland in preparing a pre-emptive attack; communist
historians argue that the Entente was schooling the Poles for
an assault on Russia. Neither make fair comment. It is the
duty of armies to prepare for the defeat of the enemy. In a
situation where hostilities had already been in progress for a full
year, the Polish and Soviet commands would have been guilty

of gross dereliction of their duty if they had not made preparations. Generals are expected to fight. It is the job of politicians,
if they can, to catch the dogs of war and put them on the leash.

One problem that was settled in the winter of 1919–20 was
that of Poland's relations with the Entente. The Entente
decided that it would *not* support a Polish attack on Soviet
Russia in the way that Kolchak and Denikin had been
supported. It is worth examining the problem carefully, since
it perplexed politicians at the time and has perplexed historians
ever since.

Soviet historians have always assumed that the Polish
campaigns were an integral part of Allied Intervention. In
Soviet parlance, the Polish-Soviet War is referred to as *Tretiy
Pokhod Antanty* (The Third Campaign of the Entente). Kolchak,
Denikin, and Piłsudski appear as three wicked uncles succes-
sively duped by the Entente into attacking Russia. Piłsudski
conspires with Wrangel, just as Kolchak conspired with
Semyonov and Denikin with Yudyonich. The organizers and
paymasters of the campaign are the imperialists of Britain,
France, and the United States, whose military missions actively
prepare the Polish army for the attack and provide it with
food, arms, and money. Poland always appears as *panskaya
Pol'sha* (lordly Poland); Poles are never referred to as Poles,
but as *belopolyaki* (White Poles).

This curious melodrama can be traced specifically to Stalin,
who first coined the phrase *Tretiy Pokhod Antanty* in a long
article devoted to the periodization of the Civil War which
was published in *Pravda* on 25 May 1920. It was further
ornamented in Stalinist times and erected into the orthodox
Soviet version. Despite a few hesitant attempts to question its
validity, it still holds sway in Soviet historiography.[30] It
originally gained currency, and still enjoys a certain plausi-
bility, because there were people in the Allied countries eager
to play the parts assigned to them. What these people wanted
and what they actually achieved were two different things,
however. They did not get their way. They were baulked
partly by Piłsudski's obstinate refusal to co-operate but
principally by Lloyd George's masterful transformation of
Allied policy at the end of 1919.

Lloyd George's position needs some clarification. He was not an imperious dictator. He was a minority leader in a coalition government, who had to pay inordinate court to the contrary opinions of his Conservative colleagues like Churchill and Curzon. He worked by cunning, not by frontal attack, and it took time. Until the withdrawal of the Americans from the Supreme Allied Council and Clemenceau's fall from power in France at the beginning of 1920, he had no special influence among the Allied leaders. Although he hated the Soviet system as much as anyone, he had a sneaking admiration for revolutionaries. Lord Curzon once remarked that 'the trouble with the P.M. is that he is a bit of a Bolshevik himself. One feels that he sees Trotsky as the only congenial figure on the international scene.'[31] Lloyd George was unable in the early stages to prevent Intervention, but consistently argued that it was a waste of time and money. He believed that it would strengthen the Bolshevik régime and arouse the Russian people's natural fear of foreigners. He proposed that Bolshevism should be killed by kindness—that by reopening trade and thus restoring Russia's prosperity the Allied powers could benefit themselves and at the same-time remove that state of chaos and hardship on which Bolshevism thrived. Although he declared his personal opposition to intervention in Russia as early as 16 April 1919, when he said in the Commons that he would 'rather see Russia Bolshevik than Britain bankrupt', it was November before his policy was adopted by the Cabinet, and January 1920 before it was adopted by the Entente as a whole.

Lloyd George's position gradually improved as intervention failed. In the autumn of 1919, when British expenditure in Russia had reached £94 million without showing any results, he was able to persuade the cabinet to deny Churchill any further funds. On 9 November, speaking at the annual Guildhall Banquet, he announced a new initiative to reopen trade with Russia. On 12 December, he joined with Clemenceau in supporting the static concept of the 'barbed wire fence' round Soviet Russia, as opposed to the previous active concept of intervention. Finally, on 16 January at a conference in Paris, he succeeded in persuading the Allied leaders to undertake 'the exchange of goods with the Russian people whilst maintaining their boycott of the Bolshevik government'.[32] It was this occasion which prompted the famous outburst of the *New York Times:* 'This reversal of world policy overnight bears the unmistakable signature of the artist...Mr. Lloyd George, whose brilliant improvisations display the agility of a Rocky Mountain goat'.[33] From that point on, Lloyd George was in sole command of Allied policy.

Allied attitudes to Poland underwent a parallel transformation. In 1919, the interventionists assumed that Poland, as an Allied country, would participate in Allied intervention. In particular, they expected Poland to collaborate with Denikin. In September, Paderewski submitted a scheme whereby a Polish army of 500,000 men would march on Moscow at a cost to the Allies of £1 million a day. But a meeting of the Supreme Council on 15 September categorically rejected it. Clemenceau objected on the grounds that a Polish invasion would rally all Russia to the Bolsheviks; Lloyd George 'suggested that Paderewski should be told the Allied powers did not want him to act;' Mr Polk for the United States, said that his country was 'not ready to find money to enable them to wage war.'[34] In October, as already detailed, the British Cabinet refused Poland's request for military aid. On 8 December, the Supreme Council approved a provisional frontier between Poland and Russia, later called the 'Curzon Line'.[35] On 12 December, in conformity with the 'barbed wire' policy, Poland's function was defined 'as a barrier against Russia and a check on Germany'.[36] The final clarification was made on 15 January when the Polish Foreign Minister, Patek, visited Lloyd George in person. Lloyd George's secretary made the following note of their conversation:

PM meets Patek at breakfast. From his extravagant claims for Polish boundaries scents that an early offensive is in the wind. Utters a word of warning as to the consequences of provocative action of the kind. Disclaims all responsibility.[37]

After a further meeting on 26 January, the Cabinet approved the following principles of British policy:

1. The Border states must take responsibility themselves concerning war or peace.

2. H.M.G. could not advise war since it would incur responsibilities which it could not discharge.
3. Great Britain entertained feelings of the most sincere friendship for Poland.[38]

To be precise, Allied policy sought to discourage Poland from attacking Russia whilst yet providing her with the means of defence. Without formally forbidding a Polish offensive, they emphasised that it could not enjoy their support.

Allied military assistance to Poland was only matched to limited, defensive purposes. The French military credit of 375 million francs may sound enormous. In fact it was far from generous. 375 million francs would not have covered one day's expenditure on the French army during the World War; it represented a sum which, on Paderewski's estimate of September 1919, would have been exhausted in five weeks by the cost merely of feeding and clothing the existing Polish army; it was equal to only one sixth of the sum expended by the British government in 1919 on Denikin. No serious logistics expert can suggest that 375 million francs was intended to finance a Polish invasion of Russia. Furthermore, Allied assistance for Poland was directed more against German revanchism than against Bolshevik revolution. Poland was to be 'a barrier against Russia and a check on Germany', *not* a check against Russia and a barrier against Germany. On the same day that the Supreme Allied Council rejected Paderewski's plan to use the Polish army against the Bolsheviks in Russia they authorized its use, if necessary, against the Germans in the Baltic States.[39]

It is important not to underestimate Piłsudski's independence from the Entente. He was quite capable of accepting military assistance from the Allies and of using it for purposes which they had categorically forbidden. Whenever they tried to impose conditions on their assistance, he replied that Poland could do without it. As France and Great Britain knew to their cost, Piłsudski tolerated no interference, least of all from patronizing allies. He was the leader of the anti-Entente wing in Polish politics. He came to power without Allied knowledge or consent. His main rivals for office were the Allied-sponsored National Democrats, whose sense of outrage was only partially quelled by the compromise of Paderewski's coalition ministry. Paderewski's resignation on 30 November 1919, which was largely occasioned by his inability to bridge the gulf between Piłsudski's policies and Allied demands, ushered in a period where feeble ministers were easily bullied and overruled. In their moments of deepest frustration, the Allied governments were willing to believe that Piłsudski was in league with Lenin.[40]

It is equally important to understand the claustrophobia reigning in Russia. Neither the Bolshevik leaders nor the Soviet public were aware of the niceties of Allied policy. All they saw was Soviet Russia surrounded on every side by armies bent on her destruction. It was the most natural thing in the world for them to assume that the armies were operating in collusion.

Soviet historians continue to support the theory of the collusion of the 'imperialist' powers with Poland in 1919–20. Their conclusions are the result of dialectical thinking. They would argue that any scientific interpretation of the war must take into account the total balance of forces. They minimize the role of political will and individual opinions. They would contend that Poland was inescapably bound to the Entente by ideology, by finance, by military aid, and by the common hostility to Bolshevism. They would maintain that anything which strengthened Poland automatically increased her capacity to fight against Soviet Russia. They regard the work of the American Relief Administration, for instance, whose work was exclusively civilian, as an invaluable contribution to the Polish war effort—claiming that by providing food and care for four million Poles in 1919–20, the ARA automatically freed Poland's own resources for the use of the Polish army. Their arguments are, of course, logically correct. Their weakness lies in their irrelevance to the springs of political action and in their failure to put the Allied contribution to the Polish-Soviet War into any true proportion. Their concern with the total balance of forces implies that Poland was supported by the entire military and economic capacity of the Entente, whereas in effect only an infinitesimal fraction of that capacity was made available.

The role of the Allied military missions is full of contradictions. The British mission in Warsaw was highly embarrassed by the Cabinet's refusal to send the supplies requested. It degenerated to a source of military intelligence on Russia for the War Office. Its chief, General Adrian Carton de Wiart VC, was a wasted asset. This indestructible warrior, who had lost an eye in Somaliland in '98 and a hand at Ypres, who had been shot through the lung in South Africa, through the skull and the ankle on the Somme, through the hip at Passchendaele and through the leg at Cambrai, possessed all the qualities best designed to appeal to the Polish officers among whom he was sent. He was wealthy, aristocratic, cosmopolitan, Catholic, heroic, and indefatigably foolhardy. He was one of the few men to enjoy the confidence of the reserved Piłsudski. He first came to Poland in February 1919 as the British member of the Allied Mission to East Galicia. From then on, his life was a series of escapades. There was the occasion when he was involved with General Mannerheim, future president of Finland, in seconding a dueller at the Myśliwski Club in Warsaw, and another soon after when he was compromised in a gun-running operation from Budapest using stolen wagon-lits. In October 1919, he crashed his plane while flying over Lithuania and in May 1920 crashed it again when trying to reach Kiev. At Mława in August 1920, he fought off a detachment of marauding Cossacks from the running board of his observation train, having at one point in his enthusiasm fallen onto the track. According to the ethos of the day, he was more Polish than the Poles. After the war he stayed in Poland as a private citizen, occupying himself with one-handed duck-shooting on an estate in Polesie presented to him by his former ADC, Prince Charles Radziwiłł.

The French Military Mission enjoyed quite the opposite reputation from the British. Unlike Carton de Wiart, its chief, General Henrys was regarded by the Polish Staff as a feather-brained busybody. He was studiously ignored by Piłsudski. He was eager for *la gloire*, and earnestly intrigued for a Polish offensive in the east, regardless of the caution expressed by his own government in Paris or by the Allied diplomats in Warsaw. In contrast to its chief, however, the French mission commanded considerable respect and influence through the activities of its 400 officer-instructors. These men, distributed among the cadres of the Polish Staff, were entrusted with the task of training the officer corps in the art of military science and in the use of the French army manuals. Typical of them was a young captain, Charles de Gaulle. Newly released from internment as a prisoner of war at Ingolstadt in Bavaria, de Gaulle had been anxious for active service; as the son of a patriotic Catholic family, he was attracted by the prospect of an anti-Bolshevik campaign in Poland. In May 1919, he joined the 5th Chasseurs Polonais at Sillé-le-Guillaume and in the body of Haller's army travelled with them to East Galicia. At the end of that campaign, he was transferred to Rembertów near Warsaw where, in the former school of the Tsarist Imperial Guard, he lectured on the theory of tactics. In July and August 1920 he was attached for a short period to a Polish combat unit, and raised to the rank of major. In 1921, he was offered a permanent commission in Poland, but preferred to develop his ideas and experiences by returning to France as a lecturer on military history at Saint-Cyr.

The failure of the Mikaszewice negotiations in December 1919 produced a flurry of political activity. Although peace had not yet been definitively abandoned, both sides were considering alternative arrangements.

Soviet Russia followed a double policy. One part of the policy called for an immediate strengthening of the Western Front. Marchlewski on his return to Moscow from Mikaszewice sounded the alarm. He thought the reports of poor morale in the Polish army were much exaggerated. 'If the Poles get the order, they will march,' he said, '...and such is the state of our Western Army, that they will march into Smolensk and Gomel as if on parade.'[41] Lenin heeded the warning. Without waiting for the final defeat of Denikin, he sent the following note to the War Council:

27 Feb. 1920—All the indications are that Poland will present us with absolutely impossible, even insolent conditions. It is essential that all our attention be turned to strengthening the Western Front. I consider it imperative, that exceptional measures be taken to effect a lightning transfer of whatever we can from Siberia and the Urals to the west. It is necessary to issue the slogan 'prepare for war with Poland.' Lenin[42]

The second part of the Soviet policy was a diplomatic 'peace campaign'. On 22 December 1919, the Commissariat for Foreign Affairs sent the following note to Warsaw:

As early as April of last year the Russian Soviet government gave the representative of the Polish Republic, Mr Więckowski, repeated assurances of its immutable desire to terminate the bloodshed between the peoples of Russia and Poland... Our proposals for peace received no reply and during the following months the Polish army advanced into the territory of Soviet republics allied to Soviet Russia.

The Soviet government learned with great surprise, therefore, that on 28 November in answer to a question in the Polish Sejm, Assistant State Secretary Skrzyński replied not simply that the Russian Republic had never proposed peace but even that it was threatening Poland with invasion...Wishing to set aside any misunderstandings, the Soviet government repeats its earlier assurances of its firm desire to end the conflict with Poland. The Soviet government formally proposes to begin negotiations as soon as possible with a view to concluding a just and lasting peace.

Peace between Poland and Russia is a vital condition for the development and prosperity of both countries...The Soviet government expresses the hope that the peaceful intentions, evidenced by the majority of the Polish people, will prevail and will facilitate the termination of hostilities which only serve foreign interests.

The Soviet government proposes that the Polish government indicate the place and time for negotiations to begin, with a view to the conclusion of a peace treaty between the two republics.

People's Commissar for Foreign Affairs, Chicherin.[43]

Not having received a reply, on 28 January 1920 Chicherin sent a more specific note signed by Lenin and Trotsky. It contained a promise that the Red Army would not cross a line corresponding in the main to existing fronts. At the same time, the Central Executive Committee of the Soviets was persuaded to address a public appeal to the Polish nation. It stressed the common interest of the Russian and Polish 'working people' and their common history of war, foreign exploitation, and Tsarism. It contained the following statement:

We, the representatives of the Russian proletariat and peasantry, have always openly acted before the whole world as fighters for communist ideals. We are deeply convinced that the working people of all countries will follow the same road as that on which the Russian working people have already embarked.

But you are deceived when our common enemies say that the Russian Soviet government wishes to impose communism on Poland at the point of the Red Army's bayonets. A communist régime is only possible where the assembled majority of the working people have stated their desire to progress under their own power...At present, the communists of Russia intend only to protect their own land, their own peaceful and constructive work. They are not thinking, nor can they think about the forcible imposition of communism on foreign lands. The reorganization of Poland in the interests of the Polish toiling masses must be seen to be the work of those same toiling masses.

[Signed] Kalinin, Chairman, Central Executive Committee.[44]

This statement was to be remembered in Poland in the summer.

The tactics of the Soviets' peace campaign were based on their rooted belief that the Allied governments were pushing a reluctant Piłsudski along the warpath, and not vice-versa. The belief can be documented not only in Soviet propaganda, but equally in private letters, such as Marchlewski's. It was a belief which totally ignored the radical change in Allied policy, which Lloyd George had recently engineered. The Soviet notes carefully avoided any personal embarrassment to Piłsudski. They aimed to discredit those elements in Polish politics which were connected with the Entente, particularly the National Democrats, and to leave Piłsudski free to make peace with the backing of popular and radical opinion. The tactics were misplaced. Unbeknown to the Bolshevik leaders, it was Piłsudski, impressed more by the actions of the enemy's generals than by the words of his diplomats, who was dragging the reluctant Allies towards war.

Polish historians have traditionally explained the Soviet double policy in terms of innate 'Bolshevik aggression'. But it is equally explicable in terms of the Bolsheviks very real fears. Bolshevik reactions were conditioned by two years of blockade and bullying. They had been attacked so often, that they automatically braced themselves for the expected blow. Their generals reacted with customary bravado, their diplomats with their customary mixture of sweet reasonableness and impudence. These were ingrained Bolshevik defence mechanisms.

The effect of the Soviet peace campaign on Polish politics was the opposite of that intended. Far from facilitating a *rapprochement* between Piłsudski and the Left, it drove him into the arms of the National Democratic Party. The Soviet notes were accompanied in Poland by a wave of strikes organized by the communists and a vociferous press campaign for peace mounted by the socialists. In its frustration, the Left turned on the Government. It appeared that the internal accomplices of Bolshevism were trying to subvert the Republic. Piłsudski was given no alternative but to suppress the strikes, to ignore the socialists, and to suffer the applause of a party who were quite unsympathetic to his real intentions.

Piłsudski's dilemma in the spring of 1920 was acute. He was far from confident in the ability of his army to survive if the war continued; he had no illusions about its fate if the Red Army struck first. He could not easily make peace, so long as peace could be interpreted as appeasement of the strikers; he could not easily make war, without flouting the advice of the Allies. He hated the threat of war which accompanied the discussions about peace. As he told a correspondent of *Le Petit Parisien*:

> Unfortunately, my impression of Bolshevik behaviour is that peace is out of the question. If someone puts a knife to my throat I have an unpleasant feeling. I am not a man to whom one can speak in such a manner.
>
> I know the Bolsheviks are concentrating large forces on our front. They are making a mistake, thinking they can frighten us and present us with an ultimatum. Our army is ready.[45]

His natural warrior's instinct told him to fight his way out of an intolerable corner The honourable move was to fight and to go down fighting. The military considerations were more comprehensible to him than the political, and he knew that eight weeks would suffice for the Red Army to mobilize overpowering superiority At some point in February or March he made the choice within himself to launch the pre-emptive attack he had long considered But he brooded, and he hesitated. Whilst preparing for war, he still prolonged the talk of peace. He had reached exactly the same state of indecision which had beset the Soviet leadership for months past.

In such a situation, the Soviet peace notes were lost in a welter of mistrust. Neither side was prepared to suspend its military preparations as a sign of good faith. The Polish Foreign Minister, Patek, was harried to make a definite reply, first by a communication of the Ukranian Soviet Republic on 22 February and then by a reminder from Moscow on 6 March;[46] but he clearly had no conception of what he should say. He eventually responded on 27 March, sending a note marked 'Très urgent' in reply to Chicherin's of 22 December.[47] He suggested that *pourparlers* should begin on 10 April in the Polish bridgehead town of Borisov on the Berezina. Chicherin countered with a demand for a ceasefire and for a different rendezvous, preferably in Estonia.[48] From then on, the correspondence deteriorated into a meaningless wrangle over whether Borisov was, or was not, a suitable place to talk. On 20 April in Warsaw and on 23 April in Moscow, bulletins were issued where each side blamed the other for the breakdown.[49] Although the Foreign Ministry in Warsaw did prepare its peace terms, they were never communicated to Moscow. Similarly, the Poles never received any indication of what the Soviet terms might be, beyond the worrying news that the line of 28 January was no longer acceptable.[50] The failure of the proposed Borisov *pourparlers* is often put forward as the point of no return in the drift to war. This is not so. The correspondence between Chicherin and Patek was an elaborate pantomime designed to reassure the professional diplomats that their existence was not entirely superfluous. They had lost control of events long since. Even if, for form's sake, the Polish and Soviet negotiators had actually met at Borisov, it is inconceivable in the prevailing atmosphere of deep suspicion that they could ever have reached an agreement.

Already by the middle of April, the Polish army had been raised to a state of readiness. On the 14th, all Polish officers were withdrawn from training schools and sent to the front. On the 17th the General Staff issued the order for the army to take up forward positions within the week.

The Red Army was less prepared. Although their numbers were swelling rapidly, the final groupings, as determined by the order of War Council of the Western Front of 10 March, had still not been effected. The Western Front Command was still waiting for its shock troops. The First Cavalry Army, (Konarmiya) which had driven Denikin into the sea at

Novorossiysk in February, only began its westwards march on
1 April. It had a thousand miles to cover. The Red Army
could not be completely ready for eight weeks at least. This
delay gave the Poles their hope of salvation.

Meanwhile, Piłsudski was solving a long-standing problem
of private diplomacy. In his mind, he was building a Federation
of Border States, and he badly needed an accomplice. He went
to great lengths to find one. In September, he had sent General
Karnicki to Denikin's headquarters to explore the prospect of
co-operation. The mission persevered for several months and
was vigorously encouraged from London, first by Churchill's
letters then by visits to Warsaw by Major-General Greenly in
November and Sir Halford Mackinder in December. But it
soon became obvious that the 'great white hope' had no intention whatsoever of encouraging even Polish independence, not
to mention a whole federation of breakaway Russian provinces.
In January 1920 Piłsudski turned his attention to the Conference
of Baltic States at Helsinki. His delegates supported a proposal
for forming an anti-Bolshevik military convention. He enjoyed
good relations with Finland, whose President, Mannerheim,
knew Poland well from his days as a Tsarist general and who
had recently revisited his old haunts in Warsaw. His standing
in Latvia was high, in consequence of the Dunaburg campaign.
But Estonia, which made peace with the Soviets on 2 February,
was only lukewarm, and Lithuania, inconsolable over the fate
of Wilno, was virulently hostile. The Lithuanians were
beginning to realize that their only hope of recovering Wilno
was to side with the Soviets. Again, although the conference
persevered for several months, its deliberations were fruitless.
Between 16 and 20 January, Piłsudski received Savinkov and
Tchaikovsky, the representatives of Prince Lvov's Russian
delegation in Paris. Although these gentlemen were somewhat
more reasonable than Denikin had been, the contemporary
news of Denikin's last stand at Baltaysk robbed them of their
claims to represent any authority in Russia outside the Crimea.
Soon after, Piłsudski received Take Ionescu, Foreign Minister
of Rumania, who, whilst expressing general sympathy, was not
prepared to provoke the Bolsheviks by joining any anti-
Bolshevik venture. Early in February, Piłsudski sent Titus

Filipowicz to Georgia with a view to exploring the disposition of the Menshevik governments of the Caucasus. He found them fighting for their life. When Azerbaijan fell to the Reds in April, Armenia and Georgia were stranded. The only possible ally whom Piłsudski is not known to have contacted is Nestor Makhno, whose anarchist bands had recently destroyed Denikin's rear in the southern Ukraine and who might conceivably have relished the traditional Cossack role of Poland's freebooting ally on the flank of the Muscovites. Thus by a process of elimination, Piłsudski was left with Semyon Petlura.

Petlura's politics did have some watery resemblance to Piłsudski's own. He was a Ukranian nationalist, devoted first and foremost to the independence of his country; his social philosophy was socialist and radical; he condemned the exploitation of the Ukraine by Russian landowners and foreign capitalists; he was as much a warlord as a politician, who had defended his ideals sword in hand. His movement first emerged in Kiev in 1917 after the February Revolution. In January 1918, his Directory was represented at the conference of Brest-Litovsk and at one stage recognized by the Bolsheviks as the legal representative of the Ukraine. In 1919, having been ousted from the Civil War by each of the successive factions, he ended up first in an enclave at Kamenets Podolsk and finally in Polish protective custody. But in three years of political life he failed to meet the challenges of all with whom he came in contact. He was defeated by the Ukrainian Reds in 1918, deposed by the Germans and decimated by Denikin. The French distrusted his criticisms of foreign investment, fearing nationalization, and the English deplored his clash with Denikin. Of all the Ukrainian factions, Petlura could boast the least vigour and the weakest following. His only virtue was that he had survived. With his shining black hair smartly brushed back, neatly parted and incongrously surmounted by a British brass hat, he looked the perfect image of a rising corporal, and as such he suited Piłsudski's purposes. The winter of 1919–20 witnessed the inexorable reconquest of the Ukraine by the Reds—Kiev in December, Rostov in January, Odessa in February. The Ukrainian wheatlands were the most valuable granary of Eastern Europe; the Donbass coal and steel region its most formidable industrial complex. With the Ukraine, Soviet Russia could reforge the economic and political predominance of the Tsarist Empire; without it, she would be reduced to a shivering northern rump, incapable of feeding and equipping her people. With the Ukraine, Piłsudski's Border Federation had a real chance of prosperity and survival. Poland, as chief sponsor, could command a network of trade and commerce stretching from Finland to the Near East. Poland might recover the glory of her medieval past when, or so the story goes, as arbiter of a realm vaster than the Holy Roman Empire, she ruled over Cossacks and Tartars and drove the cringing princes of Muscovy to their lair. Without the Ukraine, the Border States would be so many barbs on an Allied fence.

It is essential to be precise about the moment at which Piłsudski succumbed to the alliance with Petlura. He succumbed much later than most historians suppose. It was an afterthought, not a long planned move. When on 17 April 1920 he gave the vital order to launch the offensive against Kiev, he still had not treated with Petlura. Soldier that he was, he first put the army in order, committed himself to the attack and then, only then, gave thought to the political details. He was confident that the Polish army could reach Kiev. But what would happen after Kiev was captured? The Poles could not garrison the Ukraine; they could not pursue the Red Army into the heart of Russia. They had to find someone to form and maintain an independent Ukrainian state friendly to Poland.

Piłsudski undertook the alliance with Petlura in the frame of mind of a man who, having set out to cross the Sahara, will hire anything with a hump. The Polish federalists demanded a federation; the new Polish landlord of the Ukraine needed a caretaker. Ataman Petlura, who in Piłsudski's earlier search for a collaborator had been constantly rejected, now at the eleventh hour, became Poland's official ally.

The political agreement was signed on 21 April 1920 in Warsaw:

The Government of the Polish Republic on the one hand and the Government of the People's Republic of the Ukraine on the other, deeply convinced that each nation possesses the inalienable right to self-determination...have agreed to the following propositions:

I

In view of the right of the Ukraine to an independent state existence within the frontiers which to the north, east and south shall be agreed with her neighbours, the Polish Republic recognizes the Directory, headed by Ataman Semyon Petlura, as the supreme authority of the Ukrainian People's Republic.

II

The frontier between the Polish Republic and the Ukrainian People's Republic shall be defined as follows: River Zbrucz-former Austro-Hungarian frontier to Wyszegrodek-the Krzemienieckie Heights-eastern boundary of Równe district and of the former Minsk Province-River Pripet. The districts of Równe, Dubno and Krzemieniec, at present in Poland, will be the subject of later, more precise agreement...

III

The Polish Government acknowledges as Ukrainian such territories to the east of the frontier described in Art. II and up to pre-Partition Polish frontier of 1772, that Poland already possesses or will gain from Russia by military or diplomatic means.

IV

Each Government undertakes not to sign any international agreement directed against the other.

V

The national-cultural rights which the Polish Government guarantees for its citizens of Ukrainian nationality, shall be guaranteed to no lesser degree for Ukrainian citizens of Polish nationality.

VI

Economic and commercial agreements shall be confirmed between Poland and the Ukraine. The agrarian question in the Ukraine shall be determined by a Constituent Assembly. Until the Constituent Assembly is convened, however, the position of Polish landowners in the Ukraine shall be the subject of a special understanding.

VII

A military convention, which shall form an integral part of this present agreement, shall be concluded.

André Livytsky	Jan Dąbski
(Permanent Secretary for	(Permanent Secretary for
Foreign Affairs,	Foreign Affairs.
Ukrainian People's Republic)	Republic of Poland)[51]

The economic treaty was, of course, never implemented, but a draft exists to show what was in mind.[52] The Polish government sought to secure the free transfer of goods, a number of profitable concessions and the improvement of communications. Poland was to import from the Ukraine without restriction food products, iron ore, manganese, scrap, rags, wool, bristles, hides, sugar, linen, hemp, livestock; the Ukraine was to import agricultural machinery, tools, oil, and textiles. The Polish government was to receive concessions at Karnavatka and Kolachevskoye, both important iron ore mines in Krivoy Rog, and preference in the development of phosphate deposits at Vankovka in Podolia. Elaborate arrangements were designed to enable Polish trains to exploit the existing Ukrainian railways, and three new lines were to be built. Poland was to enjoy concessions in the ports of Kherson, Nikolayev, and Odessa, and a plan was to be prepared for a Vistula–Dnieper Waterway. All Polish concessions were to be covered by 99-year leases. This hardly amounted to an attempt to turn the Ukraine into a Polish colony. But in view of the fact that Krivoy Rog turned out in the next decade to be one of the richest ore fields in the world and Dniepropetrovsk a kingpin of the Soviet Five-Year-Plans, it is interesting to speculate what might have happened had the Poles become their master.

The military convention was signed on 24 April.[53] It provided for combined operations, for the subjection to Polish command of all Ukrainian forces up to the Dnieper, for the provisioning of the Polish army on Ukrainian soil by the Ukrainians, for the arming of the Ukrainian army by the Poles, and for the eventual withdrawal of all Polish forces. As with the political treaty, it showed all the signs of last-minute haste.

For Piłsudski, the Ukrainian treaties provided the necessary ritual to bless his sword. But he could not wait for their provisions to be put into effect. He arrived at his headquarters at Równe on 22 April. Before the ink of the treaties was dry, the offensive was underway. The rhinoceros had charged.

CHAPTER THREE

THE INVASION OF THE UKRAINE

With the Kiev operation, one reaches the stage at which the Polish–Soviet War is usually supposed to have 'broken out'. On this point British writers carelessly follow the prejudices of Russians. Thus, in 1919, when the Polish–Soviet War was vital only to Poland, they pretend it did not really exist; in 1920, when it became vital to Russia also, they suddenly discover an 'outbreak'. E. H. Carr, for instance, is persistently wayward on Polish matters. Nor is it an accident. In 1920 Carr visited Poland in his capacity as an observer for the Council of Allied Ambassadors and is on record as telling his superiors 'not to take the new nations of Europe too seriously' and advising that their affairs 'belong principally to the sphere of farce'.[1] When he reappears thirty years later as a leading historian of Soviet Russia, it is not surprising to find him among those who talk of 'the outbreak of war with Poland in May 1920'.[2]

The Kiev operation transformed the scale, the intensity, and the stakes of the war entirely. It has a unique character which is impossible to convey by maps and diagrams. It was certainly much grander than the operations of 1919. Yet it was something frail and fleeting compared to the massive movements of the First World War or even to the later events of 1920. It provides the spectacle of border warfare in its purest form. Speed and dash were at a premium. 'We ran all the way to Kiev', a Polish veteran commented, 'and we ran all the way back'. (See map, p. 107)

The exact balance of forces in the Ukraine in April 1920 can not be calculated with any certainty. The opposing staffs did not know what it was, and spent much time after the war contesting each other's calculations. According to Kakurin and Melikov, the total number of men available to the Red Army for service on the South-West Front on 20 March was 82,847. But of these only 28,568 were fighting men (*boytsy*). Two armies were ranged against the Poles, the XII and the XIV. The former, with 13,731 bayonets and 1663 sabres, was not a strong force, whilst the latter, with 4590 bayonets and 204 sabres, was hardly up to the establishment of a division.[3] According to Kutrzeba, the Polish Army enjoyed a superiority of three divisions. The Soviet authors of *Grazhdanskaya Vojna* (1930) claim that the Poles enjoyed a superiority of 52,000 to 12,000.[4] One must remember, however, that with on average only one soldier for each square mile of the theatre of operations, total numbers are meaningless. It is sufficient to know that the Polish concentrations were more than adequate in face of their objectives.

The Polish forces were concentrated in five groupings. In the north, the 4th Infantry Division with the Group of Colonel Rybak was in touch with the Fourth Army in Polesie. In the centre was the Third Army Group of General Śmigły-Rydz at Novograd and General Listowski's Second Army at Shepetovka. Behind them, at Rogachev, were the two brigades of General Romer's Cavalry Division. In the south, on the Dniester was General Iwaszkiewicz's Sixth Army. Śmigły-Rydz's Attack Group, consisting of the 1st Legionary Division, the 7th Infantry Division, and 3rd Cavalry Division, supported by artillery, three platoons of armoured cars, and two columns of motorized transport, was to provide the main strike force, whilst General Romer's cavalry was to deliver the initial tactical blow aimed at the railway junction of Kazatin. In front of them, the Soviet XII Army of Mezhaninov based on Kiev held the 150 miles between the Pripet and the Boh. The tiny XIV Army of Uboryevich based on Zhmerinka, guarded the Dniester.

Soviet difficulties were seriously aggravated by a mutiny which broke out on the eve of the offensive. The mutineers belonged to two of the Red Army's three Galician brigades. They were men recruited the previous year among the Ukrainian population of East Galicia to fight the Poles. But they were brought up to an area round Khmelnik, where Petlura's 'Premier', Isaak Mazeppa, had maintained the vestiges of the Directory's authority. When on 23 April one of

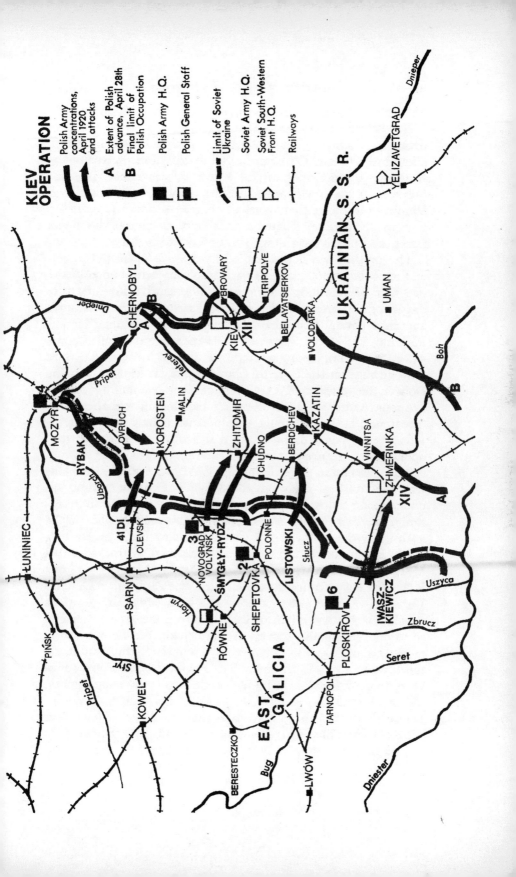

KIEV OPERATION

A	Polish Army concentrations, April 1920 and attacks
B	Extent of Polish advance, April 28th
	Final limit of Polish Occupation
■□	Polish Army H.Q.
□	Polish General Staff
▬▬	Limit of Soviet Ukraine
□	Soviet Army H.Q.
⬠	Soviet South-Western Front H.Q.
	Railways

UKRAINIAN S. S. R.

Dnieper

YELIZAVETGRAD

CHERNOBYL

BROVARY

TRIPOLYE

UMAN

KIEV XII

BELAYATSERKOV

VOLODARKA

Pripet

Teterev

Dnieper

MOZYR

OVRUCH

KOROSTEN

MALIN

ZHITOMIR

CHUDNO

BERDICHEV

KAZATIN

Boh

RYBAK

Uborc

4† DI

OLEVSK

NOVOGRAD VOLYNSK

3

POLONNE

ŠMYGŁY-RYDZ

2

SHEPETOVKA

LISTOWSKI

Słucz

VINNITSA

ZHMERINKA

XIV

ŁUNINIEC

SARNY

Horyn

RÓWNE

6

IWASZ-KIEWICZ

Uszyca

PIŃSK

PINSK

Styr

Pripet

KOWEL

BERESTECZKO

Bug

EAST GALICIA

LWÓW

PLOSKIROV

TARNOPOL

Zbrucz

Seret

Dniester

Petlura's Ukrainian divisions was moved to the front in the body of the Polish Second Army, the Galicians found the bonds of national solidarity pulled more strongly than Bolshevik discipline. The 2nd Galician Brigade which formed part of the XII Army, went over to the Polish side *en masse*. The 3rd Galician Brigade which was in the XIV Army's reserve at Vinnitsa turned on their Russian comrades. Some 11,000 men were involved. They formed a sizeable proportion of the Soviet forces, and paralysed the whole at a critical moment.[5]

The mutiny was accompanied by a wave of partisan raids on the Soviet rear. Kutrzeba estimated that some 12,000 White irregulars were still operating in the Western Ukraine after the dispersion of Denikin. Even more serious were Makhno's anarchist bands, centred on Gulaypolye east of the Dnieper. Makhno was at the height of his career. He controlled some 55,000 men who, having wrought havoc to Denikin's rear, were now turning on the Soviets. On 25 April, at Marinka on the Donets, they massacred a regiment of the Ukrainian *Trudarmiya* (Labour Army). A rash of bridge-blowing in the Kiev area threatened to bring Soviet transport to a halt and the XII Army was obliged to carry out a series of search-and-destroy operations to secure its communications.

The dislocation of XII and XIV Armies was in a curious way the cause of their salvation. When Piłsudski sprang his offensive on 25 April, the Soviets were in no state to resist. Śmigły-Rydz's Third Army swept into Zhitomir at dawn on the 26th—fifty-five miles and twenty-four hours from the starting point. His motor columns, advancing along field tracks instead of the paved road, achieved maximum surprise. Colonel Rybak's Group rolled into Korosten the same day. General Listowski reached Berdyczew on the 27th when also Romer's cavalry fought its way into Kazatin. On the extreme flanks of the front, seeing the success of the centre, the Fourth Army moved out of Polesie up to Chernobyl and the Sixth Army in the south walked into Zhmerinka. The Soviets staged a number of rearguard actions—at Malin, at Chudnov on the Teterev, which delayed General Listowski for a day, and in Kazatin, where they tried in vain to save their artillery. Their losses were considerable. Forty per cent of the 7th Rifle Division fell at Malin when they charged a Polish cavalry brigade with bayonets. The confusion was enormous. The 44th Rifle Division lost all contact with its staff, its artillery and its ammunition. Its remnants were found wandering two days later. The XII Army command in Kiev lost all contact with the frontline units. Comrade Muralov, the Army's political officer, was sent out in an aeroplane on the 28th to find out where they were. But with the exception of several badly battered units, the main body of the Soviets was able to withdraw. Had they been better prepared, they might have been tempted to stand and fight and thus have risked destruction.

From the Polish point of view the results were only moderately encouraging. They had gained an enormous tract of territory; but had failed to trap the enemy. They had split the XII Army from the XIV, and opened the way to Kiev, but they found themselves floundering in the void. To take stock of the situation, a halt was called. The Polish centre was re-constituted. Śmigły-Rydz's and Rybak's Groups were merged, and the 15th Infantry Division, which had distinguished itself at Chudnov, was added to them in exchange for the 7th. It was hoped that the Soviet XII Army would try to pull its scattered units together, and thus present a target worth attacking.

This satisfaction was not granted. When the advance was restarted after a week's rest, the Poles found that their way had not been barred. Mezhaninov, seeing the advantages of his involuntary retreat, had decided to continue it voluntarily. A patrol of Polish hussars succeeded in penetrating Kiev on 3 May. They rode into the city centre from the northern suburbs on a commandeered tramcar. Having captured an astonished Soviet officer waiting at a tramstop, they left as quickly as they had come. The XII Army evacuated Kiev on 6 May, and the next morning the main Polish forces marched into the un-defended streets. Their troops carried flowers in the muzzles of their rifles, their columns and transports passing in parade among citizens and shoppers who paid scant attention to the fifteenth change of régime in three years. A skirmish occurred at the suspension bridge which spans the Dnieper, but after a short exchange the 1st Legionary Division crossed the river and dug in round a left-bank bridgehead ten miles deep. For the first time in two and a half centuries the Polish Army had passed victorious through the Golden Gates of Kiev.

Piłsudski expressed satisfaction. He claimed that right-bank Ukraine had been occupied for the loss of 150 dead and 300 wounded. The bitterest loss to himself was that of his aide-de-camp, the 7th Brigade's Chief of Staff, Stanisław Radziwiłł, who was bayoneted and killed by the Bolshevik charge at Malin. Yet, as Piłsudski later admitted, there were grounds for uneasiness. The capture of Kiev was a hollow victory. He had entered an empty Russian capital without so much as a Borodino. If the Poles were to stay a month or two in Kiev, their hard-won initiative would pass to the Soviets. If they were to press on, they had nowhere to go. Only sixty miles beyond the Dnieper lay that fateful reminder to all who had pressed on in the past—the field of Poltava.

To administer the Ukraine was more difficult than to conquer it. Although the Poles arrived in the spirit of liberators, they soon became the 'occupiers'. They aroused neither enthusiasm nor hostility. According to the British military observer on the spot, both Poles and Bolsheviks were much preferred in Kiev to Denikin.[6]

The Polish occupation of the right-bank Ukraine revealed few features in common with their practices in Byelorussia. There was no attempt to garrison the province; huge areas, especially in the Zaporozhye, were never even visited by Polish troops. The Straż Kresowa and the administrators of the Z.C.Z.W. were not set to work. Piłsudski's 'Proclamation to the Citizens of the Ukraine' was far less ambitious than his proclamation issued in Wilno almost exactly a year previously:

To all inhabitants of Ukraine!
On my order Polish forces have advanced deep into the Ukrainian lands.

I formally delare that the foreign invaders, against whom the Ukrainian people have risen sword in hand to defend their homes from rape, banditry and looting, will be removed by the Polish forces from territories inhabited by the Ukrainian nation.

The Polish forces will remain in the Ukraine for such time as may be necessary to enable a legitimate Ukrainian government to take control.

From the moment that a national government of the Ukrainian

Republic has established its state authority and has manned the borders with forces capable of protecting the country against a new invasion, and the free nation is strong enough to settle its own fortunes, the Polish soldier will return beyond the frontier, having fulfilled his honourable task in the struggle for the freedom of nations.

Advancing with the Polish forces are the fighting sons of the Ukraine who under the leadership of Ataman Semyon Petlura have found help and shelter in Poland...

The Polish forces assure care and protection to all inhabitants of the Ukraine without distinction of class, race, or creed.

I appeal to the Ukrainian nation and to all inhabitants of these lands, patiently bearing the privations of war, to assist the Polish Army in its bloody struggle for their life and freedom with all means at their disposal.

Józef Piłsudski, Commander-in-Chief, Polish forces. 26 April 1920. Army Headquarters.'[7]

Everything political was left to Petlura. As the British minister in Warsaw assured London: 'The Poles will not stay in Ukraine longer than they have to. The landed proprietors are not in control. There is no Polish minister in the Ukrainian Government.'[8] The claim, repeated by E. H. Carr among others, that here was an attempt to create 'a satellite of the Polish Empire',[9] is an exaggeration.

Petlura was entirely inadequate for the task assigned to him. He was given six weeks by the Poles to establish an administration and to recruit an army. But there is no evidence that he made any progress whatsoever. He was as unwelcome to Makhno in the central Ukraine and Wrangel in the Crimea as he was to the leaders of Soviet Ukraine in Kharkov. In the event, his régime did not even survive the probationary six weeks.

Unless one regards Piłsudski as a complete political inalphabète, one must accept the view that he used Petlura merely as a labour-saving device. No doubt he would have rejoiced had the Ukrainian national movement succeeded. But he did not count on it. His main intention was to win time and space for Poland in the coming life-and-death struggle with the Soviets. This interpretation is borne out by the behaviour of the Polish forces. Having occupied Kiev, they carefully shunned all political distractions. They turned their backs on the Ukraine, and re-formed to face the threatening situation in the north. Śmigły-Rydz's strike force was dismantled. The Second Army was dissolved altogether. The remaining elements of the Third and Sixth Armies and Romer's Cavalry Division were merged into a single group under General Listowski. These were not the dispositions of a military command earnestly intent on supporting a shaky political ally in its newly won territory.

In the capitals of Europe, the occupation of Kiev was greeted with a mixture of delight and resentment. Any new blow at the hated Bolshevist régime caused delight. But another *fait accompli*, undertaken by Piłsudski against the advice of the Allied leaders, caused immense resentment. Lloyd George commented: 'The Poles are inclined to be arrogant and they will have to take care that they don't get their heads punched'.[10]
In London, the British government refused to make official comment. Lloyd George was abroad at the San Remo Conference. Churchill was sullenly silent. He was dismayed that Piłsudski should invade the Ukraine alone when in the autumn he could have invaded it in unison with Denikin to much greater effect.[11] Curzon, the Foreign Secretary, was embarrassed. His refusal to make a public statement gave rise to a bitter controversy with Lord Robert Cecil, chairman of the League of Nations Union, who filed a formal complaint against 'the deplorable events now taking place in Central Europe' where 'for months past Poland has been notoriously preparing to attack Russia'.[12] Curzon replied that since the Soviets did not recognize the League, the League could not possibly be invoked to defend the Soviets. 'In any case, this episode does not constitute an outbreak of war, it is merely a phase of a war which has been going on for some time'.[13] To Curzon's immense annoyance, this private correspondence was sent without his consent to Lord Northcliffe and published in *The Times* on 17 May. Even worse, it was communicated to Paderewski in Paris.[14] Although the likelihood of a positive British response to the Kiev Campaign was always small, Cecil's attempt to pressurize Curzon ruled it out altogether. The only flicker of a response came from King George V who on

3 May sent a telegram to Piłsudski complimenting the Polish Republic on its national day.

In Paris the French government also failed to respond. The clash of interest over Poland which might have developed with Great Britain was more potential than real. Millerand's new ministry was caught between the extreme demands of the military and of the militant left. The beginning of May saw a series of massive strikes. Millerand was happy enough to leave Allied policy to Lloyd George.

The Kiev Campaign did evoke vociferous protests. The 'Hands Off Russia' Committee first made headway at this time. On 9–10 May, the *Jolly George*, a ship loaded with munitions bought in England by the Polish government, was boycotted by London dockers. A British Labour Party delegation recently returned from Moscow swelled the chorus of outrage. But at this stage, if the noise was great, the effect on the government was minimal.

In Warsaw the occupation of Kiev inspired a sudden wave of confidence. The Sejm addressed the following telegram to Piłsudski:

The news of the brilliant victory achieved by the Polish soldiers under your leadership, fills the whole nation with joyful pride. In recognition of this bloody and heroic labour which brings us nearer to peace and puts new ramparts round the power of the Polish State, the Sejm in the name of a grateful fatherland sends you, Chief and Leader of the army of heroes, its heartfelt thanks.[15]

Piłsudski returned to Warsaw on 18 May to a state reception and a solemn Mass. Only the Polish communists protested. May Day processions in Warsaw, Łódź, Czętochowa, turned into anti-government demonstrations. In Poznań, a railwaymen's strike on 26 April turned into a week-long pitched battle with the authorities. Success on the eastern front released the pent-up anxieties of supporters and opponents alike.

On the Soviet side of the front, the occupation of Kiev caused consternation and bewilderment which quickly passed. It was quite unexpected, as shown by the unprepared state of the XII and XIV Armies, and its political purpose was far from clear. The Soviets knew that Petlura was a political nonentity, and did not believe that a hard-bitten campaigner like Piłsudski could think otherwise. They soon realized that they were faced with some sort of diversion.

In a speech on 29 April, Lenin weighed two explanations. On the one hand, he supposed that the Kiev campaign might be intended to divert attention from Wrangel in the Crimea. This might explain its southerly direction. On the other hand, he supposed that it might be intended to interrupt Red Army preparations in the west. 'We ought to recognize,' he said, 'that this has been done to strengthen the barrier and to deepen the gulf, which separates us from the proletariat of Germany.'[16] The words betray his hope of crossing the barrier.

After the initial surprise the Kiev campaign caused no real alarm among the Bolshevik leaders. Lenin assured his colleagues that they could 'regard the new adventure with the utmost calm.'[17] The Soviets could count on the full support of the working masses of Europe and would emerge victorious. Kalinin, the President of the Central Executive Committee of the Soviets, was still more explicit:

I believe the Polish lords by marching on the Soviet republic are only digging their own graves...I believe that within a month the Polish gentry will feel the heavy hammer of the Russian working class; and if we deliver the first blow, the Polish proletariat will deliver the second and final one...The western capitalists have sought to strangle Soviet Russia with Polish hands; but they will only succeed in founding yet another Soviet state through which we will gain close relations with the proletariat of the west.[18]

In the military sphere, there was relief that the blow had fallen where it had. Sergey Kamenev, the Commander-in-Chief of the Red Army, described it as 'convenient'. In his orders to the South-West Command on 29 April, he urged that the Polish army be lured forward, in order 'to suspend it in mid-air'. The aim was to 'rivet' the Poles in Kiev, and thus give the Red Army time to complete its own offensive in the north.[19]

The public reaction of the Soviet leaders was quite different. The Polish offensive gave them a moral and political advantage which was not to be squandered. Although Kiev lay not in the Russian Republic but in the Ukrainian Republic, the call went out for the defence of *Russia*. The appeal by the Communist

Party's Central Committee on 29 April was addressed, not just to the working class to defend the Soviet Republic, but to 'all workers, peasants, and honourable citizens of *Rossiya*', that vast, vague, mystical empire which the Revolution was supposed to have destroyed. It succeeded in appealing both to the old-fashioned patriots and to the new-fangled revolutionaries. Its language was heavy with talk of ancient rivalries and foreign invasions, with allusions to 1610 and 1812 and 1914:

Honourable citizens! You cannot allow the bayonets of the Polish lords to determine the will of the Great Russian nation. The Polish lords have shamelessly and repeatedly shown that they care not who rules Russia but only that Russia shall be weak and helpless.[20]

After the defeat of Kolchak and Denikin, there was a large fund of unattached patriotic opinion ready to respond to the call for unity. The Ukrainian communists, who for three years had been the implacable foe of Ukrainian nationalism, now called on the whole population to defend the Ukrainian 'fatherland'. At the same time, every care was taken to keep the class-enemy in view. Lenin specifically decreed that 'all articles about Poland and the Polish war are to be passed by reliable editors who shall be personally responsible. Do not overspice it; that is, do not fall into chauvinism, and always distinguish the lords and capitalists of Poland from the workers and peasants.'[21] Hence this curious mixture, curious fifty years ago, of Russian nationalism and Soviet internationalism—a mixture which pervaded the Red Army for the first time in 1920 and which has characterized Soviet attitudes ever since.

Soviet propaganda was also directed abroad. A chorus of mingled voices harmonized an oratorio of righteous indignation. The protests of Soviet diplomacy and Comintern[22] were joined by those of newly formed communist parties and by innumerable resolutions despatched from factories and workers' committees throughout the length and breadth of Europe. The appeals for peace matched the pacifist mood of a war-weary continent. Whatever were the military advantages for Poland of the Kiev campaign, the cost in international good-will was high and was never recovered. It was the price Poland had to pay for winning the race for the spring offensive.

In Kiev itself, the advantage daily turned in the Soviets' favour. Polish dispositions were static. The Ukrainian People's Republic, having been delivered into this world, proved stillborn. Soviet reinforcements flooded in. The XII Army, reduced in two weeks' fighting to 2,511 men, was withdrawn to Nezhin and reinfused with entirely fresh units—notably the 25th 'Chapayev' Division from the Urals and Murtazin's Brigade of Bashkir cavalry. The XIV Army which had fallen back on Cherkassy received the Kotovsky Cavalry Brigade. All existing formations were brought up to strength. On 12 May, there occurred the last twitch of the Polish offensive when Brovari on the perimeter of the left bank bridgehead was captured. Thereafter the initiative passed to the Red Army.

Throughout May control of the Dnieper was hotly contested. For some eighty miles between Chernobyl and Tripolye, the river followed the frontline; to the south, it provided the Soviets with their principal means of communication. The Soviets maintained a 'Dnieper Flotilla' of shoal-draft monitors, which carried a task force of a thousand marines.

To combat the Flotilla, the Poles sent their 9th Air Squadron into Kiev, their heavy, Breguet biplane bombers, strafing the convoys, driving them onto the shoals and rapids, and duelling with the gunboat escorts.

The overall situation was dominated by the imminent arrival of the First Red Cavalry Army. Even today it is difficult to distinguish legend from reality regarding this most glamorous of Soviet formations, and to its commander, Semyon Budyonny. It is almost impossible to reconstruct the awe and terror—testified by Polish and Soviet witnesses alike—which attended their approach.

The First Cavalry Army (the Konarmiya) was the most successful innovation of the Civil War. Formed in November 1919, it was the logical outcome of warfare with the White armies, in which the Reds had proved themselves equal to everything except the Cossack cavalry. By massing all available sabres into one formation, it enjoyed not only the famous Cossack mobility and *esprit de corps* but also overwhelming weight and numbers at any point where it was applied. It waged a form of Tartar *blitzkrieg*. It welcomed all who could ride and obey, who were ready to saddle and march to any point in the continent where the Revolution was in danger. It was the ultimate antithesis of the original localized, class-conscious, footslogging Red Guards of 1918.

Semyon Mikhaylovich Budyonny typified the best of the men he served. He was a man who had thrived on hard times through his skill as a soldier and by force of personality. The son of a poor farmer in the Rostov province, he joined the 43rd Cossack Regiment in 1903 and served in Manchuria before graduating from the Petersburg Riding School. In the summer of 1917, chairman of the soviet of his mutinous regiment, he found himself at Minsk, where Frunze and Myasnikov were organizing resistance to Kornilov. From there he made his way as a Red cavalry commander. He first attracted notice at Tsaritsyn in December 1918, when his daring and enterprise recommended him to Voroshilov. He was the obvious choice to lead the 'Konarmiya'. Very tall, very athletic, he was a breathtaking horseman, who led from the front. His fine Asiatic features, his superb black moustache, curled and groomed like the mane of a showhorse, his steady almond eyes revealed the perfect man of action—a prime animal, a magnificent, semi-literate son of the steppes. 25 April 1920, the day the Kiev campaign was launched, was his fortieth birthday.

The troopers of the Konarmiya had little in common with Bolshevik politics, except that they were fighting on the same side. Most of them were former Cossacks, partisans, and bandits, won over in the course of the Red Army's victories. Yet they understood Revolution perfectly. They approached the thoughts of Lenin and the concepts of Marxism more with awe than with understanding. There were one or two literates, like Isaak Babel in the 1st Brigade of the 6th Division, or Zhukov, the future Marshal. But by and large they were more distinguished in heroics than in dialectics. In the eyes of the Poles, they were the reincarnation of the hordes of Genghis Khan.

Despite the primitive nature of its politics, the Konarmiya was not politically unimportant. It was the creation and chosen instrument of the small, and ambitious faction of Joseph Stalin—a faction which was destined to dominate and destroy the Bolshevik Party as ruthlessly as the Bolsheviks had dominated and destroyed the revolutionary movement as a whole. The Konarmiya's command and political direction grew out of the circle of friends at Tsaritsyn, who under Stalin's inspiration had defied Trotsky and the plans of the party. They were the 'homespun communists', 'the simple soldiers', 'the patriot proletarians'. They detested intellectuals, professionals, officers, bureaucrats, Jews, westernisers, foreigners, in fact most of the people who ran the Bolshevik Party. They disliked orders and mistrusted theories. They were, in Stalin's words, the 'good fellows' who got things done. Budyonny, the sergeant-major who raised his own Cossack army, was a perfect foil for Kliment Yefimovich Voroshilov, the mechanic of Lugansk, whose men in 1918 had forged a mechanized army with their own bare hands. These two, the commander and the political officer, lived, rode, and slept side by side. Their destiny was yoked together for more than forty years.

The transfer of the Konarmiya from the Caucasus to the Polish front had been decided at the Smolensk meeting of 10 March. At that time it was at Maykop, having recently dispersed the remnants of Denikin's Volunteers. It left on 3 April. A fortnight later it began to cross the Don into Rostov. Here it was faced with a dramatic challenge. In the prison at Rostov lay a certain Dumenko. Five months earlier when Rostov was being sacked by the Red Army, Dumenko, a former cavalry commander, had murdered his commissar. Now when the Konarmiya returned, Dumenko's former comrades raised a riot and demanded his release. Budyonny faced the mob in person, ordering them to choose between him and the prisoner. The riot was quelled. Dumenko was shot. The march continued. After Rostov the army divided into columns: Gorodovikov's 4th Division, Timoshenko's 6th, Morozov's 11th, and Parkomenko's 14th. Their four armoured trains, three air squadrons, and other support services were despatched by rail through Central Russia. They themselves went overland. Leaving Rostov on 23 April they gave themselves a fortnight to reach the Dnieper. They travelled in column, resting and riding by turns. They pulled the sick and tired behind them in carts, along with the artillery. They shot the horses lamed by the pace at the rate of a dozen a day. In the daytime the front ranks carried letter-boards on their backs to teach the ranks behind to read. In the evening, they bivouacked in the open, singing their songs:

По весенной жидкой топи
Отдыхаем Мы в Майкопе,
Читимся и моемся
На ученья строимся.

Отдыхать бы так подольше,
Да нужны Мы против Польши·.
С белыми попутчики
Балуют пилсудчики.

Много верст до них от Дона
Но не просим Мы пардона.
Коль до красных дело им,
Мы те версты сделаем.

(In the watery thaw of spring, we are resting at Maykop, reading and cleaning up, and trying to learn. Oh to rest like that some more! But we're needed to fight in Poland, where the Piłsudchiks are having a ball with their White companions. There are many miles to reach them from the Don, but we beg no excuses. Once we Reds know what it's all about, we shall cover the miles.)[23]

At the end of April, with news of the Polish offensive, they received orders to quicken their pace. They were in Makhno country, where for months past a murderous war for the life and soul of the peasantry had been in progress. Cheka squads were touring the villages, hanging partisans and installing soviets. Makhno was following them, shooting communists and ambushing Red Army forage parties. On 28 April the 14th Division stormed Gulaypolye, 'Makhnograd' itself, routing a force of some 2,000 partisans. The Konarmiya rode on regardless, like a ship of the line driving through a fleet of fishing smacks. At last, north of Yekaterinoslav, on 6 May, they began to cross the Dnieper. On 13 May the 6th Division brushed through a Petlurist force at Chigirin. The columns were now converging on Uman, where they were due to assemble and refit. In the seven weeks since they left the Kuban, they had spent thirty days on the march and had covered 750 miles.

The Konarmiya possessed nearly 16,000 active sabres. By Civil War standards it was a large force. But by recent European standards, it was minimal. In 1914 the Tsarist Army had possessed forty cavalry divisions, with 300,000 sabres. 'If I had those 300,000,' Budyonny was said to have sighed, 'I would plough up the whole of Poland, and we would be clattering through the squares of Paris before the summer is out.'

Polish intelligence knew they were coming, but it was not until 25 May that an Albatros spotterplane of the Kościuszko Squadron actually caught sight of them. The pilot was vastly impressed. Having glided down to investigate what he took to be a sand-storm, he discovered the Konarmiya masked in the clouds of dust raised by thousands of hooves. The troopers were trotting eight abreast, their sand-brown cloaks streaming in the wind, black astrakhan caps tilted forward over their eyes, sabres shining in the sun at their belts, carbines bristling at their backs. When he returned the next morning, he found them seventy-five miles further on. Without knowing it, he had seen two different divisions of the Konarmiya. His flight report, which mentioned a cavalry army of 30,000 marching at seventy-five miles a day, could have done nothing to lessen Polish apprehensions.[24]

Plans for the Soviet counter-offensive in the Ukraine were finalized in the third week of May. The obvious point for attack lay at the juncture of the two principal Polish groupings, between the Third Army centred on Kiev-Byelatserkev and the Sixth Army at Zhmerinka-Vinnitsa. It was for this purpose that the Konarmiya had been assembled in the area of Uman. To assist the central thrust, preliminary attacks were to be launched by a task force of the XII Army under Golikov and by a specially formed 'Fastov Group' under Yakir, commander of the 45th Division. Golikov was to cross the Dnieper north of Kiev and send his Bashkir cavalry to cut the vital Korosten railway; Yakir was to advance frontally on Belatserkev, in conjunction with a descent of the Dnieper flotilla on Tripolye. The small XIV Army in the south was to push forward only if the other operations were successful. The offensive was timed to start on 26 May. (See map, p. 121 opposite.)

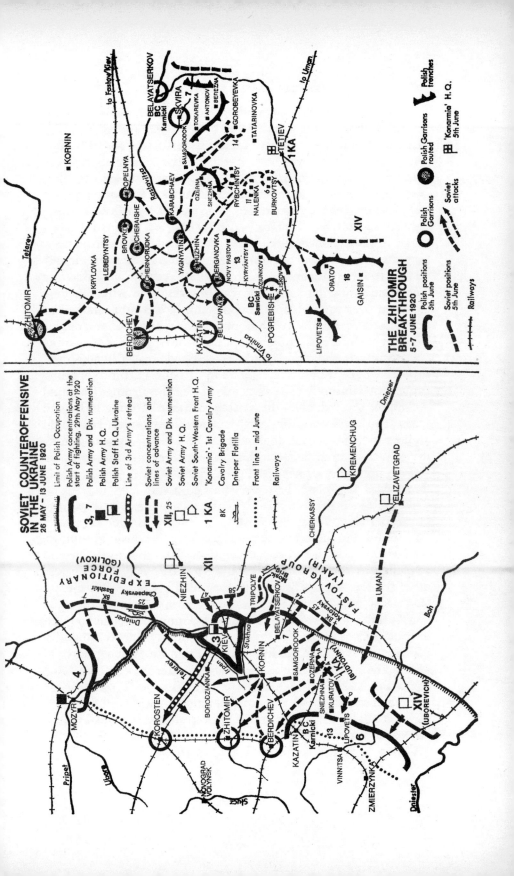

SOVIET COUNTEROFFENSIVE IN THE UKRAINE
26 MAY – 13 JUNE 1920

Limit of Polish Occupation

Polish Army concentrations at the start of fighting, 29th May 1920

3, 7 Polish Army and Div. numeration

Polish Army H.Q.

Polish Staff H.Q., Ukraine

Line of 3/d Army's retreat

Soviet concentrations and lines of advance

XII, 25 Soviet Army and Div. numeration

Soviet Army H.Q.

Soviet South-Western Front H.Q.

1 KA 'Konarmia': 1st Cavalry Army

BK Cavalry Brigade

Dnieper Flotilla

Front line – mid June

Railways

THE ZHITOMIR BREAKTHROUGH
5-7 JUNE 1920

Polish positions 5th June

Soviet positions 5th June

Railways

Polish trenches

Polish Garrisons

'Konarmia' H.Q.

Polish Garrisons routed

Soviet attacks

Polish Garrisons

In later years, this plan was attributed to the genius of
Stalin. Although the Commissar for Nationalities did arrive
at South-Western Front HQ at Kremenchug on 29 May and
did attend the ensuing battles, there is no reason to believe
that he had any part in the preparations, nor indeed that the
plan bore any marks of genius. Kakurin, writing in 1922,
quotes the relevant final order, No. 358 of 23 May, in full;
it was signed by Trotsky.[25] Budyonny, writing in 1965,
makes no mention of Stalin. He recalls having received the
Konarmiya's initial orders on 20 May and having been highly
dissatisfied with them, so much so that Yegorov and Berzin,
commander and political officer of the South-Western Front,
travelled over to see him.[26] In Budyonny's view the plan was
uncomfortably vague. It made no stipulations about the exact
location of the Polish units nor of the Konarmiya's Red Army
neighbours. It did not provide the Konarmiya with infantry
support. Budyonny asked for two divisions, but Yegorov
could not comply. The work of Soviet intelligence was as
incompetent as that of the staff was hasty. The Poles were
screening their lines with partisan bands. Budyonny would not
know what he was up against until he made contact. These
initial blemishes in the plan were to mar its eventual success.

The primitive provisions for a radio link illustrate how
flimsy was the bond between the command and the commanded. Once the Konarmiya had broken through, it would
be out of touch. Yet it alone would possess up-to-date information about the Polish forces. Hence it was agreed that the
Konarmiya's radio station at Yelizavetgrad should serve as a
co-ordinator for all Soviet intelligence. A system of coded
messages was hurriedly arranged; 'Kasbek is out for a stroll-
28-Falcon' meant '4th Division engaged in Sector 28 - Budyonny'; 'First Violin sleeps-32-Kite' meant '6th Division resting
in Sector 32 - Voroshilov.'[27]

On 25 May, the Konarmiya was visited by Mikhail Ivano-
vich Kalinin, Chairman of the Central Executive Committee
of the Soviets. He decorated the 21st and 22nd Regiments of
the 4th Division, both veteran formations, with the Order of
the Red Banner. It was a clear sign that Moscow set great store
on events in the Ukraine.

On 27 May the Konarmiya groped its way forward. After

two days of skirmishing with the partisans, Timoshenko's 6th
Division charged the Polish trenches at Kuratov, followed on
31 May by a day-long attempt to storm the barricaded town
of Lipovets. Neither attack succeeded. The 6th Division lost
its political officer, Pishchulin, and a hundred or so casualties
in each of its three brigades. They failed to find the enemy's
flank, and were surprised by the steadiness of the Polish
infantry under cavalry attack. In the night of 2 June, a surprise
counter raid by the Poles captured two of the Konarmiya's
armoured trains, the *Death to the Directory* and the *Nikolay
Rudnev'*. The Konarmiya's only success occurred when the 4th
and 14th Divisions lured General Karnicki's cavalry into an
encirclement and forced him to withdraw. (See map, p. 121)

On 2 June the Konarmiya's commanders assembled for a
conference on tactics. They all agreed that the methods which
had routed Denikin were inadequate against the Poles. A
cavalry charge on trench positions was pointless. They decided
that the best way to dislodge entrenched infantry, was to
approach them in dismounted and scattered formation, to
apply an artillery barrage and then to despatch small task
forces against each of the fortified strongpoints. Mounted
cavalry was only to be used to turn the flanks. Counter-attacks
were not to be frontally resisted, but were to be drawn into the
cross-fire of artillery posts and machine-gun nests drawn up
behind the frontline.[28]

Budyonny's personal experiences on the day of the breakthrough, 5 June, are most illuminating. Three of the four
divisions were to lead the attack, the 14th on Samgorodok,
the 4th on Ozerna, the 11th on Snezhna. The 6th was in
reserve. Budyonny spent a sleepless night, kept awake by the
uncertain prospects, by Voroshilov, who always developed a
severe headache on such occasions, and by the rain. At dawn
he rode out of his bivouac at Tatarinovka in time to see the
4th Division definitively repulsed. His cavalry was still too
eager. Having galloped forward in the cover of some armoured
cars, they found they could not live in the forward areas.
Budyonny then rode over to the 14th Division, whose 1st
Brigade was advancing with more circumspection. They had
chosen an area of marshy ground to the south of Samgorodok,
blotted out with early morning mist and lying on the extremity

of the Polish positions. They surprised a patrol of uhlan scouts and gave chase. Budyonny himself overtook one of the uhlans who had fired at him, knocked him out of the saddle from behind, and, surviving a further misaimed shot from the grounded rider, disarmed him with the flat of his sabre, and brought him in for questioning. He had found an ideal way across the Polish lines. When the decisive clash occurred, he was able to fire in some cases directly along the Polish trenches. The cavalry edged safely past. The front had been pierced.

In the course of the day, the other divisions had the same success. Having mounted a fierce bombardment and a frontal assault without effect, the dismounted troopers of the 4th Division infiltrated Ozerna unexpectedy from the north. Towards seven o'clock in the evening, the 11th Division entered Snezhna. The Konarmiya had carved a threefold gap. It claimed to have taken 1,000 prisoners and to have 'sabred' a further 8,000. Its way was open to terrorize the Polish rear.

Seen in detail, the breakthrough of 5 June was not so spectacular as was sometimes supposed. Success was achieved more by stealth than by shock. This is not to deny either the measure of their success, or the fact that they soon reverted to their preferred style. When, in succeeding weeks, the Konarmiya smashed its way through the small towns of Podolia and East Galicia, the Cossack charge was just as much in evidence as Tartar stealth.

For the next thirty years, 5 June was to remain one of the Red Army's annual festivals—a celebration of 'the first victory of the Soviet military art over European arms'.

Budyonny's success was attended by mixed circumstances. It was favoured by the progress of the Soviet offensive as a whole. Golikov, after a poor start, had cut the Korosten railway. The Polish Third Army was thinly but definitely encircled; its 7th Infantry Division was badly battered and isolated. Confusion in the Polish command matched the panic in the ranks; Piłsudski issued orders which contradicted those of General Śmigły-Rydz on the spot. Yakir took Belatserkev. Even the XIV Army was able to advance. Success was restricted, however, by factors both foreseen and unforeseen. The Konarmiya possessed no reserves, and no infantry with which to widen the gap created; it had no supply organization capable of supporting a protracted campaign beyond the front; it had no plan to concert its activities with those of other Soviet units; it was weakened by the defection to the Poles of the Orenburg Cossacks, a regiment which earlier in the year had defected to the Red Army from Denikin. In the northern sector, the Soviet armies in Byelorussia were hardpressed and unable to extend any assistance. From the Crimea on 6 June, Wrangel made his final bid, and advanced onto the lower Dnieper. The Konarmiya was very much alone.

Budyonny's moves in the vital days following the break-through reflected his isolation. It was unthinkable that he should have tamely retreated for want of support. He could not resist a day or two of raiding. On 7 June, the 4th Division descended on Zhitomir. They achieved total surprise. The Polish garrison was put to the sword. Bridges, marshalling yards and military warehouses were wrecked. The prisons were opened. Some 5,000 Soviet prisoners-of-war were liberated. The same day, the 11th Division descended on Berdichev. A hospital containing 600 Polish wounded and their Red Cross nurses was burned to the ground. Although the military value of the raids was short-lived, the psychological effect was enormous. Every Pole west of the Dnieper was thoroughly frightened. The Warsaw government did not dare to publish the facts.[29] After the raids, the Konarmiya fell back towards Kornin to re-form and recover its bearings.

The lull which occurred between 7 and 11 June gave the Polish forces a chance of salvation which they readily seized. The Third Army had been squeezed into the triangle of the rivers Dnieper, Irpen, and Teterev, facing outwards in three directions at once like a herd of bison awaiting the slaughter. Piłsudski intended it to retreat on Zhitomir and, in conjunction with the Sixth Army, to sandwich the Konarmiya in its extended position. But the Konarmiya's withdrawal made this manoeuvre both pointless and dangerous. Śmigły-Rydz took matters into his own hands. He ordered the Third Army to retreat north-westwards on Korosten involving it in encounters with the Chapayev Division at Borodyanka, and with the Bashkir cavalry at Irsha. He ordered the evacuation of Kiev, effected on 10 June. He surprised Budyonny who expected the Poles to retreat on Kazatin. When Budyonny realized his own mistake and attacked, he found himself pursuing the Poles in the direction they had already chosen to go. He was kept at arm's length by a series of rearguard actions. The Polish Third Army withdrew safely into the northern wing of the Polish lines. The Second Army was hurriedly reconstituted under General Raszewski in the centre. The Sixth Army stepped backwards in the south. The gap was closed.

Polish historians have criticized Budyonny for throwing away his advantage as soon as it was won. Kutrzeba has argued that Zhitomir should have been held, and implied that a competent general would not have given the Third Army time to avoid encirclement.[30] Budyonny, however, probably achieved as much as was possible—a heavy blow, and a dramatic scare. The breakthrough of 5 June started a general advance of the Soviet forces in the south which continued unchecked for the next ten weeks.

As always on the Borders, an offensive given initial impetus could easily be kept rolling. Although the Soviet armies enjoyed no numerical superiority, they pushed the Poles continually westwards in a daily routine of stabbing at the weakest points. Whenever they met resistance at the numerous towns and junctions, they could always turn the flank of hurriedly prepared positions; whenever they were faced with counter-attacks, they could absorb the pressure by advancing on either side of the attackers. All the Polish actions were fruitless. The stubborn defence of Novograd Volynsk was reduced on 26 June; General Romer's enterprising cavalry sally out of Ovruch was outflanked. Stores had to be abandoned, prisoners released; aeroplanes were left behind on the ground because there was not time to repair them; units which lingered to fight were overtaken. By 10 July, the front returned to the line it had occupied a year earlier. Budyonny was in Równe, Piłsudski's headquarters at the start of the Kiev campaign in April. The Konarmiya crossed the Zbrucz:

The fields flowered around us, crimson with poppies...The standards of the sunset fluttered above our heads. Into the cool of the evening dripped the smell of yesterday's blood, the stench of slaughtered horses. The blackened river roared along, twisting itself into foaming knots at the rapids. The bridges were down, and we waded across. A majestic moon rested on the waves. The horses slipped into the water up to their saddles, and the torrent gurgled noisily among hundreds of equine legs. Someone sank, loudly defaming the Mother of God. The river was strewn with square black wagons full of confused sounds, of whistling and singing which echoed above the wisps of moonlight and the shining pools...[31]

The invasion of the Ukraine had been eliminated.

The Kiev campaign is generally taken to have been a political and a military fiasco. On the political side, there can be little doubt of this. In the Ukraine, Petlura's Directory was a total failure; in Poland, Skulski's government resigned and precipitated a lengthy cabinet crisis: in Soviet Russia, the Bolshevik leadership reaped a measure of support hitherto unequalled. On the military side, some pre-war Polish apologists have contended that the Kiev campaign was not so disastrous. Kutrzeba maintained that it successfully interrupted the main Soviet offensive, that the Polish armies in the south remained intact and that they were not prevented from making a major contribution to the defence of Poland in the high summer. His ingenious commentary on Polish troop movements shows that eight of the twelve divisions involved in the Kiev campaign participated in the Battle of Warsaw in August.[32] What he omits to mention is the fact that the Soviet Command had dealt with the invasion of the Ukraine without diverting any forces from their existing assignments. The XII, XIV, and First Cavalry Armies had all been assigned to the South-West Front in March, and proved equal to their task. In terms of deployment, the Kiev campaign was probably an irrelevance to the main trial of strength which was already underway in the north; but in terms of strategy, its effect was clear. Whereas in April Poland was threatened with invasion on one front only, now in July she was threatened from two directions at once.

An interesting feature of the Kiev campaign was the emergence of the Polish Air Force. For the first time in the war aeroplanes came into their own. They gave the army eyes. Superiority in the air was one reason why the Polish army was able to extricate itself from dangerous confrontations on the ground.

The Polish Air Force was typical of the improvised support units of the war. It was pioneered in 1919 by Captain Jaciński, and a Major Rajski who had been head of the German Air Force in Turkey. It inherited a varied assortment of machines—Austrian Albatros D-3's, Fokker D-7's, and Brandenburg trainers, and later received consignments of Italian Balillas, German A.E.G.s, French Farmans and Breguets, and British D.H.-9s, Sopwith Camels, and Bristol Fighters. Many of these were idle at Mokatów airfield near Warsaw waiting for conversions, spares, or pilots.

The squadrons which saw active service in 1919–20 were organized in the best amateur tradition. They operated from 'aviation trains' which pulled their whole organization—aeroplanes in crates, workshops, command wagons, sleeping quarters, and portable hangars—from one temporary field to the next. Their first role was reconnaissance, searching for the enemy and verifying the location of their own units. Strafing, bombing, spreading leaflets, and carrying messages were secondary roles. They sometimes landed behind the lines to ask the villagers about the enemy, and frequently crash landed through disorientation or shortage of petrol. There are stories of grounded pilots being butchered by Cossacks, being rescued on snowsleighs driven by sympathetic priests, or even being worshipped by awe-struck peasants.

The 7th (Kościuszko) Squadron was especially interesting.[33] Its pilots were all Americans, commanded by Major Cedric Fauntleroy of Chicago. They had volunteered for the prank in Poland rather than return home with their colleagues from France. When they first met Piłsudski in October 1919, he told them: 'Poland can fight her own battles. Paid mercenaries are not needed here!' But as volunteers they were accepted. In March 1920 they were detailed to Polonnoe on the Slucz, attached to the headquarters of General Listowski's Second Army. They had received a number of Balillas, armed with two bomb chutes and a machine-gun firing through the propeller at 200 rounds a minute, and capable of 5 hours' flying at 160 m.p.h. They felt immensely superior to the Soviet observers across the front who peered at the Poles from moored balloons and were easily shot down with regular monotony. They could fly to the Dnieper and back without refuelling. On 19 April one of their pilots dropped a bomb on Kiev. They played a prominent part in the offensive.

During dozens of sorties flown during the advance to Kiev, this particular squadron only once reported having sighted a Soviet aircraft, a black-painted Gotha glimpsed over Kazatin. Kakurin states that the Soviet South-Western armies possessed thirty-five aircraft, of which eighteen were assigned to the XIV Army, presumably for overflying the Rumanian frontier.[34] But it is doubtful whether they possessed the pilots to fly them.

The Soviets had no answer to the Polish Air Force. Isaak Babel, whose own troop-leader, Pavel Trunov, was killed by the Kościuszko Squadron, described the action in tones of evident respect:

Troop-leader Trunov pointed out the four specks in the sky, four bombers sailing in and out of the swanlike clouds. They were massive armoured 'planes, machines of the Air Squadron of Major Faunt-le-ro. Trunov started levelling his machine-gun...The 'planes were flying into our station ever more closely, clumsily creaking up to their full height before diving down and looping the loop, a pink ray of sunlight on their wings. Meanwhile, we were in the forest, awaiting the end of the unequal combat...The major and his bombers showed considerable skill. They dropped down to three hundred metres and shot up first Andrushka and then Trunov. None of the shots fired by our men did the Americans any harm...So after half-an-hour, we were able to ride out and fetch the corpses. We carried the riddled body of Trunov to the town of Sokal. All his wounds were in his face, his cheeks punctured all over, his tongue ripped out. We washed him as best we could, placed a Caucasian saddle at the head of his coffin, and dug him an honourable grave next to the cathedral in the municipal gardens in the very centre of the town.'[35]

CHAPTER FOUR

THE INVASION OF POLAND

THE excitement of the Kiev Campaign diverted attention from the entrance into the Polish war of the Red Army's most celebrated commander—Mikhail Nikolayevich Tukhachevsky. He arrived at Western Front Headquarters at Smolensk in the week that Kiev fell.

Tukhachevsky personified many of the contradictory trends which contributed to the growth of the Red Army. He was an aristocrat in the service of the proletarian revolution, a Russian patriot who practised an elaborate doctrine of revolutionary warfare. He was dubbed by Stalin with the aptly ambiguous title of 'the demon of the Civil War'.

In 1920, Tukhachevsky was only twenty-seven years old, the same age as his idol, Napoleon, when entrusted with the Italian campaign. He was the son of a noble family from the Penza province. His parents were strong-minded people who paid scant attention to the legend which traced the family's origin to a crusading count of Flanders who had married a Turkish captive and taken service with the Tsar. His father was an atheist, his mother a simple peasant woman. He served in the Great War as a lieutenant in the élite Semionovsky Life Guards. On 19 February 1915 he was taken prisoner during the German attack on Łómża. After three attempts at escape, he was sent to Ingolstadt in Bavaria, where the Germans kept escape-prone Allied officers, among them Charles de Gaulle. In March 1918, when the Treaty of Brest-Litovsk permitted Tsarist officers in captivity to be paroled, he absconded. His Allied comrades remembered him for his looks and for his bravado. He possessed a solid and powerful Russian physique adorned by the sculptured features and swarthy complexion of a Greek. Before departing, he was reputed to have told his fellow prisoners, 'I shall be a general by the time I'm twenty-five, or else they'll have me shot.' He achieved both distinctions. During the Civil War, he made his way by sheer ability. He appeared in Moscow in April 1918 and joined the Bolshevik Party at a time when former officers not to mention aristocrats were viewed with immense suspicion. Having served in the war department of the Central Executive Committee of the Soviets, he was despatched to the Volga. In the company of 'Butcher' Muravyov, he organized the defence of Simbirsk and Samara. After Muravyov's defection, he survived capture by the enemy and assumed command of the First Red Army. In 1919, he commanded the Fifth Army on the Eastern Front and conquered Siberia from Kolchak. His army advanced 2,011 miles in 247 days. He acquired in the process the inklings of a theory about the 'permanent offensive' and the 'expansion of the revolution'. He developed the idea that the unique proletarian character of the Red Army enabled it to win recruits from the people in the lands through which it passed and thereby to sustain an endless advance. He was tempted to believe that the Red Army could go rolling round the globe until all the proletarians of the world were united. It was with this theory in mind that at the end of 1919 Tukhachevsky was given command of the Caucasian Front to roll back Denikin, and on 28 April 1920 sent to the Western Front in the hope of rolling through Poland.

Tukhachevsky's meteoric career inevitably aroused suspicions. His origins alone sufficed to offend a large number of Russian communists who instinctively mistrusted an aristocrat and who despised the unswerving servant of Moscow. It was Tukhachevsky's fate on repeated occasions to cross the path of Stalin's friends. In 1918, he and Muravyov were fighting on the Volga in open competition with Voroshilov at Tsaritsyn. Tukhachevsky recaptured Tsaritsyn after Voroshilov had been removed on Trotsky's orders. His later Caucasian command was dominated by Budyonny's First Cavalry Army and supervised by Stalin. When in 1920, he found that the Tsaritsyn circle had manoeuvred themselves into control of the South-Western Front, he demanded that they be subjected to his orders. Voroshilov, Budyonny, and Yegorov, with Stalin behind them, were unruly at the best of times. Given independent control of the Galician operation they could seriously disrupt the co-ordinated direction of the Polish campaign. Tukhachevsky's demand, however, was not met in full. The Commander-in-Chief of the Red Army, Kamenev, ruled that the Western Front Command could only absorb the South-Western armies when the Soviet offensive reached the Bug. This compromise delayed but did not prevent the eventual clash.

As a general, Tukhachevsky was an unknown quantity. But in the course of 1920 he impressed his enemies at least as much as his superiors. Although Trotsky admitted that Tukhachevsky 'displayed extraordinary talents', he decried the 'element of adventure in his strategy'. The Commissar for War felt compelled to criticize attempts 'to create a military doctrine by means of hastily adapted Marxist formulas' and thought Tukhachevsky had made 'an over-rapid leap from the ranks of the Guards Officers to the Bolshevist camp'.[1] Pilsudski was more magnanimous:

Tukhachevsky inspired his subordinates by virtue of his energetic and purposeful work. He is marked out for ever as a general with daring ideas and the power of putting them into vigorous execution. He gives me the impression of a soldier who tends toward abstract conceptions, but who shows will-power, energy and a curious obstinacy... Generals of this type are seldom able to take the broad view since they merge their whole personality in the immediate task. On the other hand, they radiate confidence in their ability to carry out unhesitatingly whatever they undertake. Tukhachevsky handled his troops very skilfully, and anyone can discern the signs of a general of the first order in his daring but logically correct march on Warsaw.[2]

Pilsudski was praising a man who shared his own adventurous outlook.

When Tukhachevsky arrived at Smolensk, he came to a front as yet only half-organized. Although the flow of reinforcements had given the Soviet armies forming in the West a nominal superiority, only one of them was in a state to take the offensive. Yet the situation was urgent. The South-Western Front Command was in dire need of relief. At the same time, there was the distinct possibility that the Poles, having halted at Kiev, would transfer a number of their victorious divisions from the Ukraine and disrupt Soviet preparations in Byelorussia. A diversion was required. Hence Tukhachevsky's order to the XV Army to advance. It came in the nick of time. Piłsudski had already made dispositions for an attack on Zhlobin-Mogilev starting on 17 May. Had this attack taken place and succeeded, the Polish forces would have controlled the rail network linking the two theatres of operations and would have been well placed to take the unprepared Soviet concentrations from the rear.

The 'Battle of the Berezina', is less interesting, therefore, than the potential developments which it forestalled. It was essentially an improvised, preventive operation. For all that, it was hard fought. On 15 May, the XV Army with six divisions of infantry crossed the Dvina. Led by a young commander called Chuikov, it struck at a point on the left wing of the Polish line hitherto neglected. It was joined soon afterwards by the XVI Army's siege of Borisov. For two weeks the Red infantry pushed the Poles steadily back. Their pace gradually slackened, until at the end of May they ground to a halt along a ragged arc strung between the lakes and forests separating Koziany in the north-west and Lake Pelic in the south-east, seventy miles from their starting point. Despite the premature celebratory announcement in *Pravda*, Borisov did not fall.[3] (See map, p. 134)

Once they had abandoned their original intentions, the Polish command met the emergency without much difficulty. General Sosnkowski regrouped the First Army at Święciany using the reserve army from Wilno. General Skierski was ordered to prepare a second group at Lohojsk. By attacking the Soviet arc on its opposite extremities, they made to isolate its centre.

Tukhachevsky played cautiously. Having saved Zhlobin and Mogilev and won himself a fortnight's respite, he preferred to retire. On 8 June, he pulled his troops back to the rivers Auta and Berezina, whose banks formed a more economical and more natural line of defence. He still had his preparations for the main offensive to complete. Already Budyonny's breakthrough at Samgorodok had turned the thoughts of the Polish army once more to the south. For the next month, the line in the north was stationary.

In the early summer of 1920, the Bolsheviks were faced with a situation which they had long foreseen, but for which they

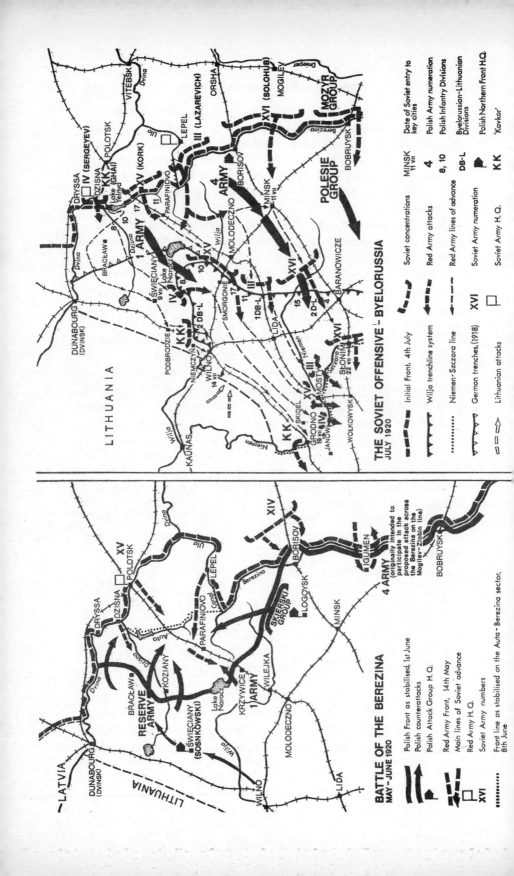

THE SOVIET OFFENSIVE¹—BYELORUSSIA
JULY 1920

LITHUANIA

DUNABOURG (DVINSK) · DRYSSA · DZISNA · IV (SERGEYEV) · POLOTSK · VITEBSK · BRACŁAW ■ · KK · Lake Yelnya · V (KORK) · KK (GHAI) · LEPEL · ULA · III (LAZAREVICH) · ORSHA · Dvina · Dvina · 8 · 10 · 17 · 11 · 1 ARMY · PARAFINIOVO · 4 ARMY · BORISOV · MOGILEV · XVI (SOLOHUB) · Dnieper · MOZYR GROUP · ŚWIĘCIANY · 9 vii · Lake Narocz · 8 · 10 · IV · XV · SMORGONIE · MOLODECZNO · MINSK 11 vii · Berezina · BOBRUYSK · POLESIE GROUP · PODBRODZIE · KK · 2 DB-L · 17 · 11 · III · 1 DB-L · XVI · BARANOWICZE · NIEMCZYN · WILNO 14 vii · LIDA · 15 · 2 D-L · 4 · XVI · Wilja · SKIDEL · III · XV · Szczara · St. ONIM 22 vii · Niemen · MOSTY · SŁONIM · GRODNO 19 vii · IV · JANÓW · WOŁKOWYSK · KK · KAUNAS · Niemen · Willja · Willja

Legend:

▬▬▬	Initial Front, 4th July
▬▬▬	Wilja trenchline system
·········	Niemen-Szczara line
▼▼▼▼	German trenches (1918)
⇨ ⇨	Lithuanian attacks
⟋⟋	Soviet concentrations
⟍⟍ (arrow)	Red Army attacks
▬ ▬ ▬ (dashed arrow)	Red Army lines of advance
XVI	Soviet Army numeration
☐	Soviet Army H.Q.

MINSK 11 vii	Date of Soviet entry to key cities
4	Polish Army numeration
8, 10	Polish Infantry Divisions
DB-L	Byelorussian-Lithuanian Divisions
▲	Polish Northern Front H.Q.
K K	'Kavkor'

BATTLE OF THE BEREZINA
MAY—JUNE 1920

LATVIA

DUNABOURG (DVINSK) · LITHUANIA · WILNO · DRYSSA · DZISNA · POLOTSK · XV · Dvina · Ula · Dzisna · Dvina · BRACŁAW ■ · KOZIANY · RESERVE ARMY (SOSNKOWSKI) · ŚWIĘCIANY · Lake Narocz · Auta · PARAFINIOVO · LEPEL · canal · Berezina · BORISOV · XIV · KRZYWICE · 1 ARMY · WILEJKA · Wilja · MOLODECZNO · LIDA · MINSK · SKIERSKI GROUP · LOGOYSK · IGUMEN · 4 ARMY (originally intended to participate in the proposed attack across the Berezina on the Mogilev-Ziobin line) · BOBRUYSK

Legend:

▮▮	Polish Front as stabilised, 1st June
▮ (arrows)	Polish counterattacks
▲	Polish Attack Group H.Q.
▼▼	Red Army Front, 14th May
▮ (thick arrows)	Main lines of Soviet advance
☐	Red Army H.Q.
XVI	Soviet Army numbers
·········	Front line as stabilised on the Auta-Berezina sector, 8th June

were still mentally and physically unprepared. Once the Polish advance into the Ukraine came to a halt, they had to consider their own offensive. Having sustained the first blow of the season, they could reasonably justify their offensive as a measure of self-defence. But they had great difficulty in accepting the ideological propriety of the emotions which attended it and in defining its nature and aims. They plunged into lengthy discussions which were concluded in July less by the attainment of unanimity than by the irresistible temptations of military success.

The wave of patriotic feeling, first aroused at the end of April by Piłsudski's attack on Kiev, continued unabated. It turned the Polish war into a popular event. It stirred the sympathies of many Russians who hitherto had refused to serve the Soviet regime. Most prominent of these was Alexey Brusilov, former Russian Commander-in-Chief under the Provisional Government and the only Tsarist general of the World War to lead a successful offensive. In 1920 Brusilov was a white-haired invalid, crippled two years earlier when the house in Moscow where he was hiding from the Red Terror was struck by a shell. He now emerged and offered his services. His letter to the Soviet Command, and later an appeal to his former subordinates, was published in *Pravda*:

Forget the wrongs you have suffered. It is now your duty to defend our beloved Russia with all your strength and to give your lives to save her from irretrievable subjugation.[4]

Brusilov was appointed chairman of a specially founded advisory council of military experts.

Patriotism was an attitude which few Bolsheviks admired and which none of them had expected to operate to their advantage. Patriotism had seduced the workers of the world into the fratricidal slaughter of the Great War. Patriotism was a false god of the bourgeoisie who used it to lure the proletariat into self-inflicted sacrifices. Patriotism had been roundly condemned by all the leading Bolsheviks whose arguments on the subject distinguished them from most of Europe's other socialist movements. Patriotism was a quality which the Polish enemy possessed in ample measure. Yet in May 1920, patriotism was drawing Russian men to the ranks of the Red Army in exactly the same way that it had drawn them to the service of the Tsar in August 1914. The paradox was agonizing. The political problem, whether to encourage the trend or to suppress it, was acute; it taxed the minds of Party theorists for weeks, and made a lasting impact on Soviet ideology. The first reaction was to pretend that it did not exist. Early in May, *Pravda* published a number of articles arguing that the Polish war did not have a national character at all. Poland under Piłsudski was going through the same phase as Russia under Kerensky, and the war against her was no more than an extension of the Civil War. 'The war with Poland', wrote Grigory Sokolnikov in a leading article on 9 May, 'is a class war, and is as far from being a national war as Heaven is from the Earth'.[5] The longer the war continued the more inappropriate this viewpoint appeared. Russian journals and Red Army propaganda were putting out a stream of jingoistic slogans as violent as anything which could be found in the Polish press. Lenin had to issue stern warnings on the dangers of chauvinism.[6] Trotsky suspended the Red Army journal *Voyennoye Delo* ('Military Affairs') for publishing an article which had contrasted the 'inborn Jesuitism of the *Lyakhs*'* with the 'honourable and open spirit of the Great Russian race'.[7] The task of reconciling past theory with present reality was entrusted to Karol Radek, who as a Pole was specially aware of the force of patriotism and who made three lengthy contributions to *Pravda* on 'The Character of the War with White Poland'.[8] Radek admitted that both national and social aims were present in the conduct of the Polish war, but explained that the national element was more apparent than real since it derived from a coincidence that the latest capitalist enemy happened also to be a foreign enemy. He distinguished between Russian chauvinism, which bore hatred towards everything Polish, and 'healthy patriotic instincts'. The latter, he said, could be observed in the peasant who feels the need to protect the land he now possesses, in the worker who seeks to defend the power which is now in his hands and even in certain 'circles of the intelligentsia which so far have been hostile towards us'. He concluded that 'between our

---

* '*Lyakh*' was an abusive term for the Poles.

patriotic and our internationalist tasks in this war there are no serious differences and no contradictions'. He went further:

Since Russia is the only country where the working class has taken power, the workers of the whole world ought now to become Russian patriots...We are sufficiently strong not to worry about these patriotic themes deafening our orchestra or drowning our singing of the 'Internationale'.[9]

The ideological debate monopolized the mind of the Soviet government to the detriment of an equally necessary review of their practical aims. Trotsky was the only Bolshevik leader to formulate a coherent view of the Polish war and of its implications for Soviet policy as a whole. Paradoxically, his long-standing apprehensions about the war led him to demand absolute priority for it once his army was irrevocably committed. Having constantly maintained that a direct confrontation with the European powers would be extremely hazardous, he was now bound to insist on a supreme effort if disaster was to be avoided. His opinion, contained in his sixteen theses *On the Polish Front and our Tasks*, was approved by the Revolutionary War Council on 30 April:

1. The imperialists of the Entente, who are conducting trade talks with Soviet Russia, have nonetheless maintained their ties with White Guard Poland, Finland, and Latvia. Hence it may be concluded that uncertainties and antagonisms reign in the imperialist camp concerning the best way to strangle Russia of the workers and peasants.

2. One group of the capitalist countries, where the techniques of mass production are highly developed, hoped to destroy our socialist economy by establishing an exchange of goods with the *kulaks* through the medium of White Guard co-operatives. The other group, which relies more on heavy industry and on war industries, seeks to gain its ends by military action and by the direct seizure of Russia's natural riches. Individual governments and individuals within each government fluctuate between these two views in accordance with their particular capitalist connexions and their estimate of the military situation.

3. White Guard Poland has no independent policy, but is driven on by greed and cowardice. The attack on the

Ukraine may be seen as an attempt to satisfy the Entente's demands for raw materials at Russia's expense whilst conserving Poland's own resources.

4. A new wind is blowing. Fresh military adventures against Soviet Russia will be encouraged by the revolutionary situation in Germany and by the realization that trade with Russia will not destroy the Soviet system but on the contrary will actually strengthen it.

5. The Polish bourgeoisie was well aware of these considerations when it attacked the Ukraine.

6. The territorial policies of Finland and especially of Latvia are formulated in Warsaw in conjunction with the Polish government.

7. The whole question of foreign trade and of future relations with our western neighbours will be determined by the outcome of the Polish war.

8. The Polish bourgeois republic has given proof that it will not and can not co-exist with Soviet Russia. It has fallen into its own trap. The gentry and bourgeoisie of Poland will be rounded up by the Polish proletariat who will then proceed to turn their country into a socialist republic.

9. The war will be fought in a specially strained and vicious atmosphere. The Polish government, which is hand in glove with the old foxes of social-patriotism, is whipping up against us not only the brutal hatred of the great, middle and lesser *kulak-bourgeoisie* and the haughtiness of the Polish gentry, but also the nationalistic prejudices of the masses....This does not affect our commitment to the independence of Poland one iota.

10. The Polish war must be treated, not as the private problem of the Western Front, but as the foremost problem of all Russia.

11. All state, Party, and professional organizations must explain our policy to the entire population, even in the furthest depths of the countryside. Workers and peasants, men and women, must all understand and feel that the Polish war is their war, a war for the independence of socialist Russia and for her union with proletarian Poland and with the proletariats of all the world.

12. All measures for improving transport and communications must be intensified.
13. Our enemies interpreted the formation of labour armies as a sign of military weakness. They were mistaken. The majority of these forces must be released from their present duties and transferred to the Western Front.
14. All local and party organizations must consider how best they can co-operate with the Western Front.
15. Everywhere and anywhere, meetings and conferences must be called to explain the Polish war to the non-party masses.
16. All national commissariats must draw up plans for assisting the Western Front.[10]

Trotsky's theses are notable for the logical way in which their practical recommendations were developed from a purely theoretical evaluation of the policy of the Entente. His analysis of the exclusively economic motivation of Allied designs is quaint in the extreme, but his observation concerning their contradictions was nicely relevant. By exaggerating the military nature of Allied hostility to Bolshevism and by minimizing the Polish government's capacity for independent action, he inevitably convinced himself that Armageddon was at hand. He was so transfixed by the enormity of the coming struggle that he was quite incapable of looking beyond it. His theses contain no proposals for the terms of an eventual settlement and no precise conception of the 'proletarian union' of the future. He assumed that Poland would be liberated by her own people and not by the Red Army of Russia. His only recognizable war aim was to survive. His directive of 9 May— the first to Tukhachevsky in his new command—stated that the Western Front was the most important of all and 'far more important than the Eastern or Southern Fronts'.[11] To emphasize the point, he set off on a tour of inspection. Starting from Smolensk, he drove to the frontline at Rechitsa on the Upper Dnieper. On 10 May he was in Gomel, where he made a hair-raising speech about the threat of espionage and about the supposed atrocities of the enemy. He told his audience that the Poles took no prisoners and that they were in the habit of hanging or shooting all who fell into their hands, including the sick, the wounded, and 'non-party men'.[12] On 11 May he was at Nezhin, at the junction of the Western and South-Western Fronts. On 15 May, he was back at Mogilev in time to launch the Battle of the Berezina in person.

Stalin's views were down-to-earth and definite. He foresaw two difficulties in the Polish campaign. Firstly, he was worried by the organization of the Red Army's rear:

> When we have talked of the chances of Russia's victory and have said that those chances are growing and will grow still further, it does not follow that victory is already in our pocket. . . . The above mentioned victory can only have real meaning in conditions where our forces are properly organized, where they are supplied regularly and accurately, where our agitators are able to spread burning enthusiasm among the troops, where our rear is cleansed of filth and corruption and where it is consolidated both morally and materially. . . [13]

His second worry concerned the nature of the future Polish constitution. Everyone was blandly talking about a 'Soviet Poland' and of 'hoisting the Red Star over the citadel in Warsaw', without ever stopping to think what was actually involved. Stalin's experience as Commissar of Nationalities warned him against treating the historic nations like Poland, Germany, or Hungary in the same way that the Bashkirs or the Ukrainians had been treated. In a letter to Lenin on 16 June, he proposed that Poland should be accommodated, not in the existing Russian Soviet Federation, but in a wider *confederation* of Soviet states.[14] On one point he was quite clear. He was sure that neither Soviet Russia nor the Entente would allow the Border States to enjoy a genuinely independent existence:

> Three years of Revolution and Civil War have shown that without the mutual support of Central Russia and the Borderlands, the Revolution is impossible, the liberation of Russia from the claws of imperialism is impossible. . . The so-called independence of Georgia, Armenia, Poland, Finland, and so on, is only a deceptive appearance masking the complete dependence of these—pardon the expression—states on this or that group of imperialists.[15]

Lenin displayed fewer doubts than any of his colleagues. He was not at all upset by the paradoxes revealed in the public debates. He scorned Trotsky's caution. He took little notice of Stalin's misgivings and practical suggestions. He said that Soviet Russia would only talk peace with 'Polish workers and peasants'.[16] He was very angry with Radek, who dared to express the opinion that the Red Army would not be welcomed by the workers and peasants of Poland. He turned instead to another Pole, Unszlicht, who told him what he wanted to hear.[17] So long as the Polish war was progressing favourably, he let it run its course. Indeed, his confidence increased. The successes of Budyonny in Galicia and the massive build-up in Byelorussia seemed to confirm his optimism. When in the middle of July, the diplomatic situation demanded a formal ruling, he did not hesitate. He insisted that the Red Army advance into the heart of Poland with all possible speed. On 17 July, he impressed this vital decision on the Politburo without much difficulty. He overruled Trotsky's advice, proferred on behalf of the Supreme Command, to halt the offensive and await developments. He carried the five other members with him. By that time Tukhachevsky was more than half way to the Vistula.

The month of June 1920 saw the transformation of the Soviet Western Front, so that in July, after nearly four months' preparation, the Red Army was at last to launch its attack on Poland. For the first time in its existence, the Soviet Republic attempted to marshal a large part of its total forces on a single front and for a foreign campaign.

Encouraged by Brusilov's example, the Soviets decided to conscript all former Tsarist officers and NCOs. A commission headed by Glezarov supervised their drafting. By 15 August, 314,180 of them were in service.[18] They represented a sizeable increase in the numbers of trained and skilled men available. It is significant that all of Tukhachevsky's army commanders— Kork, Lazarevich, Sołłohub, and Sergeyev—were former Tsarist colonels.

Those who could not be conscripted were urged to volunteer.

Volunteers are needed! You, young men of the proletariat! You, conscientious peasants! All you in the intelligentsia who are honourable men! Russian officers, who have understood that the Red Army is saving the Freedom and Independence of the Russian nation! The Western Front calls you all. TROTSKY.[19]

One who answered the call was Vladimir Mayakovsky. This

problem child of the revolutionary movement, whose epic poem '150,000,000' expressing his feelings during this period was to be condemned by Lenin as 'hooligan communism',[20] forsook poetry for a while and joined the war effort. He took a job at *Rosta*, the Soviet Press Agency, where he applied his talents to the design of propaganda posters. On 19 May, he addressed his fellow workers in a lecture on the union of art and poetry in propaganda.[21]

Large numbers of civilians were involved in war work. A state of emergency was declared in twenty-four provinces of western Russia. Absolute priority was given to munitions and transport. Bolshevik party members were mobilized *en masse*. By August, sixty-five per cent of the party's membership, 280,000 communists, were serving in the ranks.[22]

Even the deserters returned. On the assurance that there would be no reprisals, about one million men out of the estimated two-and-a-half million who had drifted away from the Red Army during the winter found their way back.[23]

The Red Army multiplied mightily. By 1 August, it exceeded the five million mark. These were rightly classified as 'mouths' or 'eaters' (*yedoki*), since they consumed a quarter of the country's wheat supply for 1920 and far outnumbered the weapons available. Only one in nine could be classified as a 'fighting man' (*boyets*). Even so, in the course of 1920 almost 800,000 men were sent to the Polish war, of whom 402,000 went to the Western Front and 355,000 to the armies of the South-Western Front in Galicia.

The overall balance of forces is impossible to ascertain. The Soviet manpower pool in the West seems to have stood at 790,000. Tukhachevsky had so many men that he did not know what to do with them, so there seems little point in trying to count them exactly. He himself claimed to have some 160,000 fighting men to hand, whilst Piłsudski counted his opponents at between 200 and 220 thousand. Kakurin quotes figures of 90,509 bayonets and 6,292 sabres in the Soviet line and 86,000 bayonets and 7,500 sabres on the Polish side, of whom 37,000 were actually in position.[24] At all events there was a considerable Soviet superiority, probably 50,000 men, in the frontline area. The Soviet forces on the Western Front were divided into five armies—the IV Army of Sergeyev with four infantry and two cavalry divisions on the Dvina, the XV Army of Kork with five infantry divisions at Polotsk, the new III Army of Lazarevich with four infantry divisions and a cavalry brigade at Lepel, the XVI Army of Dovojno-Sołłogub with five infantry divisions on the Berezina, and the Mozyr Group of Chwesin with two combined divisions on the southern wing. They were opposed by three Polish armies, the First of General Żygadłowicz, the Fourth of General Szeptycki, also commanding the front, at Borisov, and the Polesie Group of General Sikorski on the Pripet. (See map, p. 134).

Tukhachevsky's problem was not one of manpower but of organization. He needed to raise the transport and supply far above Civil War standards. Some 7,400 carts were assembled for the IV Army alone; the XVI Army requisitioned 16,000. Field kitchens and food stores were prepared. Railway tracks were repaired, and strategic bridges, such as the Dvina bridge at Polotsk, completely rebuilt. The artillery was strengthened. Some 595 guns were brought up, giving a threefold superiority. A powerful and mobile strike force had to be fashioned. This was done in the form of the 3rd Cavalry Corps, the 'Kavkor' commanded by Ghaia Dmitriyevich Ghai.

Ghai was well known to Tukhachevsky. Like him, he was young, handsome, and confident. Born as Gaik Bzhishkian, at Tabriz in Persia in 1887, the eldest son of an exiled Armenian socialist, he had changed his name whilst serving in the Tsarist army. He lived several years in Tiflis where as an adolescent journalist, he used his first revolutionary pseudonym, 'Bandor' (worker), and earned himself five years in jail. In 1914, as a youth of 21 he was conscripted. He commanded a battalion on the Turkish front and was twice decorated for bravery, with the St George Cross (IV Class) and the Order of St Anne (IV Class). He was invalided out, for wounds incurred during his escape from Turkish captivity, and for a short period in February 1917 directed the activities of the 'War Patrol Command' of the pre-revolutionary Red Guard in Moscow. A further spell of convalescence sent him back to Samarkand, where early in 1918 he formed a detachment of armed workers. Unable to withstand the local counter-revolution, he led his men out into the wastes of Kazakhstan, whence after an epic trek across the Ural Mountains, he fought his way into Samara.

From that point on, the legend grew steadily. For much of the Civil War he served under Tukhachevsky. He commanded the famous 'Iron Division' on the Volga and eventually the First Red Army—'first in number and first in prowess'. In 1919, he was recalled by Tukhachevsky to the Southern Front to form the Caucasian Cavalry Corps of the X Army. When Tukhachevsky moved to the west in 1920, it was not surprising that Ghai was summoned to follow.[25]

Ghai reached his headquarters at Polotsk on 3 June 1920. His Kavkor was attached to the IV Army, and was to be forged from two existing cavalry divisions, the 10th, under N. D. Tomin, from the Urals, and the 15th (Kuban) Division commanded by V. I. Matuzenko. Infantry support was provided by the 164th Rifle Brigade. These were Tukhachevsky's shock troops. In due course they earned from the Poles the title of the 'Golden Horde of Gay-Khan'.

The role assigned to the Kavkor was of the utmost importance. Operating on the extreme right wing of the Soviet advance, they were to get under the edge of the Polish carpet, as it were, and to turn it up for rolling back by the weight of the following armies. The process was facilitated by three factors—by the vast expanse of the battle zone which as always favoured the speed and mobility of an attacking force, by the proximity of the Lithuanian frontier which acted as a shield and refuge, and by the character of the Polish defence. The Polish Command had conceived a system of 'defensive lines'. These were to be manned by strong garrisons, which could summon help from the reserve forces to any hard-pressed point. It was a typical First World War conception, relying on the fire-power of the trenches and the speed of the rail-borne reinforcements. In the event, it was to prove unsuited to Border conditions. The Poles had too few men to man the trenches adequately; their artillery was scattered, and outgunned at critical sectors; the railways were overladen, and too few and far between; the distances were too great for reinforcements to arrive in time. The Kavkor always got there first, forcing the Poles to abandon their positions often before they had the chance to defend them. Ghai was to seize the initiative from the start and to dominate the campaign until he was deep in Poland.

Tukhachevsky was ready at the beginning of July. His famous Order of the Day radiated confidence:

To the West !
Order to the forces of the Western Front
No. 1423   Smolensk   2 July 1920

Soldiers of the Red Army!
The time of reckoning has come.
The army of the Red Banner and the army of the predatory White Eagle face each other in mortal combat.
Over the dead body of White Poland shines the road to world-wide conflagration.
On our bayonets we shall bring happiness and peace to toiling humanity.
To the West!
The hour of the attack has struck.
On to Vilna, Minsk and Warsaw! March!
Commander-in-Chief, Western Front, Tukhachevsky; Members of the Revolutionary War Council, Smilga, Unszlicht; Chief of Staff, Schwarz.[26]

The grand offensive was launched on 4 July. A huge artillery barrage at dawn heralded the general advance. Ghai rode out from Dzisna. His task was to pierce the Polish line in the region of Lake Yelna and to raise havoc in the rear. He first encountered the 10th Infantry Division of the Polish First Army, which held firm and obliged him to turn to the north. He then met the 8th Infantry Division, whose command could not decide whether to stand and fight or whether to retreat to the German trenches. Ghai simply overtook them, and, reached the German trenchline near Bracław unchallenged. He could now ride south, and on 9 July entered Święciany, won at the cost of fourteen dead and thirteen wounded. He was two days ahead of schedule, and only forty-five miles from Wilno. The weak resistance of the Polish Army on other sectors may be attributed to the shock produced by Ghai's initial success. 'Rumours of the deep advance of our cavalry spread quickly among the Polish soldiers', Sergeyev wrote, 'and assumed fantastic proportion...A single word about the movement of our cavalry from the north panicked the Poles into throwing away their positions which faced the front to the east'.[27] Meanwhile, on the night of 6–7 July, the XVI

Army crossed the Berezina. The III Army cut the Molodeczno railway at Parafiniovo, then wheeled round to join the attack on Minsk, which fell on the 11th. The first Polish line had been broken.

Ghai was already thinking about Wilno, the main prize of the Borders but an objective which by rights should have waited. In Święciany he met a fourteen-year-old Byelorussian Young Communist called Vasya who offered to discover the state of Wilno's readiness. Vasya was driven over the Lithuanian border by Ghai's chauffeur, whence by night marches through the woods and a series of lifts in peasant carts, he was able to evade the Polish patrols and enter Wilno unnoticed. Staying in the homes of communist sympathizers and talking with soldiers in the streets and cafés, he learned that the city was only defended by a small garrison of some 2,000 men, by one of the Lithuanian-Byelorussian divisions digging in round the bridge over the Wilja, two reserve battalions, three cavalry squadrons and the Legion of Polish Women. Having obtained a Polish uniform and yet another lift, this time in a Red Cross transport heading for the frontline, he managed to approach the Soviet positions, got himself captured, and reported to the Red command in time for the attack.[28]

Ghai was also helped by the Lithuanians, who claimed Wilno as the future capital of their republic and were willing to go to considerable lengths to obtain it. On 9 July, they started diplomatic talks with the Soviet government and launched a series of armed raids across the demarcation line against the Polish army. They further disrupted Polish dispositions and encouraged Ghai to take his chance.

Ghai, in fact, had little time to choose. His exposed position in Święciany was being threatened by increasingly severe counter-attacks. His cavalry was obliged either to retreat or to advance. He advanced.

The approach to Wilno was covered by the River Wilja. Four frontal attacks by the Soviet 15th Division had been beaten off with heavy losses. Ghai, therefore, tried a ruse. Leaving the division's 1st Brigade in dismounted order to draw the enemy's fire, he led the four other brigades to a wooded stretch of the bank, from which they made a surprise attack in force. By the evening, the Wilja had been crossed in three places. The attackers then split into several parties, one riding round to Novotroki to approach the city from the south-west, one closing from the west, another marching from Niemczyn in the north and the main body pushing forward from the east. They quite disorientated the Polish defence. The Polish commander General Barszczuk was still moving troops towards the Wilja quite unaware that he was surrounded on all sides.

The fall of Wilno on 14 July had important consequences. In the diplomatic sphere, the Soviet and Lithuanian governments reached agreement. Wilno was to be given to Lithuania. The Soviet gesture helped to allay the fears of all the Baltic States. In the military sphere, the Polish army was forced to retire still further. There was no point now is defending the German trenches. The second Polish line had been broken.

The next phase of the offensive closely resembled the previous one. The Poles intended to stand on the line of the Niemen and Szczara. Sikorski's Group was holding the bank of the Ogiński Canal; the Polish reserve army was being moved from Białystok in two groups, one to the Niemen, the other to the Szczara in the region of Mosty. The chief fortress of their defensive line, Grodno, was at its western extremity, like Wilno, and thus exposed to the attentions of the Kavkor. At dawn on 19 July, Matuzenko's 15th Division raced into Grodno unannounced, and collided with the feeble garrison of General Mokrzecki. A violent battle ensued, which at first seemed likely to end in the punishment of Matuzenko's rash and lonely raid. Tomin's 10th Division, was pinned down in Skidel; the infantry of the IV and XV Armies still fifty miles behind. For two days the issue swayed in the balance. The divisional commanders begged Ghai to let them withdraw. The Poles sent every spare soldier to the Grodno sector. In the process they weakened the opposite, eastern extremity of their line. On 22 July, while the battle for Grodno still raged, the III and XVI Soviet armies crossed the Szczara. By the end of the week Matuzenko, relieved now by the infantry, broke out of Grodno to the west and effected the encirclement of the city. Grodno yielded 5,000 prisoners and, what was more important to the Kavkor, a Polish livery stable containing 500 fresh saddle horses. According to Ghai's own account, in Matuzenko's original charge 300 uhlans were sabred. Another 500, an entire Polish regiment, were drowned when they tried to swim their laden mounts in panic across the swift-flowing Niemen. The town's railway station was burned to the ground and the riverside quarter reduced to ruins. The third Polish line had been broken.

The battle at Grodno was the first occasion on the Western Front when the Red Army encountered tanks. On 19 July, the cadets of Grodno's military academy, advancing behind the fire of four Renault tanks, had forced two brigades of the Kavkor's 15th Division to retreat. In his memoirs, Ghai recalled the comments that were made: 'Tanks, Comrade Corps Commander! How can one sabre them when they're made of steel?' 'Bayonets are no use; in any case you can never get near them!'[29] There were in fact two companies of tanks in Grodno, some thirty vehicles in all. One company was never unloaded from its transport train, and could only fire from a stationary position on the flat cars in the marshalling yard. The second company formed the only active operational group left in the city. It was eventually surrounded and forced to retreat through the streets to the riverside. One by one, the tanks were disabled, by direct hits, by collisions, by lack of petrol, by breakdowns. Only two crossed the last burning bridge over the Niemen to rejoin the the Polish lines. As Ghai concluded, 'an armoured tank is nothing to frighten a skilled cavalryman'. He expressed a view which prevailed for two more decades.[30]

The Soviets had reached their Rubicon. Just beyond Grodno lay the Curzon Line. To advance further was to defy the Powers—to invade Europe. Tukhachevsky did not hesitate. His instructions were to press on. On 23 July, he ordered that Warsaw be occupied by 12 August at the latest.[31]

Despite the confusion of their retreat, the Polish army fiercely contested the Soviet advance. In one rearguard action, at Janów, an important cavalry engagement occurred. The 13th (Wilno) Uhlans, having covered the withdrawal of General Żeligowski's divisions across the Niemen, were ordered to screen their further retreat. They possessed no maps, and relied on the reports of peasants for the whereabouts of the enemy. At one moment a herd of stampeding bullocks was mistaken for a posse of Cossacks. On 25 July, they encountered the 15th Division of the Kavkor and charged. It was one of those rare occasions where lance and sabre clashed in splendid isolation. The Poles came off best. Their commander, Mścisław Butkiewicz killed his Soviet counterpart in hand-to-hand combat. They annihilated the leading squadron and delayed the march of the whole division by two or three days. They were surprised by the Kavkor's mediocre resistance, and by its defensive and 'unchivalrous' use of machine-gun *tachanki*. They revived the hope that all was not yet lost.[32]

The fourth and last defensive line, that of the Narew and the Bug, proved a stiffer obstacle than any of the others, mainly because of the state of the troops. Wearied attackers and wearied defenders could only fight a weary battle. In the week after the fall of Grodno, the Kavkor dissipated its energies, scouring the East Prussian frontier. The XV and III Armies were clearing the central area round Białystok and Bielsk. Piłsudski described the conditions of the Polish forces 'as a kaleidoscope of chaos'. Different units of the various divisions and armies were thrown together, sometimes joining up, sometimes splitting apart, always retreating. Piłsudski described how far their morale had sunk:

The incessant peristaltic movement of the enemy's greater numbers, interrupted from time to time by sudden leaps and bounds, a movement lasting for weeks on end, formed the impression of something irresistible, like a heavy, monstrous, uncontainable cloud... Under the influence of this moving storm, the State snapped, morale reeled, the hearts of the soldiers quailed.[33]

When the battle was rejoined on 29 July there were no dramatic manoeuvres. The Kavkor attacked Łómża on the Narew, but without its usual flair. Łomża resisted for a week. The XVI Army at Brest-Litovsk showed more dash. Storming the fortress with waves of infantry, they took the town with the collusion of local communists who had occupied the telephone exchange. But as soon as they crossed the Bug on 1 August, they were caught by a sudden counter-blow at Biata by Sikorski's Polesie Group and propelled back across the river. The III Army crossed the Bug in the central sector, but was soon halted at Sokołów. The Red Army had indeed broken the last Polish line of defence but more by the weight of numbers leaning clumsily on a demoralized enemy that by any disciplined exercise of the military art.

Once in Poland the Kavkor took new heart. While the other Soviet armies shambled forward, Ghai sped westward once more. On 4 August, he took the fort at Ostrołęka, and butchered the newly assembled cavalry group of General Roja. Przasnysz, Bieżuń, Sierpc fell in turn. At last in the second week of August the Red cavalry stood on the banks of the Vistula. The 10th Division reached the township of Bobrowniki, twenty-five miles from Toruń. On 17 August the 15th Division stormed the bridge at Wtocławek and cut the vital railway between Warsaw and Danzig. Poland had been well and truly invaded. (See map, p. 196)

The vagueness of Bolshevik political plans for the West stood in marked contrast to the precise ambitions of the Polish communists. For the Bolsheviks, the proletarian revolution in Poland was a troublesome but necessary stage on the road to their real goal in Germany and beyond; for the Polish communists, it was the be-all and end-all of their existence. The Polish Communist Workers' Party considered itself the junior partner but not the lackey of Moscow. It possessed a vibrant tradition of its own. It was dominated by left-wing communists who were dreaming of the same extreme and idealist programmes with which their colleagues of the Lit-Byel had so disastrously experimented. Although they were opposed in principle to the formation of a sovereign Polish state, they were worried by the recent manifestations of Russian patriotism in the Bolshevik Party and naturally wanted to keep control of the Polish communist movement in their own hands. Yet such was their standing in Moscow and their meagre support in Poland itself that nothing could be achieved without subordinating their wishes to those of their Bolshevik patrons. During the Soviet occupation of Poland, they suffered the exasperating fate of seeing their own organization subjected to the rigorous control of Moscow and their chances of political success seriously damaged by the clumsy politicking of the Red Army. In 1920 they received their first hard experience of life between the anvil of Catholic Poland and the hammer of Soviet Russia.

On 3 May the second 'All-Russian Conference of Communist Poles' opened in Moscow. The ninety delegates represented both local sections and army units. The war with Poland was the topic of the day. Resolutions were passed to mobilize all Polish party members, to intensify propaganda, and, most significantly, to merge the Conference's Commisariat of Polish affairs into the Bolshevik Party's own Polish Bureau.[34]

As a result of the conference the 'Polizdat' (Polish publishing house) started business in Kharkov later that month. At first it served the propaganda section of the South-Western Front and eventually of the entire Polish campaign. It turned out three newspapers, *Glos Komunisty* ('Voice of The Communist'), *Żolnierz Revolucji* ('Soldier of the Revolution') and *Wiadomoście Komunistyczne* ('Communist News'). In Smolensk, the news-sheet *Młot* ('The Hammer') was published by the Western Front Command in editions of 280,000, larger than that of any newspaper in Warsaw.

In the early summer months, Soviet propaganda fell on relatively fertile ground. Unlike their comrades on the southern front, the Polish soldiers in Byelorussia had occupied purely defensive positions for some nine months. They knew neither the exhilaration of an offensive nor the assurance that they were defending the homeland. Boredom and weariness bred pacifism and anarchy. Although desertion never reached the gigantic proportions current in the Red Army, the Polish command was worried. Bolshevik propaganda was circulating among men returning from leave, even among the wounded in field hospitals. On 2 July, General Szeptycki reported from Minsk:

Soldiers returning from leave and the latest reinforcements are agitating widely against the war, condemning its aimlessness. They say that 'Piłsudski has sold himself to the squirearchy...' Today, two rankers of the 22nd Infantry Regiment., Stanisław Dąbrowski and Stanislaw Królikowski were shot, in consequence of the sentence of a court martial which condemned them for mutiny and illegal agitation.'[35]

There were repeated incidents of insubordination. On 26 June part of the 29th Infantry Regiment tried to cross to the enemy lines *en masse*. Singing the 'Internationale', they climbed out of their trenches and headed into no-man's land. They were stopped by fire from behind. Yet the Soviet command wrongly attributed Polish desertions to widespread sympathy for the communist cause. Discipline was worst in the Silesian and Poznanian regiments and the 'Podhalański' (Alpine) Divisions from the Tatras, whose politics were far from progressive. The Polish soldier simply wanted to go home. In later stages, when the war was brought to the gates of Warsaw, the mettle of these Polish soldiers and their devotion to duty was shown to be superior to that of the Red Army.

When the Red Army crossed the Bug and at last reached territory which the Bolshevik leaders were willing to recognize as Polish, the political campaign expanded rapidly. Special 'Soviet Departments' were created in all Red Army units. Their task was to found communist cells in each of the occupied villages, estates, and factories. A revolutionary committee (*revkom*) was established in each of the occupied towns. According to Julian Marchlewski, this initial attempt to instal a communist system had disastrous consequences.[36] It was directed by Russians, who assumed that Russian and Yiddish ought to be the official languages of revolutionary Poland. To the Polish civilian, the Red Army's 'liberation' was indistinguishable from the countless military occupations of the past. The revkoms attracted the most opportunist elements in Polish politics, and resisted subsequent efforts to put them under the control of civilian, communist authorities following on the Red Army's heels. At Łómża, the revkom was run by an assortment of anarchists, Zionists, and conservative National Democrats.

On 23 July in Moscow, the Bolshevik 'Polish Bureau' resolved to form a 'Provisional Polish Revolutionary Committee', the Polrevkom, to which administrative and political powers in the liberated territories were to be transferred. The committee was 'provisional', in that final authority was theoretically reserved for the Polish proletariat, and in particular, after the occupation of Warsaw, for the Polish Communist Workers' Party. Its chairman was Julian Marchlewski.

The Polrevkom first assembled on 24 July in Smolensk. It worked from a train which carried a printing shop, an editorial office, a command carriage, and a motorized transport column. On 25 July it was in Minsk, on 27 July in Wilno, and on 30 July in Białystok, where its headquarters were installed and a public proclamation issued:

> On Polish territories freed from the yoke of Capital, a Provisional Polish Revolutionary Committee, composed of comrades Julian Marchlewski, Feliks Dzierżyński, Feliks Kon, Edward Próchniak and Józef Unszlicht, has been established. The Provisional Committee, having taken the administration into its own hands, has set itself the task, pending the formation in Poland of a permanent peasants' and workers' government, of laying the foundations of the future Polish Soviet Socialist Republic.
>
> To this end, the Provisional Committee
> (a) has removed the previous gentry-bourgeois government
> (b) is constructing factory and farm committees
> (c) is creating municipal revolutionary committees
> (d) is declaring all factories, land and forests to be national property administered by municipal and rural workers' committees
> (e) guarantees the inviolability of peasant holdings
> (f) is creating organs for security, supply, and economic control
> (g) assures complete safety to all citizens who loyally observe the dispositions and orders of the revolutionary authorities.[37]

On the same day, Marchlewski telegraphed Lenin:

> The magnificent Red Army, having broken the enemy's resistance, has advanced onto Polish territory as an active companion-in-arms of the Polish proletariat in its struggle with its bourgeois oppressor... Guided by the example and experience of Red Russia, we hope in the near future to put a thankful end to the liberation of Poland and to unfurl the Red Banner of Revolution over this fortress of imperialism. We greet the leader of the worldwide proletariat.
>
> Long live the Red Army, liberator of the working class of the whole world!
> Long live the Third Communist International!
> Long live the Revolution![38]

Although Marchlewski was the titular head of the Polrevkom there can be little doubt that its moving spirit and guiding hand was Feliks Dzierżynski. Dzierżynski was the senior Pole in the Bolshevik Party, and in 1920, chairman of the All-Russian Extraordinary Commission, the Cheka, the revolutionary political police. During the Civil War he specialized in eliminating the enemies of the Revolution in frontline areas. He toured the provinces, descending from his armoured train to dispense summary justice on station platforms to the unsuspecting subjects of the new Soviet power. In Białystok in August 1920, he was both prince and paymaster. He was the personification of Moscow's blessing, the essential link between the Polrevkom and the Bolshevik Polish Bureau and between the civilian and military authorities. From 9 August to 10 September, he was political officer of the War Council of the Western Front. He maintained his own private line with Lenin and Moscow; he co-ordinated the parallel political activities of the Western and South-Western Front Commands. His own department was the source of the milliard rouble credit advanced to the Polrevkom by the Soviet government.[39]

Dzierżyński's return to Poland in 1920 was poignant indeed. Poland had been the scene of his many tragedies, the stage for one of the most dramatic revolutionary careers of all time, the homeland which he had last seen six years previously through the grille of a convict wagon. Born in 1877, the son of a gentleman farmer at Oszmiany near Wilno, he had been a social outlaw from adolescence. Expelled from the gymnasium for the crime of speaking Polish—'that dog's language', as his Russian headmaster explained—he turned to socialist agitation. While still at school, he started the Lithuanian section of the Polish Social Democratic Party, and eventually joined 'the ruling five' of Róża Luksemburg's movement. He was a socialist and an internationalist, as much at home in Russia as in Poland, but never before 1917 a Bolshevik. From the day he was first arrested in Kaunas in July 1897 to the day of his release by the amnesty in Moscow in March 1917, he was constantly a convict or a wanted man. He spent fifteen of those twenty years in prison. He was thrice exiled to Siberia, and each time escaped. His personal life was crushed by political misfortune. His wife was a party widow, living alone in Cracow He was forced to watch the rape of his mistress by prison warders, but never set eyes on his only son, born in 1913 in Warsaw's female penitentiary. His intelligent pointed features were scarred by a toothless mouth, allegedly disfigured during the rape as he smashed his face in desperation against the iron bars of his cage. To cover the gaping gums his lips were always pursed, his nostrils distended, his lower eyelids slightly stretched, presenting an air of unnatural tension and unease. He lisped as he spoke, and always moved in haste. His tirelessness was legendary. To his friends he became 'Iron Feliks', to his enemies 'Bloody Feliks'; Lenin called him 'Feliks —the Good Heart'. To himself, he was the Robespierre of Soviet Russia, totally committed, totally incorruptible. He was a poet and a musician, who for consolation recited Mickiewicz and played the violin. Despite the lurid legends of his exploits, whether in the snows of Siberia, in a burning Moscow brothel or in the torture chambers of the White Guards, he has been described even by one of his most virulent detractors as 'an extremist with an open mind'. In Warsaw, he was known, feared, and awaited with apprehension. Stanisław Patek, Foreign Minister of Poland till June 1920, had been his defence lawyer before the war on several hopeless, occasions. Józef Piłsudski went to the same school. As Dzierżyński waited at Białystok for the assumption of power in Poland, both he and Polish leaders must have recognised the awesome symmetry of a terrible career turned full circle in the space of a few months.

The programme of the Polrevkom started with a mass meeting in Białystok on 2 August. Speeches were delivered by Marchlewski, Tukhachevsky, and a representative of the Bolshevik Central Committee, I. Skvortsov-Stepanov. These were followed by a demonstration of railwaymen who had decided to support the new authorities.

The Polrevkom was closely supervised by the Bolshevik Polish Bureau. The two worked side by side in the confiscated palace of the Branicki family. The Polish Bureau took the important decisions, whilst the Polrevkom confined itself to mainly administrative affairs.

The Polrevkom functioned for three weeks and two days. Its limits followed the frontline in the west and south, the East Prussian frontier in the north and the recreated Byelorussian SSR beyond the Bug in the east. The Polish *wojewódstwa* (counties) were renamed *obwody* (circuits) which to some ears sounded more democratic. Local administration was in the hands of the sixty-five revolutionary committees. Polish replaced Russian as the official language. All the main industrial enterprises were nationalized—although as yet there was no state to administer them. The eight-hour working day was introduced. Elections were prepared but never held. A Union of Communist Youth appeared, and a Central Trade Union Commission. Revolutionary tribunals were created 'to counter political and economic crimes and banditry'. A militia was recruited exclusively from workers and peasants. Steps were taken to protect 'cultural objects and historical monuments'. A 'Declaration for Freedom of Conscience' was issued.

On 6 August Dzierżyński telegraphed Lenin that 'we consider the most important problem to be the organizing of a Polish Red Army and we hope to found a proletarian force in the very near future'. On 9 August he told Marchlewski to compose an appeal to Polish working men, on the basis of which a Polish Volunteer Regiment was formed. In the two weeks before its disbandment the regiment attracted a total of 175 men.[40] Tukhachevsky took measures of his own to organize a more substantial, regular Polish Red Army. The language of command was to be Polish, and the soldiers were to wear the distinctive *rogatywka* hat surmounted by a red star. Otherwise everything was to be identical with the Soviet Red Army. It was to draw on all the Poles scattered through the Soviet divisions, and also on the large numbers of prisoners soon expected. The staff of this First (Polish) Red Army, headed by its commander R. Łagwa and its commissar S. Budkiewicz, were stationed at Minsk. At the end of the war, it was evacuated to the Urals, and its leading soldiers, like Karol Swierczewski had to wait for later occasions to distinguish themselves.

Careful attention was paid to political security. Before leaving Moscow, Dzierżyński arranged for all Poles working in the Cheka to be drafted into the special service units of the Western Front. There is evidence to suggest that Lenin considered shooting 100 Poles for every communist executed by the Polish authorities.[41] The Cheka increasingly diverted its men against infiltration by German agents, who were crossing the East Prussian frontier in the guise of Spartakists and, much to Dzierżyński's dismay, 'were being given a warm welcome from our gullible comrades.'[42]

An attempt was even made to establish 'soviets' within the Polish army. The suggestion came from Stalin, and on 11 August Dzierżyński telegraphed Lenin to report that it had

1. Polish watch on the Horyn River, 1921

2. Joseph Pilsudski,
Head of State

3. Kazimierz Sosnkowski,
Chief of Staff

4. Joseph Haller,
OC Warsaw Front, 1920

5. Lucjan Zeligowski,
'an incomparable mutineer'

6. Michail Tukhachevsky,
OC Western Front, 1920

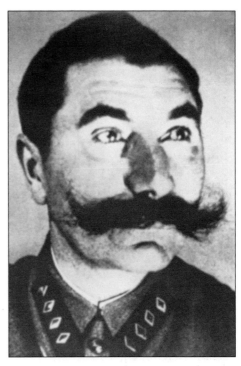

7. Semjon Budjonny,
OC 1 Konarmiya

8. A.I. Yegorov

9. Ghaia Dmitriyevich - 'Ghai-Khan'

10. V.I. Lenin,
General Secretary RSDP

11. J.V. Stalin,
Commissar for Nationalities

12. L.B. Trotsky,
Commissar for War

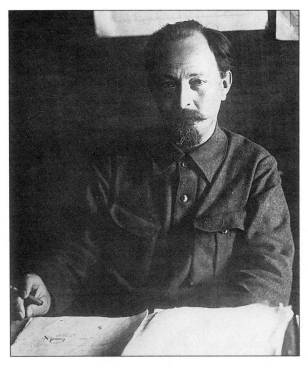

13. Feliks Dzierzyński, founder of the Cheka

14. Karol Radek,
Lenin's adviser on Polish affairs

15. Isaac Babel,
journalist and writer

16. Alexandre Millerand,
Prime Minister of France

17. David Lloyd George,
Prime Minister of Great Britain

18. Archbishop Achille Ratti,
Papal Nuncio (later Pope Pius XI)

19. Major Charles de Gaulle,
French Military Mission

20. Polish frontline trench: River Pripet, 1919

21. Patrol watch on the upper Dniepr: Polish soldiers in French uniforms

22. Soviet Nieupoort fighter, 1919–20

23. Polish women's machine-gun unit, Lwów, 1919–20

24. Polish Uhlans behind enemy lines, Ukraine, 1920

25. A Polish armoured train

26. Soviet soldiers in regulation 'Tartar caps'

27. 'The Polish Church
Militant'

28. The Prior of the
Lavra Monastery,
Kiev, with a Polish
sentry.

29. Polish scouts on frontline reconnaissance

30. General Haller: spotting enemy positions

31. Two Polish horsemen

32. Polish cavalrymen

33. A Mayakovsky poster:
1) If we don't defeat the White Guards completely,
2) The White Guards will rise again.
3) If we defeat the Polish squire, then fold your arms,
4) Wrangel will raise his hand against the worker.
5) So long as the Red Banner is not secured, it's not for us to cast our guns aside.

34. Poland as a French pig 'dressed in Paris': in the pig's trotter 'The Frontiers of 1772'

35. 'Out of the way!' A Communist Polish poster

36. The Polish Army enters Kiev, 8 May 1920

37. Ataman Semeon
Petlura, the Ukrainian
leader, salutes General
Edward Rydz-Smigly,
Kiev, May 1920

38. Marshal Joseph
Pilsudski with General
Edward Rydz-Smigly,
Battle of the Niemen,
September 1920.

39. A Polish legionary unit fords a river in the Ukraine

40. Retreat over the Bug, July 1920

41. The Red Cavalry: Soviet 'Konarmiya' troopers, 1920

42. The Polish Cavalry: a regiment of Uhlans

43. Jewish volunteers prepare a defence line near Warsaw

44. Polish soldiers dig in

45. The *Polrevkom* (Polish Revolutionary Committee), 10 August 1920: Feliks Dzierzyński, Julian Marchlewski, Feliks Kon

46. The Second Congress of the Communist International (Comintern), Moscow, July-August 1920. View of the platform with Lenin (*centre*), Kamenev (*right*), Zinoviev (*left*) and Stalin (*background, second from left*)

47. The Interallied Mission: Lord D'Abernon (*left*), General Weygand (*centre*)

48. Weygand wonders what his Polish colleagues are discussing

49. Red Army delegates cross the frontline

50. Talks about talks: Poles (*left*), Soviets (*right*)

51. Bonawentura Snarski's peasant partisans (some in pre-1917 Tsarist uniforms)

52. Independent Workers' Battalion in Warsaw

53. Captured Soviet standards:
'Proletarians of all countries unite' and 'All hail to the October Revolution'

54. General Sikorski interrogates young Soviet deserters

55. Soviet prisoners of the Polish Army

56. After the Battle of Warsaw, August 1920

57.–58. Polish prisoners of the Red Army

59. Red Army men in captivity

60. Bolshevik massacre: Polish prisoners allegedly used for sabre practice

61. Uhlan's grave:
'Corporal Jerzy Bakowski, 4th Hussars, killed in the charge at Burnicki,
near Zwiahel, 5 October 1920, aged twenty-five years'

62. Workers' anti-war demonstration in Warsaw calling for
'bread and work' and 'social revolution'

63. The peace conference at Riga, October 1920

64. Last rites

been adopted. It had some small effect, especially among the Warsaw regiments.[43]

In a largely rural area, the foremost political problem was the agrarian question. The support of the peasantry was essential to the success of the expected revolution. Lenin took a personal interest in these matters, and was understandably dismayed when the Polrevkom failed to follow his advice. On 14 August, Lenin sent Karol Radek to Białystok to enquire why the Polrevkom's manifesto made no mention of the agrarian question. On 19 August, Lenin cabled Radek:

I beg you, go straight to Dzierżyński and insist that the landowners and kulaks are destroyed ruthlessly and a bit more quickly and energetically, also that the peasants are effectively helped to take over seigneurial land and forest.[44]

Dzierżyński, however, was unable to convince his colleagues of the necessity of following Lenin's advice. The majority of the Polrevkom scorned the idea of slavishly imitating Russian policies. They opposed the immediate redistribution of confiscated land, on the grounds that it would obstruct their scheme for collectivizing agriculture. The Polrevkom showed itself to be more communist than the Bolsheviks, or, in Lenin's phraseology, to be suffering from 'the infantile disease of "Leftism" '. On 15 August, Dzierżyński had wired Lenin: 'The question of land policy will be fully examined when we arrive in Warsaw, whither we depart today'.[45]

Lenin was not satisfied. Having heard that the peasants in the Siedlce area had taken matters into their own hands, he addressed a last appeal, 'to Dzierżyński, Radek, and all other members of the Polish Central Committee':

If the small-landed peasantry in Siedlce have started to seize the estates, it is all the more reason why a special decree of the Polrevkom should be published, to the effect that a part of the landed estates will be given without fail to the peasants, in order that the poor peasantry and farm labourers be thereby reconciled. Please reply.[46]

There was no time for a reply. The Polrevkom did not reach Warsaw. It left Białystok on 20 August, the day before Lenin's last telegram was received. Its land policy was never settled.

A public declaration *Do włościan polskich* ('To the Polish Peasantry'), made several promises about the inviolability of peasant holdings and the liquidation of all peasant debts, but in the face of the Red Army's forced requisitioning it can have inspired but little confidence.

As even official communist historians now admit, the failure of the Polrevkom was due to the simple fact that it did not enjoy the respect or confidence of the people it sought to liberate. It operated in the wake of military operations whose destruction and brutality had already alienated the civil population. It operated under the patronage of a Russian army. It operated among people for whom national independence was far dearer than social revolution. It sought to import an ideology entirely alien to the prevailing beliefs and attitudes of the time. It did not even follow the advice of its Soviet patrons, whose bayonets provided its only means of survival. It quite failed to attract those social elements who should logically have welcomed its arrival. The peasantry were offended by requisitioning; the proletariat by the repression of all existing working-class parties. In the history of 'the field of class struggle', the Polrevkom was a sickly seed cast on the stoniest ground.

The political campaign on the South-Western Front developed along similar lines. The Galician Revolutionary Committee, the 'Galrevkom' with its seat in Tarnopol, resembled the Polrevkom in all essential respects. Its president was Vladimir Zatonsky, onetime minister of the Ukrainian SSR and now political director of the XIV Army. It enjoyed a considerable measure of independence. It regarded itself, not as a branch of the Ukrainian, Polish, or Russian communist movements but as the forerunner of an entirely separate Soviet republic, the Galician SSR. Surviving as it did from 8 July to 21 September 1920, it had time to organize its affairs. It succeeded in establishing a new administrative structure, a new system of justice, and education and a new militia. A Galician Red Army was inaugurated. Soviet currency was introduced. Polish, Ukrainian, and Yiddish were instituted as official languages of equal status. One would not have gathered from its ambitious pronouncements that the two most important areas of East Galicia, the city of Lwów and the Borysław-Drohobych oilfield, were not under its control. The Galician

Soviet Republic was no more than an interesting experiment in a rural backwater.

The zenith of the Polrevkom and the Galrevkom was reached on 14 August. On that day, Dzierżyński drove from Białystok to Wyszków, a town on the lower Bug only twenty-nine miles from Warsaw. He was ready to enter the capital in triumph. Budyonny was besieging Lwów.

In retrospect, the Soviet political experiments in Poland in 1920 seem to present a classical example of puppet régimes imported in the baggage of an invading army. Yet the charges of malice aforethought are exaggerated. In 1920, the immediate aim of the Red Army was not to forge a new state system but to provoke a social revolution. The Bolshevik leaders had not even considered the final administrative organization of the new order in Russia itself; the Soviet Union did not yet exist; the eventual place of Soviet Poland or of Soviet Galicia was no clearer than that of the Soviet Ukraine or Soviet Germany or Soviet America. Nothing was prepared. All went by improvisation. The political experiments were undertaken in response to and not in premeditation of the given military situation.

It is probably more accurate to stress the elements of farcical self-delusion. The invasion of Poland was undertaken by politicians who had been isolated from the outside world throughout their brief careers. As founders of the first socialist state in history, they had no precedents to work from. As practitioners of an ideology still in the course of formation, they operated by guesswork, by imagination, by deduction from their Marxist textbooks. As statesmen who had only recently emerged from exile, outlawry, and the underground, they proceeded by a haphazard mixture of intuition, dogma, defiance, and sudden rushes of enthusiasm. When they arrived in Poland it was as a gang of unruly toddlers who had strayed from curiosity out of their political nursery and onto the street. If an international outrage *was* committed by the Soviets in 1920, it was due more to infantile ignorance than to dire intent.

It is a well-tried rule that war accelerates social and political change. War acts as a bellows which fans smouldering problems into flame and forces people into new decisions and new dissensions. It is not always recognized, however, that the pressures of war can sometimes act interdependently on the two sides of the front, that rising pressure on one side may mean falling pressure on the other, and that both conditions are equally perilous to social and political stability. In the summer of 1920, if Poland was suffering from political hypertension Soviet Russia was suffering from a mild attack of the political 'bends'.

The crisis in Poland was all the sharper for the contrast with the mood of apathy and complacence which had so recently prevailed. In May, the communiqués of the General Staff had talked of 'the final collapse of the Soviet forces'. Skulski's ministry was proceeding quietly. Piłsudski was riding high, even in the minds of his opponents. The National Democrats connived at his military success; the Socialist Party at its congress in May prepared to join the government; the peasant parties were preoccupied with agrarian reform. The Sejm busied itself with domestic affairs. A new law for compulsory health insurance served to calm the left-wing critics. Only the communists, a tiny extra-parliamentary minority, maintained their implacable hostility to the country's leaders. Then, quite suddenly, the trend was reversed. First the battle of the Berezina, then the fall of Kiev, and finally throughout June and July the daily reports of half-concealed defeats, of rivers crossed, of towns lost—Zhitomir, Równe, Minsk, Wilno, Grodno, Białystok—convinced even the dullest citizen that his own home and livelihood could soon be in danger. On 9 June, Skulski's government resigned, to dodge the wrath to come. The press awoke. On 16 June a leading conservative daily, *Rzeczpospolita*, called for a régime of national unity, and for the subordination of the Chief-of-State to the Sejm. For a fortnight there was no government.

On 23 June the National Democrat, Władysław Grabski, agreed to form a stop-gap cabinet. He recalled Prince Eustachy Sapieha from the legation in London to revitalize the Foreign Ministry. On 30 June, in view of increasing tension, he proposed the formation of a Council for the Defence of the State (Rada Obrony Państwa), a supreme body which would formally unite members of the government with nominees of the Sejm, of the Chief-of-State, and of the army High Command, and which would be entrusted with the highest decisions of national policy. It was a proposal which, although it sealed the fate of the proposer, nonetheless solved the constitutional crisis. The parties of the left and centre, were willing to support the Rada Obrony Państwa but demanded that they themselves control the cabinet. As the socialist leader, Ignacy Daszyński told the Sejm:

The best institution for the defence of the nation is a government of the workers and peasants.... I appeal to you not as members of parties but as people threatened by a great and common catastrophe. If the worker has to make ammunition, and the peasant has to give his corn, his only horse, and his son to the army, then let him feel that the government in his own.[47]

On 1 July, the Sejm voted unanimously. The Rada Obrony Państwa held its first meeting that same evening. It had eighteen members: Piłsudski, in the chair; Trąmpczyński, the Marshal of the Sejm; three ministers—Daszyński, Skulski, and Sapieha; three generals—Haller, Sosnkowski, and Leśniewski; and ten deputies drawn from each of the main parties. Its first act was to order the arrest of persons suspected of 'anti-state activity'. During the next three months until its disbandment on 1 October, it held twenty-four sessions. It alone provided a framework for that essential unity of purpose which Poland's normal governmental machinery could not have engendered. Within its compass, a major political confrontation between Piłsudski and the National Democrats, passed off smoothly. In the session of 19 July, Piłsudski offered to relinquish all his offices.[48] Having received his vote of confidence, he then turned the tables on his critics. The National Democrat chief, Dmowski, once the self-appointed crown prince of the Republic, resigned, never to return to a position of authority. Grabski stayed on as Premier to complete the round of negotiations with England and France then in progress. On 24 July he too resigned. The way was open for the formation of the coalition ministry which, in harness with Piłsudski, fought the war to its end. The net result of the crisis was to check the centrifugal tendencies of Polish politics and for a time to forge a system in which inter-party differences were forgotten.

The composition of the Coalition Ministry reflected the progressive elements in parliamentary Polish politics of the day. The Prime Minister, Wincenty Witos, leader of the Piast Party, was a peasant from Galicia, a *kulak* as the Russians might have called him, who had prospered by his own cunning, a man who still wore smock and breeches when receiving foreign ambassadors. The Vice-Premier, Daszyński, was a dedicated socialist, a veteran of many strikes and arrests, a silver-haired lawyer who had renounced his aristocratic title, a man unashamedly striving for the triumph of the proletariat. The conservative ministers—Skulski, Grabski, and Sapieha—were administrators of experience and moderate temper. These are the men whom Soviet writers have always characterized as 'the government of squires', and others as 'the government of colonels'. Modern Polish historians explain that the coalition ministry of 1920 was 'a gesture of the dominant social classes to the demands of the popular masses'.[49] Gesture or not, the government of Witos and Daszyński was rightly seen as a government of the people.

The invasion of Poland from the east inevitably weakened the central government's influence in the continuing territorial disputes in the west and north. The situation was easily exploited by Poland's neighbours. On 11 July, the Polish vote in the East Prussian Plebiscite was lower than expected. Allenstein (Olsztyn) and Marienwerder (Kwidzyn) voted to remain in Germany. On 28 July the Council of Allied Ambassadors in Paris arbitrarily divided Teschen Silesia in two, awarding the coalfield and steelworks to Czechoslovakia. This decision which excluded 130,000 Poles from their homeland, could hardly have been tolerated by a Polish government in normal circumstances. On 19 August, a rising in Silesia was launched by a population despairing of protection from Warsaw against repeated German provocations.

Throughout the summer months Poland was swept by a wave of excitement. The approach of the Red Army intensified everyone's emotions. The propertied classes, fearful for their property, grew more possessive; Catholics fearful for their religion grew more religious; revolutionaries, in expectation of the revolution, grew more revolutionary; the police, in face of disturbances, grew more repressive; patriots grew more patriotic. Polish society polarized rapidly. Indifference was impossible. The authorities divided the nation into reliable citizens and potential traitors. In the middle of July, they launched a campaign of preventive arrests. Their main victims were communists, trade unionists, and Jews.[50] On 20–21 July, several working-class districts of Warsaw were sealed off by the military. Six hundred people were arrested. Trade union leaders were taken in for questioning. The weavers' union and metalworkers' union were suppressed, their offices shut down. The Jewish Bund was proscribed; Jewish soldiers, some of them volunteers, were separated from their regiments and withdrawn from the front; Jewish nurses were dismissed from the Polish Red Cross; the Jewish Hospital in Warsaw was surrounded and twenty people led away on suspicion of communist sympathies.[51] Most of these unfortunates, some three thousand in all, were sent to the only place large enough to receive them—the camp for Soviet prisoners-of-war at Dąbie near Cracow.

The social excitement of 1920 was reflected in Poland's cultural life. The theatrical sensation of the season was provided by Stefan Żeromski's play *Pod Śniegem* (Under the Snow). The play describes the conflicts within a landowning family, whose older members resist the efforts of the son to improve the lot of the peasants. It ends with the murder of the whole family by marauding Bolsheviks. When first produced in Lwów, it caused a riot; in Cracow it raised prolonged applause. In Warsaw, an operetta called *Commandant of the Uhlans*, in which a castle is rescued from the Reds to the accompaniment of patriotic songs and traditional dances, played to packed houses for weeks on end. Adam Asnyk wrote a historical drama on the theme of Kościuszko's defeat of the Russians at Racławice in 1794. The composer Lachmann contrived to base his *Resurrectionis Iesu Christi Missa* on the melody of the national anthem. This last monstrous idea, of a Mass set to a mazurka, was expressive enough of Poland's spiritual turmoil.

In Soviet Russia, a less acute condition had a quite different cause. There, the favourable progress of the Polish campaign brought welcome relief. For two whole years the country had been gripped by civil war. Differences of opinion within the Bolshevik Party had been suppressed; schemes had been shelved, policy subjected to the rigorous demands of 'War Communism'. Now the pressure was off. The alert sounded at the fall of Kiev soon faded away. The Polish campaign provided an important stimulus to a mood of relaxation already somewhat in evidence. Factions, theories, and heady enthusiasms proliferated.

In the Bolshevik Party itself, serious ideological opposition made its appearance. 1920 was the year of the 'Workers Opposition'. As from the Ninth Party Congress in March, a group headed by Tomsky the trade union leader, Shlyapnikov, the former Commissar of Labour, and Aleksandra Kollontay, the apostle of free love, began to criticize the conduct of policy. Their initial protests concerned the principles of industrial management but their wider criticisms concerned the growing power of the state, of the party within the state, and of the continued predominance of intellectuals within the party. Their slogans—'workers' control', 'freedom of speech', 'freedom for criticism'—represented a fundamental challenge to Leninism, and even spread to the army, where the old call for elected commanders was revived. They earned the splendid label of the 'Syndicalist and Anarchist Deviation'.

1920 also proved to be the indian summer of the extra-party opposition. The Socialist Revolutionaries and the Mensheviks basked in the open for the last time. In May, the Socialist Revolutionary leader, Chernov, addressed a public meeting in Moscow during which he compared socialism with primitive Christianity and the degeneracy of Bolshevism with that of the medieval Church. In August, the last Menshevik Party conference was held in Moscow.

In the economic sphere, a debate blossomed on the virtues of planning. In March 1920, the magic phrase 'a single economic plan' was mentioned first by Trotsky. Lenin conceived his passion for electrification.

The relative freedom enjoyed by oppositionists and debaters was also enjoyed by the bureaucrats. 1920 saw the proliferation of the state and party machines. The employees of the party secretariat multiplied from 150 to 750. New departments of purely bureaucratic significance appeared, like Rabkrin (People's Commissariat of Workers' and Peasants' Inspection) and the Commission of Control, for the consideration of complaints against party officials. Their purpose was to check the growth of bureaucracy; their use, in the hands of bureaucrats, was to encourage it. Men like Stalin, who were principally interested in political organization, used this time to consolidate their own position, arming themselves for the moment when discipline would be asserted once more. Stalin unobtrusively but relentlessly, was laying the foundations of his future power. As a member of both the Politburo and the party's Organizational Bureau, 'Orgburo', he had a dominant voice in the appointment of party personnel; as chairman of Rabkrin, he became the party's watchdog over the state, with an important say in the Commission of Control; as chairman of the newly centralized Council of Nationalities, he put his tentacles into all the non-Russian territories towards which Soviet power was now spreading; as the Central Committee's favourite political troubleshooter, he gained respectable access to all the intrigues of the day; as the political member of the War Council of the South-West Front, he had direct influence on the activities of the Red Army and the progress of the Polish war. Stalin played little part in the debates of the national Soviet, the party congress, or Comintern. He had little significance as a policy maker. But in the summer of 1920 he had already made himself the leading *apparatchik*, the obvious candidate for the post of general secretary of the party.

The developments most directly relevant to the Polish war, were those in the field of international communism. Comintern, the international association of communist parties, was in no state to lead the worldwide revolution, which the Polish war was now supposed to be provoking. Since its foundation a year earlier, it had remained an entirely *ad hoc* body having no formal constitution or rules. Its members sported the most variegated opinions about its function and aims. There were several delegations from each of the European countries, most of them at odds with each other, and some, like the British, unsure whether they ought to be affiliated or not. In the words of its chairman, Zinovyev, it was 'nothing more than a propaganda association'. Lenin realized that Comintern must be put in better order. He felt that the main obstacle lay in the views of the 'Leftists', meaning dogmatic communists who refused to compromise on their theoretical principles. He especially feared the influence of the disciples of Róża Luksemburg, who were sceptical about the maturity of the proletariat in Poland and Germany and who might have opposed the further advance of the Red Army into those countries. He himself was now confident that the Bolshevik Revolution was soon to be imitated throughout Europe, and scanned the horizon for omens. Having identified the Kapp Putsch in Berlin in March 1920 as 'Germany's Kornilov Affair', he was convinced that Germany's October could not be long delayed. Zinovyev gave Lenin's analysis more practical expression. 'It is necessary', he wrote in the Comintern's journal of 14 June, 'to put a reliable guard on the gate of the Communist International'. No doubt Zinovyev saw himself as the *concierge*.

It was in this ambiguous atmosphere, of divided counsels and common elation, that the second Congress of Comintern assembled in Moscow on 21 July. The debating floor was dominated by Russian speakers, by Zinovyev, Bukharin, and Lenin in particular. Their emphasis on unity and organization carried the day. It was resolved that each party affiliated to Comintern must adhere without reservation to the 'Twenty-One Conditions', a document largely drafted by Lenin in person. Any party which was not prepared to obey the rules and follow the common programme was to be expelled. A constitutional statute was drawn up, establishing the annual congress of Comintern as the sovereign assembly of the world-wide proletariat and envisaging the election of a central executive committee. An 'International Trade Union Council' (Mezhsovprof) was created. A suggestion to appoint a general staff of the International Revolution, made in a letter from Tukhachevsky at his headquarters on the Western Front, was not adopted, but is indicative of the prevailing mood. The end product of the congress was a new organization, modelled in the image of the Bolshevik Party but intended eventually to supersede it.

The momentousness of the occasion was symbolized by a huge map of Europe hung in the congress hall. Every day the little red flags marking the position of the Soviet armies in Poland were moved triumphantly forward. Zinovyev described the scene:

Every morning the delegates stood with breathless interest before this map...The best representatives of the international proletariat followed every advance of our armies with palpitating hearts... Everyone realized that if the military goal set by our forces was achieved it would mean an immense acceleration of the international proletarian revolution.[52]

By the time the congress closed on 7 August, the little red flags were surrounding Warsaw. Many delegates departed in the expectation that they would return the following year, not just as party members but as representatives of ruling governments.

To the Allied governments in London and Paris, the Red Army's invasion of Poland came as a rude surprise. It was a contingency for which no one had planned. The Allied leaders had complacently assumed that the Bolshevik regime was far too feeble to promote a foreign war. When fixing their policy towards the Polish-Soviet conflict at the beginning of the year, they had only considered the prospect of a Polish invasion of Russia. Their undertaking to defend Poland from the Bolsheviks had never been made in specific terms and could only be implied from their commitment to uphold the Peace Treaty as a whole and from general statements to defend all 'the countries bordering on Bolshevist territory'.[53]

For Lloyd George, whose personal supremacy in Allied counsels was now firmly established, the Polish crisis came as an acute embarrassment. It was the sort of crisis which demanded the united Allied front which he alone could inspire. It could not be side-stepped; yet it was quite unwanted. It threatened to kill his policy of trade with Russia which, with the arrival in England on 31 May of Leonid Krasin and his Delegation of Soviet Co-operatives, was just beginning to come to life. It threatened to revive his struggle with Churchill, whose interventionist designs he had defeated with such difficulty. It threatened to disturb the calm of his coalition government and the tenor of British relations with France. It presented him with so many pitfalls that his only safe policy was to do nothing for as long as possible.

Lloyd George was abetted by a curious technical snag. The frontier between Poland and Soviet Russia had never been established. The provisional frontier proposed by the Supreme Allied Council on 8 December 1919 was recognized neither by the Poles nor by the Soviets. It was impossible in 1920 for anyone to say precisely if and when the Polish eastern frontier had been violated. Coming from the east, the first city of importance to be met with which all governments accepted as indisputably Polish was Warsaw itself. If the Allied governments chose to be pedantic, they had no obligation to defend Poland until its capital had fallen. As many Poles gloomily suspected, their republic would have to be destroyed before their Allies thought of saving it. Poland's corpse would be the only admissible evidence of assault.

Lloyd George's involvement in the Polish crisis, was not the result of 'a British initiative'. He was pushed into the dispute against his better judgement. His meetings with the Polish Premier, Grabski at the Spa Conference in Belgium were arranged by Polish not by British request. The appearance of Grabski on 6 July pleading aid, thrust the issue upon him. He felt from the start as if he was acting under duress—a fact which goes a long way to explain his harsh behaviour.

The Spa Agreement of 10 July was certainly a humiliating document for Grabski to sign.[54] Despite his belief, later shown to be perfectly correct, that the Soviets intended to destroy the Polish Republic as then established, Grabski was required to support 'H.M.G.'s declaration that the Soviets desire to make peace'. He was required to relinquish Wilno to Lithuania, and to submit the future of East Galicia, Teschen and Danzig to the will of the Allied powers. In return, he received a very vague assurance from Lloyd George 'to assist in Poland's defence, if her territory was infringed, with all means available'. The assurance left Lloyd George free to interpret the meaning of 'Polish territory' and 'all means available' as *he* thought fit.

It is not always realized that Lloyd George tried to press the unfortunate Grabski still further. Yet the transcript of their conversations at the Villa Fraineuse in Spa shows that he tried to browbeat Grabski into renouncing Wilno and East Galicia for good. After telling his secretary, Philip Kerr, to trace Poland's ethnographic frontier on the map, he announced bluntly that 'Wilno is not a Polish problem'. He was equally severe over East Galicia. When Grabski insisted that the people of East Galicia had a right to self-determination, he pointedly asked why, if Poland were strong enough to protect both itself and the people beyond its frontiers, did Poland turn to the Allies for help. The conversation was rescued by the intervention of the Foreign Secretary, Lord Curzon, who guided the argument away from the rights and wrongs of a final settlement. Grabski agreed to start negotiations with the Soviets for a ceasefire. The final settlement was referred to a London conference.[55]

An important factor in Lloyd George's behaviour was his knowledge that French resolution was weak. A talk with Marshal Foch and Prime Minister Millerand two days earlier had confirmed his suspicions that Great Britain could not count on the support of France in any new military involvement in Eastern Europe. The French always talked of the need to fight Bolshevism, but never did very much. Lloyd George set out to trick them into revealing their true intentions. In contradiction of all his other statements on the subject, he deliberately gave the impression that he was planning to send British troops to Poland. 'If we allowed the Bolsheviks to trample the independence of Poland out of existence under the hooves of Budyonny's cavalry,' he declared, 'we should be eternally dishonoured. . . . If the Englishman's sense of fair play were roused, Britain would be prepared to make considerable further sacrifices for Poland.' Finally he posed the crucial question: 'If Britain were to send men for stiffening the Polish army, would France be ready to send cavalry?' Before the piece was even finished, Foch had blurted out 'Pas d'hommes!'; Millerand merely shrugged. Lloyd George had his answer. If the French with their greater continental interests were not prepared to fight, he was not going to do their fighting for them.[56]

The Spa meeting had two immediate results—the 'Curzon Line Telegram' to Moscow and the Interallied Mission to Poland. Both were Lloyd George's handiwork; both were fruitless; both are extremely curious when examined in detail.

The Curzon Line Telegram described a ceasefire line along which the Polish and Soviet forces were to halt pending the proposed London conference. It was sent to Moscow, not direct from Spa, but from the Foreign Office in London on instructions forwarded from Spa. (Curzon, except for the fact that it was sent in his name as Foreign Secretary, had nothing to do with it.) The ceasefire line was to consist of the Supreme Allied Council's provisional Polish-Soviet frontier of 8 December 1919 extended in the south across Galicia to the ridge of the Carpathians. It has since been established that the text describing the Galician section of the line, apart from being ambiguous, differed in the telegram from the text describing it in the Spa Agreement. Whereas the telegram described a straight north-south division of Galicia between Przemyśl and Lwów, the Spa Agreement mentions a line 'coinciding with the military front as at the moment of understanding'. The telegram in fact proposed that the city of Lwów should remain on the Soviet side of the ceasefire line, whereas the Spa Agreement left it in all probability on the Polish side. At some point, between the signing of the Spa Agreement on the afternoon of 10 July and the despatch of the telegram on the morning of 11 July, someone, somewhere, had changed a most vital detail. The American scholar who first examined the discrepancy attributed it to 'a mistake' committed by a hurried Foreign Office clerk unfamiliar with the geography of Eastern Europe.[57] This is possible, but not very likely. Thanks to the work over three previous years of Lewis Namier, himself an East Galician, the British Foreign Office possessed more detailed maps and information about East Galicia than about almost any other province on earth. The mystery deepens when one realizes that the 'mistake' in the Curzon Line Telegram coincides precisely with 'the straight ethnographic divide between East and West Galicia' as described by Namier in a private memorandum which is to be found in Lloyd George's personal files.[58] A detective would have good grounds at least for suspecting a connexion between the two. Certainly the text as received in Moscow must have conveyed the impression that the Allied leaders were *not* inclined to support Polish territorial claims. It encouraged the Soviets to make light of the threat of renewed Allied intervention. The Curzon Line Telegram, disinterred by Soviet diplomats in 1943 to justify their later claim to Lwów, was destined to influence the diplomacy of the Second World War more positively than the diplomacy of the Polish-Soviet War. For the time being, in Chicherin's reply to

Curzon of 17 July, its proposals were rejected outright and hurriedly buried.

Chicherin's reply poured contempt on Allied diplomacy.[59] In it, he attacked the hypocrisy of the British government 'which now professes its desire for peace but failed to give any evidence of such a desire at the time of the Polish invasion of the Ukraine'. He mocked the League of Nations, to whose Covenant Curzon had made reference:

> The so-called League of Nations has never informed the Russian government of its establishment or its existence...The Soviet government cannot in any circumstances agree to a group of powers taking on themselves the functions of a supreme court over all the states on earth...

He scorned the provisions of the 'Curzon Line', which was less favourable to the Polish nation than the Soviet proposals. He made frequent insinuations about the imminent revolution in Poland. To add a touch of holiness, he casually mentioned the newly-signed Soviet-Lithuanian treaty whose existence was still unknown in the Western capitals. He deftly parried Curzon's threat of suspending the trade talks and sent it back with interest. Knowing full well that Lloyd George set great store on the success of trade with Soviet Russia he hinted that the talks could not proceed if the British government used them as a bargaining counter in the Polish crisis. His final tilt was to say that he preferred direct negotiations with the Poles to a conference held under Allied auspices. The document was a diplomatic *tour-de-force*. Its emotional impact, on governments who at that period regarded themselves as the omnipotent arbiters of the world, was stunning. At a stroke, it destroyed all illusions that the Allied powers might control the Polish-Soviet War from afar. For the next month, Soviet diplomacy rode on the same buoyant wave of confidence and expectancy as the Red Army.

During the week that the Soviet leaders considered the Curzon Line Telegram, they convinced themselves that they had nothing to fear from the Allied powers. They interpreted the Allied proposals as a sign of weakness. As Lenin commented to Stalin: 'They want to snatch victory from our hands with the aid of crooked promises.'[60] The Commander-in-Chief, Sergey

Kamenev summarized the Soviet viewpoint in his statement of 21 July:

On both our fronts operating against Poland, instructions have been given for the energetic development of the offensive, without regard to the frontier line mentioned in Lord Curzon's telegram.

It seems desirable, however, to retard the progress of the South-West Front, at least until the attitude of the Poles to Curzon's note and the Soviet reply is clarified.

If the Poles agree to negotiate with us, it will mean that they cannot count on serious support and that we shall have the freedom to attack deep into the heart of Poland.

If, on the other hand, Poland refuses to negotiate or there are other indications that she will really be supported by her allies, we shall be compelled, while not abandoning the offensive, to take precautions against all possible dangers.

In the first place, there could be an attack from Rumania, which already possesses sufficient forces for the purpose. Our progress deep into Galicia would then be extremely dangerous. I suggest, therefore, that the south-western Front confines itself to the destruction of Polish forces on the southern flank, thus severing the Poles from the Rumanians. I further suggest that Soviet forces facing Rumania should be strengthened and that the XVI Army of the Western Front now moving on Wolkowysk should be held in reserve against a possible attack from Latvia. In this way I calculate the remaining three armies of the Western Front will be able to achieve the definitive destruction of Poland so long as she does not receive significant support over and above the expected Rumanian and Latvian attacks.[61]

Having failed to bridle the Soviets, Lloyd George still sought to rein in the Poles. Although he could not retract the Allied guarantee of Polish independence—it was repeated in Curzon's note to Chicherin of 20 July—he could still hope to escape from its incalculable consequences. To this end, he intensified the representations made in Warsaw to open armistice negotiations and, on 21 July, launched the Interallied Mission to Poland.

The Interallied Mission was Lloyd George's brainchild from the start, and was improvised in his customarily high-handed and irregular manner. Its leader, Viscount D'Abernon, British ambassador in Berlin, was casually appointed by Lloyd George on the Channel boat returning from Spa. He was to be accompanied by Sir Maurice Hankey, secretary to the Cabinet, as Lloyd George's private representative. The mission was put before the Cabinet as an accomplished fact the day before it left. Lord Curzon was not informed in advance of the secondment of his ambassador; the Army Council was given twenty-four hours to appoint its nominee, General Sir Percy Radcliffe; the French government was given forty-eight hours to appoint its two members, Ambassador Jusserand and General Weygand.

The political purposes of the mission were not confined to its formal and almost unintelligible terms of reference, namely 'to proceed to Poland . . . to advise as to the measures to be taken on questions arising out of the negotiations with regard to the conclusion of an armistice between Poland and Soviet Russia'.[62] Hankey's private letters to Lloyd George show that they aimed to replace the existing Polish government with men more amenable to Allied interests. On 21 July, whilst waiting in Paris for Jusserand and Weygand to pack, D'Abernon and Hankey dined with Paderewski and asked for suggestions. Paderewski advanced the name of Dmowski, the National Democrat leader, for Prime Minister in preference to Grabski and submitted a list of officers who might replace Piłsudski as Commander-in-Chief. He described the Rada Obrony Państwa as an 'instrument of veiled dictatorship'. These aims were quite impractical, of course. By the time the mission reached Warsaw four days later, they found that Piłsudski's position was stronger than ever and that the emergence of Witos's Coalition Ministry had put an end to Dmowski's ambitions. They were warned by the British ambassador, Sir Horace Rumbold, that any attempt to remove Piłsudski would provoke a revolution. They had no option but to leave Polish politics alone. Their intentions were limited thereafter to the supervision of Polish armistice proposals and to the installation of Weygand in a position of authority within the Polish army.[63]

The mission's journey to Warsaw was not without incident. Both D'Abernon and Weygand have related how the members of the mission, huddled in a compartment of their special train, did their homework on Poland, sorting out the difficult Polish names and learning the main facts about its recent history. Weygand says that he briefed the others, so he must be held partly responsible for their ignorance. In Prague, where their train was delayed, they telephoned President Masaryk and were invited to tea. Masaryk was not optimistic. He said that the Allies would be involved in the Polish defeat, if they tried to intervene. Bolshevism would not be defeated by bayonets. At all events, as Hankey recorded, 'there was no point in making a fight of it'.[64]

The role of Sir Maurice Hankey in the Polish crisis has never attracted attention. He was in fact the only participant in the Interallied Mission to make a definite contribution—grotesque though it proved to be. His private letters to Lloyd George and his 'Personal Report on the situation in Poland'[65] were the only detailed, on-the-spot information to reach the Allied leader in time for the *dénouement*. Hankey was a specialist in office routine; in the sphere of East European politics he was a complete ignoramus. Competence and efficiency were his touchstones, and he saw little of these in Warsaw. His version of the political situation in Poland was no less than garbled; his 'facts' were invariably inaccurate. He thought, for instance, that Piłsudski was President, leader of the Socialist Party, a friend of Lenin, an Austrian Pole, an ex-prisoner of the Austrians ... He was convinced that Piłsudski was planning a pro-Bolshevik coup to preserve his own power. After only six days in Poland, on 31 July he left for home, thoroughly disgusted. On the train, he composed his report. He described the leading Polish personalities in the worst possible light. Piłsudski was 'singularly cadaverous, with the appearance of deep depression and hair bristling in the German fashion, ... the narrow-minded, tricky and intensely vain President, ... 'who imagines himself a Napoleon'; Witos was 'a stage peasant'; Daszyński, 'pro-German, with shifty blue eyes', Rosvadosski, (Rozwadowski the Chief of Staff), 'impossible'. His final conclusions were as follows:

If Soviet Russia persists in the offensive, our efforts to save Poland will probably fail. We must do the best we can to get decent terms for Poland, to recognize that she has suffered a fate she has brought on herself in spite of our warnings, to improve relations with Germany and via Germany with Russia, and to avoid military obligations in Europe and concentrate on Overseas Trade.[66]

These excruciatingly ignorant comments are only worth
quoting at length as an illustration of the gulf between Allied
statesmen and the country which some of them still imagined
they were helping. Their effect on Lloyd George does not have
to be imagined. They confirmed what he had always believed,
that direct involvement in Poland would have disastrous and
incalculable consequences.

The helplessness of Allied diplomacy is well reflected in its
vain efforts to arrange a Polish-Soviet armistice. Chicherin's
note of 17 July proposed direct negotiations with the Poles;
his note of 24 July proposed a conference from which the
Poles would be excluded. On 6 August, he let it be known
that the Soviets' final peace terms would soon be produced;
on 9 August, he served up a preview of the terms; on 17
August he presented the terms to the Poles with important
modifications.[67] At each of these stages except the last, he
obtained Lloyd George's approval. Lloyd George had kept
the French in line with increasing difficulty. On 27 July, at his
conference with Millerand at Boulogne, he was forced to agree
to Poland's participation in any Allied conference with the
Soviets; on 8 August at the meeting at Lympne, he was forced
to define the exact nature of Allied support repeatedly promised
to Poland. Although he hedged it round with manifold
conditions, he put it at material support for twenty-two
divisions.[68] On 14 August, he lost touch altogether. On that
day the French interventionists rebelled against his policy,
precipitating their government into recognition of Wrangel
and into a rift with the British which lasted for nearly two
months. Lloyd George's control over the Poles was even shorter
lived. On 23 July, he persuaded Prince Sapieha to approach
the Soviets about an armistice by issuing 'H.M.G.'s imperative
advice'.[69] On 10 August, when he recommended the Poles to
accept the preview of the Soviet terms given by Lev Kamenev
in London, he met with a flat refusal. The British ambassador
was told by Sapieha in a most painful interview that 'Poland
will fight alone rather than accept such humiliating terms.'[70]
At that point Lloyd George's efforts collapsed. The diplomatic
dance was over. It had lasted so long only because the two
principals were anxious above all to win time, Chicherin to let

the Red Army's offensive run its course, Lloyd George to avoid the fateful decision to intervene.

In such an atmosphere of confusion, the attempts which were made by Polish and Soviet negotiators to halt the fighting, had no chance of success. It is inconceivable that the Poles would have committed themselves to an armistice in central Poland while they still had thoughts of recovery. It is equally inconceivable that the Soviets would have called off their offensive while they still had thoughts of victory. Both sides entered into armistice negotiations as a means of impressing the Entente. By doing as Lloyd George demanded, both could hope for a *quid pro quo*—the Poles for Allied support, the Soviets for Allied abstention. Each side neutralized the moves of the other, and in the absence of a military decision, no result was possible. It is a sad story of prevarication. On 1 August a Polish delegation, appointed by the Army High Command and headed by General Listowski and Dr Wróblewski, crossed the frontline and met a Soviet delegation at Baranowicze. The Poles were authorized to negotiate a ceasefire; the Soviets insisted on discussing a peace treaty. After only two days, the Polish delegation returned to Warsaw to upgrade its credentials and redefine its terms of reference. The Soviets demanded that Piłsudski himself authorize further negotiations. This was quickly arranged. But when the Polish government tried to transmit its consent to negotiations, the Soviet government's radio station in Moscow either could not or would not receive the message. The reconstituted Polish and Soviet delegations, led respectively by Jan Dąbski and K. Danishevsky, did not meet until 17 August. Since this was the day when the fate of Warsaw was being decided, it is not surprising that the Soviet hosts at Minsk locked the Polish guests inside their residence and waited for the outcome of the battle.[71]

Allied diplomacy, therefore, achieved nothing. From the point of view of Lloyd George's personal interests, this achievement was perfectly satisfactory. From the point of view of Allied interests as a whole it was little less than a disaster. Allied interests could only be satisfied by one of two things— by a Polish victory or by an end to the fighting. Lloyd George did nothing to help the former and failed to arrange the latter. In his tortuous efforts to reach an arrangement, he alienated almost all his friends and collaborators. He alienated the French by his constant readiness to believe the Bolshevik claims; he alienated the Poles by his reluctance to give them material support. He offended Lord Curzon, whose domain he usurped; the Foreign Office, whose advice he ignored; and the remaining members of the Interallied Mission, whose appeals for assistance to Poland he denied. He disappointed the Conservatives, who wanted more positive action, the opposition who wanted to bring in the League of Nations, and the socialists, who wanted to abandon Poland entirely. In the end he was quite isolated, with no-one left to talk to but Krasin and Kamenev. He lost all means of influencing the situation further. He could only wait. In the last analysis, the fate of Lloyd George, as leader of the Allied powers and perhaps as British Prime Minister, rested in the hands of the people he had done everything to discourage, the hands of Polish soldiers manning the defences of beleaguered Warsaw.

'Hands off Russia' echoed round the world in the summer of 1920. It was a slogan coined by the friends of Soviet Russia to prevent her enemies receiving support and supplies. It was first raised in Manchester in February 1919 by an obscure group of British trade unionists, who dubbed themselves the 'Hands Off Russia Committee'. It only gained general currency at the beginning of May 1920, when dockers first in Hamburg then in London refused to touch cargoes of arms destined for Poland, and when the Executive Committee of Comintern addressed its appeal 'to the proletarians of all countries'.[72] It is used in communist historiography to demonstrate how the peoples of the world, in contrast with their governments, were all on the side of the Soviets.

The significance of the 'Hands Off Russia' campaign can best be judged from its progress in Great Britain, the country where it started and where it produced its only sensational effect. The committee was in no sense representative of the British people nor even of the working class or the trade unions. Only two members, Tom Mann and Willy Gallagher, have a name in the history of British socialism. They started a campaign which, by winning popularity, eventually passed beyond their control. On 4 March 1920 they addressed a

protest to the Polish consul in London, in consequence of a
public meeting in the Kingsway Hall. 'This Committee,' they
claimed, 'is largely responsible for the viewpoint taken by the
TUC . . . If the Polish imperialists continue their present
policy, the name of the Polish Government will stink in the
nostrils of every member of the organized Labour movement in
Great Britain.'[73] This proved true when in April news arrived
of the Kiev operation. The Polish invasion of the Ukraine was
condemned by all sections of the British labour movement
without exception. It was given special prominence by the fact
that the Labour Party Delegation to Soviet Russia had
witnessed it at first hand. It first inspired practical action on
9 May when the SS *Jolly George* was prevented from sailing by
London dockers. It was formally condemned by resolutions at
the Trade Union Congress on 6 June, and at the Labour Party
Conference at Scarborough on 24 June. The climax came at
the beginning of August, when, still under the slogan of 'Hands
Off Russia', a Council of Action was formed to launch a general
strike against the government's supposed intentions of intervening on Poland's behalf. By this time however, the campaign,
which had started as the instrument of a militant, communist
pressure-group, had been taken over by a group of determined,
but essentially moderate, socialists.

The Council of Action, being one of the most muddled events
in British history, is open to many interpretations. Lenin, for
example, believed it to represent the founding of a British
soviet, which after sharing power with HM government for a
transitional period of dual authority, would proceed to organize
Great Britain's Great October. The Council of Action's
organizer, Ernest Bevin, had no such lofty aspirations, however.
He was not a Leninist, nor a communist or even a Marxist.
His Council had only one person in common with the original
committee. He was only concerned to stop Lloyd George from
involving the country in an unwanted war. He was embarrassed
by the fact that his action to save Moscow from capitalist attack
occurred at a moment when the forces of Moscow were
assaulting Warsaw. He was amazed, when he actually faced the
Prime Minister on the morning of 10 August, to find himself in
complete agreement with him. Half an hour's talk settled the
matter once and for all:

Prime Minister: Does it mean that...if the independence of Poland is really menaced, if it is really destroyed and if Bolshevist Russia does for Poland what her Tsarist predecessors did a century and a half ago, we cannot send a single pair of boots there, otherwise Labour will strike? That is what I want to know.

Ernest Bevin: Our answer is this, that the hypothesis does not hold good, that the independence of Poland is not at stake...Labour will consider its position when that occasion arises.

Prime Minister: Very well, that is quite good enough for me.

Ernest Bevin: But supposing the Polish people themselves agree upon a Constitution which did not suit the Allied Powers?

Prime Minister: I do not care what the Constitution is. If they like to have a Mikado there, that is their business.

Ernest Bevin: That is what we wanted to know.'74

Bevin walked out of Downing Street completely non-plussed. No more was heard of his Council of Action.

Lloyd George understood the Council of Action better than they understood themselves. He knew it to be the expression of misplaced fears. As he was reminded by Hankey, 'The Labour Council of Action movement is an unpleasant development, but as they are merely taking the same line as the Government . . . no-one is so capable as you of turning it to advantage.'75 He used it to magnificent advantage. He went straight from his meeting with Bevin to the Commons debate on Poland. He proceeded to denounce everyone and anyone who had ever made a positive statement about the Polish-Soviet War, lumping them all together as 'maniacs who want to widen the conflict, . . . fanatics in every country who dance to the smashing of furniture.'76 He implied that there was nothing to choose between Churchill and the interventionists and Bevin and the Council of Action. 'Lenin is an aristocrat,' he blandly announced, 'and Trotsky is a journalist. In fact my Honourable friend, the Secretary of State for War, is an embodiment of both.'77 It was typical of his whole strategy. By putting Churchill and the Bolsheviks in the same bracket, he discredited both right and left at one blow. He remained in command of the middle ground, the undoubted master of the

House. He uttered his final word on the subject a few days later: 'A socialist Party,' he said, thinking of Bevin, 'is very useful to frighten the bourgeoisie into moderation.'[78]

'Hands Off Russia' had less effect on the conduct of the Polish-Soviet War than it did on the progress of the British labour movement. Whilst providing a fleeting point of sympathy between Soviet communism and the Labour Party it also served to demonstrate their permanent incompatability. Far from uniting British socialism, it divided it. In 1920 the majority of British socialists discovered that if Soviet communism was suitable for Russia, it was not suitable for Britain. In the words of Tom Shaw, the only Labour M.P. to visit Poland in 1920, 'If I were a Russian, I would fight to defend the Soviets; as an Englishman, I would fight against their introduction in this country.'[79] The Labour Party could have no real truck with militant communists, and forced them to go their own way. It is highly significant that on 1 August 1920, the very same day that Tukhachevsky crossed the Bug and entered what to his mind was capitalist Europe, the very same day that Bevin formed his Council of Action, the original sponsors of the 'Hands Off Russia' campaign, Gallagher, Coates, *et al.*, were present at the founding assembly of the British Communist Party; Tom Mann was being elected a deputy chairman of Mezhsovprof in Moscow. British communism and British socialism parted company for good.

The pattern was repeated in almost all the countries of Europe. The Soviet invasion of Poland acted as a powerful catalyst in the rapid fermentation of the socialist parties. It gave that final stir to a pot whose contents were already separating out. The demonstrations in favour of Soviet Russia in the spring of 1920, and the strikes against arms for Poland, were quickly followed by serious quarrels and lasting schism. The British precedent was followed first in the USA then in France, Germany, Italy. At the time of the Kiev campaign, the countries where the communists had formally broken away from the socialist movement were very few; with the odd exceptions of Spain and Holland, they were all new or transformed succession states—Finland, the Baltic States, Poland, Hungary, Austria. By the time a Polish-Soviet peace was signed a year later, the only countries where the communists had *not* yet broken away were Norway, Albania, and the Vatican.

The invasion of Poland was of most immediate interest to Poland's neighbours—Rumania, Hungary, Czechoslovakia, Germany, and the Free City of Danzig. They were the next in line. All remained neutral, but none could be indifferent.

Rumania was the most directly concerned, having a common frontier both with Poland and Soviet Russia. Rumania, like Poland, had inherited territory both in the west and the east, Transylvania from Hungary and Bessarabia from Russia. Cluj (Kolosvar) was her Poznań, and Chisinau (Kishinev) her Wilno. The Rumanian government faced problems essentially similar to those of the Polish government. The Rumanian army was willing enough in principle to intervene against Bolshevism, having defied the Soviets by their seizure of Bessarabia in April 1918 and having occupied Budapest, then the capital of Béla Kun's Soviet Republic of Hungary, in the autumn of 1919. But its defensive preoccupations at home left little thought in 1920 for foreign adventures. Transylvania was not formally annexed until the Treaty of Trianon of 4 June 1920; Bessarabia, still claimed by the Soviets yet unassigned by the Allied powers, remained in dispute till the end of the year. Rumanian forces on the Dniester posed a constant threat to the southern flank of the Soviet offensive in Poland and on 24 July forced the Soviet XIV Army to turn and face them; but they themselves remained inactive. In July 1920, at the height of the Polish crisis, Rumania was paralysed by a wave of strikes which halted the railways and the postal services. The Foreign Minister, Take Ionescu, who had a friendly meeting with Piłsudski in January, confined himself for most of the summer to messages of general sympathy. His appeal on 18 August for a united policy against the Bolsheviks was overruled by the French.[80]

The Hungarian government was more enthusiastic, but less able to help. Magyar sympathies for the Poles were traditional and mutual. The Regent, Admiral Horthy, having recently assumed power by grace of the White Terror, was a dedicated crusader against Bolshevism. He made no secret of his readiness to despatch Hungarian troops to Poland, But the intervening territory of Czechoslovakia, with whom the Hungarians until 1920 had been in a state of undeclared war, made this impossible.

The Czechoslovak government adopted an enigmatic attitude towards the Polish-Soviet War.[81] As a liberal parliamentary democracy, they could not welcome the advance of Bolshevism; as the foremost client in Central Europe of France, they would not be allowed to. Yet they betrayed no special concern. Throughout 1920, the left wing of the Social Democratic Party, which in the Republic's first elections recorded the largest single vote (thirty-seven per cent), was openly establishing workers' soviets; the Communist Party was a legal organization; negotiations were in progress for opening normal relations with Russia. The Czechoslovaks had always enjoyed closer ties with the Russians than with the Poles. In Prague, Poland's stance as the sentinel of Christendom was thought rather pretentious; Piłsudski was regarded as a militarist. For most of the year, the Czechoslovak government showed no interest in Poland's predicament. Foreign Minister Beneš was using the time to exploit the dispute in Teschen, which on 28 July was settled at Poland's expense. On 21 May, a railwaymen's meeting at Breclav on the Austrian border called a halt to the flow of munitions for Poland. On 5 July, a strike on the Bohumín-Košice line produced the same effect in Slovakia. For ten weeks, Poland's main supply line was blocked. The government in Prague did not intervene. Only at the very end of July, did it begin to respond. The army was moved to Slovakia; Polish refugees from Galicia were given assistance; Bolshevik agitators were arrested; the railways were opened; Allied arms at last flowed into Poland through sub-Carpathian Ruthenia; Polish oil from Lwów flowed out. Even so, the Czechoslovak government refused to declare its support for Poland. On 9 August 1920, it issued a declaration of non-intervention and strict neutrality. There is good evidence to suggest that Beneš was planning to surrender the province of Sub-Carpathian Ruthenia and the city of Užhorod as a sop to the Soviets.[82]

Germany was of crucial importance. Germany was the Red Army's declared destination, and gave good grounds for the Bolsheviks' optimism. It was seething with social discontent and political confusion. In eighteen months since the abdication of the Kaiser, it had seen one communist revolution, two provincial soviet republics, three reactionary putsches, at least four general strikes, and five chancellors. In July 1920, the Weimar Constitution had been in force for only twelve months and the humiliating Peace of Versailles for only six. The central government was beset by the separatism of the Länder, by the close scrutiny of the Allied powers and by the constant war in the streets between armed workers' detachments and the right-wing Freikorps. When the Polish-Soviet War first attracted notice it was axiomatic that the workers should demonstrate in favour of the Soviets, that the Freikorps should propose support for Poland, and that the government should declare its neutrality. This it did, in the words of Dr Simons, the Foreign Minister, on 26 July, in a gesture of mainly internal significance. Germany in 1920 did not have a fully independent foreign policy. The Weimar Republic under Allied tutelage was incapable of intervening officially on one side or the other. But this did not mean that individual Germans and even governmental departments were barred from having ideas of their own. It can have escaped no one's notice that the advance of the Red Army threatened to destroy the Versailles settlement and thus, whatever its other consequences, to free Germany from the intolerable restraints placed upon her. As Lenin himself remarked:

That was the time when everyone in Germany, including the blackest reactionaries and monarchists, declared the Bolshevists would be their salvation.... A curious type of reactionary-revolutionary came into existence.[83]

General Seeckt, commander of the new Reichswehr, as early as Janurary 1920 had accepted 'a future political and economic agreement with Russia as an irreversible purpose of our policy', whilst still proclaiming that 'we are ready to stand as a wall against Bolshevism in Germany itself.' 'I refuse to support Poland,' he added, 'even in face of the danger that she may be swallowed up. On the contrary I count on that.'[84] Many officers thought that another revolutionary rising was the necessary prelude to Germany's escape from the grip of the Entente.

There were people in both Germany and Russia ready to exploit the invasion of Poland to their mutual advantage. Radek, having delivered his speech at the Comintern Congress on 24 July, travelled post-haste to Berlin. Tentative negotiations were already in progress. Herr Maltzan, head of the Russian Department of the German Foreign Ministry was in contact with the Bolshevik agent in Berlin, Kopp, a former Menshevik and confident of Trotsky. Hints had been dropped by Trotsky that Russia might buy arms from Germany, although Lenin specifically forbade it.[85] Kopp gave an assurance that the Red Army would not cross the German frontier. On 22 July, he forwarded a proposal from Simons to Chicherin that normal diplomatic relations should be restored. On 2 August he arranged for a representative of the German government to be attached to the Soviet IV Army, to settle any possible incidents on the German frontier. He also arranged that any Polish units who were forced into German territory should there be disarmed and interned. Ludendorff, an idol of the Freikorps, proposed to exploit the situation in a different way. In a conversation with the British chargé d'affaires in Berlin, he was presumed to have offered to lead an army of liberation into Poland, on condition that Poznania was returned to Germany and that Germany participated in the economic exploitation of defeated Russia. His démarche raised a scare in many quarters. In the Reichstag, Clara Zetkin lodged a formal protest in the name of the German left.[86] In London, the Foreign Office received an anxious query from the Polish Minister.[87] The Polish Government rightly guessed that Upper Silesia was more likely to be the aim of the Freikorps' attentions than Poznania. In any case, in Poland there was no more desire to be liberated by Ludendorff than to be liberated by Tukhachevsky.

In Upper Silesia itself some remarkable events took place. The German and Polish communities of the province were embattled in preparation for the coming Plebiscite. An inadequate Allied garrison of French and Italian troops was hard put to keep the two sides apart. On 15 August, the editor of the local German newspaper in Gleiwitz (Gliwice) decided to anticipate the fall of Warsaw without waiting for confirmation. On 16 August, a German mob appeared in the streets hailing the Soviet victory and bearing aloft images of Lenin and Trotsky. The next day a similar demonstration was organised in Kattowitz (Katowice), where the French garrison was besieged in its barracks.[88] For forty-eight hours the German terror raged unchecked. Polish citizens and Polish houses were attacked indiscriminately. A violent response was unaavoidable. Wojciech Korfanty, the Polish nationalist leader called his people to arms. It was the signal for the Second Silesian Rising. At dawn on 19 August, the bands of the Silesian POW moved through the province and occupied the plebiscite area. The French did nothing to intervene. For ten days, during the exact period when the Polish Army was fighting to save Warsaw from the Soviets, the Poles of Silesia fought to save their homes from the Germans.

In East Prussia, another Plebiscite was already complete. The voting on 11 July, influenced no doubt by the critical situation in Poland, had produced an overwhelming German success. There, the Allied garrison had been supplied by the British Army, which now showed an unseemly desire to evacuate immediately. Fears were expressed lest the Irish regiments should come in contact with the advancing Soviet forces, and therefore risk 'contamination.'[89] Sinn Fein and Bolshevism were apparently considered to be part of one and the same universal Revolution. Evacuation was concluded by the first week of August, and the Prussians were left to fend for themselves.

Danzig, too, made its plans. In the summer of 1920, the constitution of the Free City was still being prepared. Danzig was being administered as an 'Allied condominium' by a British diplomat, Sir Reginald Tower, who was nonetheless very much at the mercy of the city corporation and the Burgermeister, Heinrich Sahm. Sahm was a wanted man in Warsaw, having been charged with the transportation of forced labour from Poland during the World War. From 15 July until 24 August a dockers' strike closed the port to shipments for Poland. Pro-Soviet agitation increased, and Sahm himself was roughly handled by socialist demonstrators. On 8 August, Sahm persuaded Tower to sponsor a project to extend the Free City's territory. Both men assumed that as the Polish Republic was about to be destroyed, there was no point in safeguarding its interests.[90]

To anyone watching from a distance in the first weeks of August, the success of the Red Army's Polish offensive was already an accomplished fact. A glance at the map showed that Ghai's Kavkor, was now only ten days' march from Berlin. Sergeyev's IV Army at Działdowo was 100 miles from Danzig. They had by-passed the whole of East Prussia. Warsaw was far behind them. Tukhachevsky was close on their heels with his remaining armies, three of which were directed north of the Vistula and only one on Warsaw itself. The fate of Germany seemed a more pertinent subject for concern than the apparently inevitable destruction of Poland.

To observers on the spot, however, the Red Army's situation was less impressive. The advance into Poland had been achieved at great cost. During the month of July, losses varied from twenty-five to forty per cent. According to Kakurin, the III Army of Lazarevich shrank from 30,243 men to 23,324, Kork's XV Army from 44,796 to 27,522.[91] Kakurin's own 10th Infantry Division approached the Bug with 4,500 men, of whom a week later on the Polish bank of the river, only 2,800 could be mustered. The great majority of these losses could *not* be counted as casualties, but merely as drop-outs or deserters, soldiers who willingly or unwillingly were left behind by the pace of the advance.

Equally serious was the increasing disharmony of the Western and South-Western Fronts. Tukhachevsky's intention was for Yegorov's armies to converge on the Bug, and to advance into Poland in harness with himself. Yet by the end of July, this movement had not even started. As from 24 July, the XIV Army turned south to face the threat of a Rumanian diversion from the Dniester; the Konarmiya turned south-west and moved on Lwów. Only the XII Army on the northern flank marched in line for a rendezvous with Tukhachevsky, but found itself floundering in the marshy valley of the Stochod, where Brusilov had ground to a halt in 1916. The combined westward thrust of these three armies was henceforth weakened. Like a fork whose prongs had been twisted out of line, their power of penetration and their capacity for concerted action were severely inhibited. Their progress was considerably retarded. They were faced by an adversary who contrived to retreat in much better order than in the north. They encountered an effective Polish system of defensive 'screening' and were subjected to a series of bloody counter-attacks. Śmigły-Rydz, the Polish commander in Galicia, put garrisons of about 1,000 men into each of the strategic towns and junctions of the forward areas. He could be sure that all of them could not be attacked simultaneously, and that each, well supplied with rations and ammunition, could hold out for up to a fortnight, unless selected for special attack. Behind them, he could regroup his main forces and reinforce them with new cavalry detachments. The Second Army, disbanded in Kiev, was now reconstituted under General Raszewski, endowed with a complete division of cavalry and placed in the centre of the front opposite the Konarmiya. On 8 July, Raszewski drove Budyonny back and for a short time reoccupied Równe. The contest for the River Styr lasted for nearly a month. On 21–22 July, a raid by General Linde on the Second Army's right retook Kozin. On 2 August, the battle of Brody was launched, in which General Sawicki, leading two divisions and a brigade of cavalry, thrust deep into the Konarmiya's side.* The Polish success was frustrated by orders from above, which in consequence of the fall of Brest-Litovsk in the north, pulled all the armies in the south back to the Styr. During these weeks, Budyonny, of course was not idle. He responded with his customary vigour whenever attacked, and on several occasions cut opposing units to pieces. But his overall progress was slow. In the month of July he made fifty-seven miles, from Równe to Beresteczko. His pace did not compare with that of Ghai, who in the same period covered 400 miles. The South-Western Front was losing not only its impetus but also its sense of purpose (See map, p. 228).

Thus, despite appearances on the map and the confident assertions of the Soviet High Command, the success of the invasion of Poland still hung in the balance.

* See description, p. 37.

CHAPTER FIVE

THE BATTLE OF WARSAW

RECORDED impressions of the city of Warsaw on the eve of the Red Army's attack present a bewildering confusion of feverish activity and inexplicable lethargy. Lord D'Abernon's diary emphasises the lethargy:

26 *July* I continue to marvel at the absence of panic, at the apparent absence indeed of any anxiety. Were a methodical system of defence being organised the confidence of the public might be understood, but all the best troops are being sent to Lwów, leaving Warsaw unprotected.

27 *July* The Prime Minister, a peasant proprietor, has gone off today to get his harvest in. Nobody thinks this extraordinary.

2 *August* The insouciance of the people here is beyond belief. One would imagine the country in no danger and the Bolsheviks a thousand miles away.

3 *August* Made an expedition along the Ostrów road...I expected it to be blocked with troops and munition waggons, also with refugees. As a matter of fact there was very little traffic. Curiously enough most of the people whom I saw putting up barbed wire were Jews. This was surprising as the Jews are suspected of being an element favourable to the Bolsheviks.... The population here has seen so many invasions that it has ceased to pay attention to them.

7 *August* I visited this afternoon the proposed new front in the direction of Minsk Mazowiecki. A treble entanglement of barbed wire is being put round Warsaw at a radius of 20 kilometres, and a certain number of trenches have been dug...The work did not appear to be well designed.

13 *August* There is singularly little alarm. The upper classes have already left town, in many cases having placed their pictures and other valuables in charge of the museum authorities. Warsaw has been so often occupied by foreign troops that the event in itself

causes neither the excitement nor the alarm which would be produced in a less experienced city.[1]

Feliks Dzierżyński interrogating prisoners and refugees on
the other side of the wire at Wyszków, was conscious of greater
activity. He cabled his impressions to Lenin:

The peasants are standing aloof from the war and resisting
mobilization. The working masses of Warsaw are awaiting the
arrival of the Red Army but, owing to the lack of leadership and the
reign of terror, are not coming forward actively.... The Socialist
Party is conducting frenzied agitation for the defence of Warsaw....
Men and women are being rounded up in their thousands and sent
to dig earthworks. Barbed wire entanglements are being set up and
there have been rumours of barricades in the streets. To raise the
warlike temper of the populace, the Poles have released floods of
appeals, in which they say that one powerful blow will suffice to
repulse the tired and weakened Red Army. Everything is being
mobilized for this one blow. Women's shock brigades have been
formed. The volunteers, composed in the main of the pampered
sons of the bourgeoisie and intelligentsia are behaving desperately.
.... In general in the ruling circles there is a mood of depression.
Newspaper articles about the behaviour of the Entente are full of
irony and reproach. All the Polish cardinals, archbishops, and
bishops have appealed for aid to the episcopate of the whole world,
describing us as Antichrist...[2]

Neither D'Abernon nor Dzierżyński could see the full picture,
of course. Neither was in a position to appreciate the exact
nature of preparations being made and precautions taken.

On 13 August, the diplomatic corps retired from Warsaw to
Poznań. They had received notice that the Ministry of Foreign
Affairs could no longer guarantee their safety in the capital.
They left behind the Italians, who had orders to stick with the
Polish government, the Interallied Mission, who were fitted
out with automobiles and puncture outfits for a later escape,
and Monsignor Achille Ratti, Papal Legate, titular Archibishop of Lepanto and doyen of the corps, who thought it his
duty to brave the hordes of Antichrist in person.

The Polish government also wished to evacuate to Poznań,
at least as a temporary measure. But there was a problem.
Poznań was the stronghold of the National Democrats, whither
Roman Dmowski had withdrawn after his forced resignation

from the Rada Obrony Państwa. Dmowski had spent his time
in Poznań stirring up trouble. He organized a series of rallies
in which Piłsudski's leadership was condemned, the fall of
Warsaw predicted, and the formation of a separatist Poznanian
régime demanded. He aimed to turn Poznań into a base for
assuming power in Poland as a whole. His calculations were
astute. In the 'Ministry for the Former Prussian Partition'
in Poznań, which was virtually autonomous, and in the army of
the Western (German) Front, commanded by that old campaigner and sworn enemy of Piłsudski, General Dowbór-
Muśnicki, he possessed a sound basis for a separatist administration. He enjoyed the confidence of the Entente, who he hoped
would intervene if the Red Army overran Warsaw. On 13
August, Dmowski's movement had gone so far that Witos,
the Premier, was obliged to travel to Poznań. Witos faced the
hostile crowds in person. He made a simple speech about
national unity and the need for all Poles to stand together. He
warned that the Germans would be the first to exploit Poland's
distress and that to form a separatist Poznanian province was
the best way to invite the Prussians' return. His words made
sense. But he was obliged to make a number of concessions. He
agreed to the formation of a War Secretariat attached to the
Poznanian Ministry and to the organization of a Western
Reserve Army, commanded by General Raszewski. In the eyes
of the Poznanians, Witos and Piłsudski were on probation. If
Warsaw were saved, Poznań would remain loyal; if Warsaw
fell, Poznań would go its own way and the coalition leaders
would travel as refugees to a province ruled by Dmowski's
'Government of National Salvation'.

At this moment when Poland's political unity was beginning
to crack, her military preparedness was reaching its peak,
thanks mainly to the judicious planning and titanic efforts of
General Kazimierz Sosnkowski. Sosnkowski then Deputy
Minister of Military Affairs, had taken stock of the situation
as early as 2 July. Speaking to a conference of heads of departments of the ministry and the General Staff, he emphasized
the change in the nature of the Soviet war. It was not merely
'guerrilla warfare on an increased scale,' he said, 'but a regular
war of massed forces, where we encounter all the firepower and
mechanised aids of the recent World War, a national war,

where we face not merely the Bolshevik guards but the concentrated might of all Russia.'[3] He described the stories of Budyonny's invincibility as 'mirages and phantoms' which would evaporate as soon as a Polish cavalry corps of similar size could be mustered. The decisive period would be the next two months; the decisive factor would be morale. Sosnkowski's speech, delivered before the Soviet offensive began, was as shrewd as it was moving. It directly inspired all those measures concerning arms, transport, conscription, volunteers, discipline, and command, which in the next six weeks revitalized the Polish Army.

Polish rearmament was in a critical state. By the end of June 1920, Poland's credit for military purchases was exhausted. The French government's credit of 375 million francs had been spent; the United States government preferred to extend credit for civilian rather than military purposes; the British government showed no interest at all. The British and French military chiefs, Marshal Foch and Field-Marshal Wilson 'saw no use pouring arms into Poland until the Poles had a good government'.[4] Although the French Minister of War, Lefèvre, agreed to a further small credit of fifty million francs, the French Ministry of Finance refused to ratify it.[5] Weygand thought that Poland's best source of supply would be from the stocks remaining in Germany; but the Interallied Commission of Control was destroying such stocks as fast as they could.[6] Poland's one success occurred very late, on 26 July, when the United States undertook to equip and maintain ten Polish infantry divisions for the duration of the war.[7] Fortunately, delivery of previous purchases was still proceeding. Every train that came through brought much needed relief. Train No. 79, for instance, which left Is-sur-Tille near Dijon on 18 July with 20,000 French rifles, 40,000 British rifles, and thirteen million rounds of ammunition, in theory carried enough arms to put a hundred bullets through every soldier in Tukhachevsky's host.[8]

Transport was still a problem. The German government was held to its promise to allow a total of 150 arms trains through to Poland; but the railwaymen were reluctant and transit was slow. The opening of the line from Sighet in Rumania to Lwów, was offset by the closing of Danzig. The main route through Italy, Austria, and Czechoslovakia remained closed.[9]

Aeroplanes were in everyone's mind. Aeroplanes were not only the most modern weapon in existence and the most effective answer to the Soviet cavalry; they could reach Poland under their own power and in a matter of hours. In London, Winston Churchill asked the British General Staff whether the RAF squadrons in Germany could not be flown out from Cologne.[10] In Warsaw Horace Rumbold, the British ambassador was thinking in similar terms:

> I believe... the best thing we could do would be to send masses of aeroplanes over here. These would speedily and utterly demoralise the Bolsheviks. We ought also in that contingency to fit out a powerful bombing squadron provided with the biggest bombs and go and blot out Moscow—a perfectly feasible operation, I imagine.[11]

Neither Churchill nor Rumbold had any hope of realizing these flights of fancy, so long as Lloyd George was in command. In Paris, Paderewski, 'with tears in his eyes' told D'Abernon and Hankey to take a squadron with them to Poland in order to assure their escape.[12] On 8 August, Sosnkowski wired his military attaché in Washington 'to get hold of as many planes and pilots as you can, whole squadrons of fighter-bombers with enough armament for six weeks at least'.[13] These were thoughts of desperation. At that stage, only Alcock and Brown could have brought American planes to bear on the Battle of Warsaw. The Polish armed forces had to make do in the main with the equipment they already possessed.

Poland's human resources still held much in store. On 3 July, the Rada Obrony Państwa issued an appeal for volunteers:

> The fatherland is in need! All men of good will capable of carrying arms are called to the ranks of the army. The whole nation must resist like a solid, immovable wall. It is on our breasts that the flood of Bolshevism will be broken. May Unity, Concord, and Ceaseless Toil gather us all for the common cause. All for victory! To arms![14]

Volunteers signed on by the thousand. Men from seventeen to forty-two years were accepted for the ranks, officers up to the age of fifty. As many came forward in the next six weeks as in the previous six months. By 20 August they numbered

164,615, over 40,000 of them from Warsaw alone. A General Inspectorate of Volunteers under General Józef Haller was created, which in due course was able to field an entire volunteer army. These 'Hallerczyks', raised in anger and trained in haste, were a proud formation.

On the eve of the battle, the army's volunteers were joined by all sorts of non-official recruits. The Polish Socialist Party led the way with its military section, under deputy Tomasz Arciszewski. It raised a number of workers' battalions, some like the Workers' Regiment for Defence of the Capital (Robotniczy Pułk Obrony Stolicy) for service in Warsaw, others for the protection of factories or for raids behind the enemy lines. On 4 August, it organized the Council for the Defence of the Capital (Rada Obrony Stolicy) which co-ordinated the efforts of such bodies as the Straż Obywatelska (Citizens' Watch), a middle-class formation parading in boaters and wing-collars, and the Independent Workers' Regiment (Nienależny Pułk Robotniczy) brandishing staffs and scythes.

Voluntary recruitment was matched by compulsory conscription. In July 1920 the Polish army called up five classes, those of 1890–94 inclusive. These provided men between twenty-five and thirty years of age, who were more reliable and more easily trained than the April draft of the 1900–1 classes. Although resistance to the draft was still apparent in a few areas distant from the front—in the Bieszczady mountains, in Cracow and in the Dabrowa coalfield—conscription raised 137,152 men.

Military discipline was tightened. Deserters could expect no mercy. Persistent offenders were shot. Officers were to lead by example. Shirkers were hunted down with alacrity. In Warsaw, streets were closed and trams were searched by patrols authorized to question any civilian of military age. Persons suspected of spying, of subversion, or acting against the interests of the army, could be summarily tried by court-martial. 'The physical superiority of the enemy presents no terror to an army whose moral health is sound,' Sosnkowski told his officers: 'Battles are lost, not by numerical weakness, but by an army's internal disease.'[15]

Sosnkowski's efforts produced a marked increase both in quantity and quality. By 20 August, the nominal strength of the Polish army had reached 737,767, roughly equivalent to that of the Soviet Western and South-Western Fronts. 373,166 of these men, or rather more than half, were already trained, equipped, and placed in the field.[16] They were not raw and useless recruits. They included 28,000 cavalrymen and 33,000 artillerymen who eliminated Soviet superiority in these vital services. The volunteers were mainly students, whose intelligence, enthusiasm and education acted like a blood-transfusion to regiments which had hitherto consisted of illiterate and apathetic peasant conscripts. When, in the heat of the fighting at Radzymin on 13 August, the 11th Infantry Division refused orders, the General Staff replaced it, not with regular reinforcements of the army reserve, but with the worker-volunteers.

The growth of the army was accompanied by important changes in command. On 19 July, General Rozwadowski returned from abroad to resume his position as Chief of the General Staff. On 9 August, General Sosnkowski was appointed Minister of Military Affairs, a position which he had been occupying in all but name for months past. On 10 August, in accordance with Piłsudski's dispositions for the coming battle, a number of changes were effected in the field commands. Of special interest in this connection was the promotion of General Sikorski, to command a completely new Fifth Army.

Sikorski's standing among the field commanders was in many ways the counterpart of Sosnkowski's standing among the military administrators. Both were Piłsudski's men, associated for a dozen years or more with each of his various ventures, from the Union of Active Struggle in Lwów to the Legions of the World War; both were still in their thirties; both had given distinguished service in the first period of the Soviet campaign. Władysław Sikorski was a civil engineer by profession, who entered politics as a part-time pursuit. Before the war, he was a lieutenant in the 'Royal and Imperial' reserve and President of the Rifleman's Association in Lwów. From 1914, he was chief of the National Committee's War Department. In 1918, when the Legions were disbanded, he violently disagreed with Haller. He was interned in Hungary. In 1919, as a major-general, he was given command of the 9th Infantry Division and in 1920 of the Polesie Group. His efficiency and success made him the automatic choice for all the special assignments during the rest of the war. His business-like habits and original, independent mind recommended him to the politicians as one of the few men who could speak to Piłsudski on equal terms. His military brilliance provided the prelude to a political career which after many upheavals ended at the very summit of Polish affairs. Sikorski and Sosnkowski were the topmost pair, standing on the shoulders of hundreds of other legionary officers who at this time forced their way to the top of the officer corps, men like Marian Kukiel who, with all the authority of his twenty-five years and five feet two inches, was a full colonel in the Sixth Army in Galicia. These were Piłsudski's new captains, the life and soul of his military team.

By the first week of August, it was clear that the decisive clash of arms was bound to occur within six or seven days. The Red Army was streaming westward. The last natural obstacles had been crossed; the last rearguard actions had been fought. For the two commanders this was the crucial moment. Tukhachevsky issued his final orders on the morning of the 8th, Piłsudski on the evening of the 6th. (See map, p. 196).

Strategic planning in the prevailing conditions was a very risky business. A sound basis for making safe decisions simply did not and could not exist. Piłsudski's plan had to be laid before he knew the exact line of Tukhachevsky's advance; it was conceived before Tukhachevsky himself had decided which way to march; it was based on an assumption, later proved false, that the bulk of the Red Army was marching on Warsaw by the direct western route; it had to leave the possibilities of a feint to the north or a swerve to the south for later attention. Tukhachevsky's plan was laid in ignorance of the Polish dispositions; it was based on an assumption, which also proved false, that the Polish army would resist most strongly in front of its capital. The state of Intelligence was poor. Polish aviation was persistently blinded by cloudy weather and heavy mists; Soviet aviation failed to reach the forward areas. Reconnaissance patrols and scouts on the ground could not keep up with a constantly changing situation. Armies of 40,000 or 50,000 men might have been spotted more easily if they had marched in Napoleonic style in massed

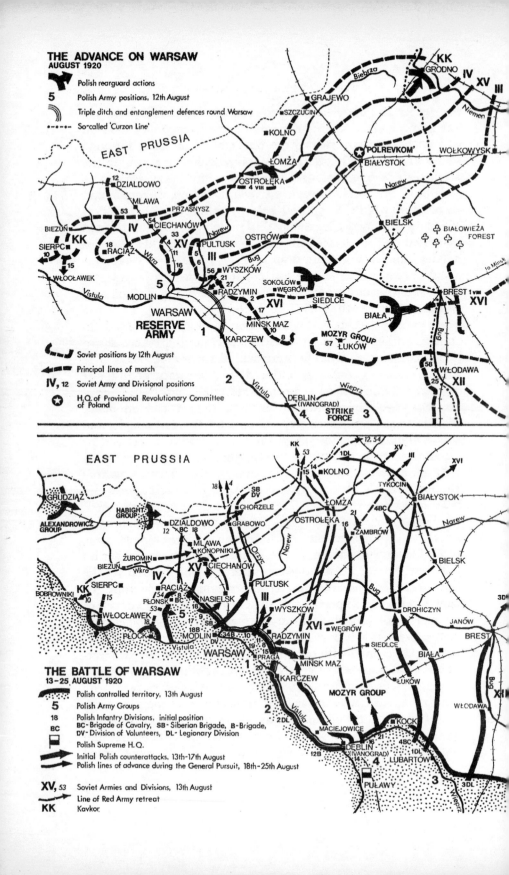

THE ADVANCE ON WARSAW
AUGUST 1920

Polish rearguard actions

5 Polish Army positions, 12th August

Triple ditch and entanglement defences round Warsaw

So-called 'Curzon Line'

EAST PRUSSIA

Biebrza
KK
GRODNO
IV XV
III
Niemen
GRAJEWO
SZCZUCIN
KOLNO
ŁOMŻA
POLREVKOM
BIAŁYSTOK
WOŁKOWYSK
Narew
12 DZIALDOWO
MLAWA
53 PRZASNYSZ
54
33 CIECHANÓW
4 OSTROŁĘKA
4 VIII
BIELSK
BIAŁOWIEŻA
FOREST
BIEZUŃ
KK
IV
Narew
OSTRÓW
to Minsk
SIERPC
18 RACIĄŻ
Wkra
XV PULTUSK
11 5
16 6
III
Bug
WŁOCŁAWEK
5
Vistula
MODLIN
56
21
27
WYSZKÓW
RADZYMIN
2
SOKOŁÓW
WĘGRÓW
17
SIEDLCE
BREST 1 VIII
XVI
WARSAW
XVI
BIAŁA
RESERVE
ARMY
1
MINSK MAZ
10
KARCZEW
8
MOZYR GROUP
57 ŁUKÓW
Bug
58 WŁODAWA
25 XII

Soviet positions by 12th August

Principal lines of march

IV, 12 Soviet Army and Divisional positions

H.Q. of Provisional Revolutionary Committee of Poland

2
Vistula
Wieprz
DEBLIN
(IVANOGRAD)
4 STRIKE
FORCE
3

EAST PRUSSIA

12, 54
KK
53
1DL
XV
III
XVI
15
KOLNO
TYKOCIN
BIAŁYSTOK
GRUDZIĄŻ
18 4
SB
DV
CHORZELE
ŁOMŻA
21
4BC
HABIGHT
GROUP
DZIALDOWO
BC 18
GRABOWO
OSTROŁĘKA
16
ZAMBRÓW
ALEXANDROWICZ
GROUP
12
MLAWA
KONOPNIKI
Orzyc
Narew
BIELSK
ŻUROMIN
BIEZUŃ
Wkra
IV
XV CIECHANÓW
4
PULTUSK
III
Bug
DROHICZYN
JANÓW
BREST
3D
KK SIERPC
54
RACIĄŻ
PŁOŃSK BC
53
NASIELSK
18
WYSZKÓW
XVI
WĘGRÓW
BOBROWNIKI
10
15
WŁOCŁAWEK
18
5
17
SB
18
18B
PŁOCK
MODLIN
34B 10
DV
11
RADZYMIN
SIEDLCE
BIAŁA
XII
WARSAW
9
PRAGA
20
MINSK MAZ
ŁUKÓW
KARCZEW
1
MOZYR GROUP
WŁODAWA

THE BATTLE OF WARSAW
13–25 AUGUST 1920

Polish controlled territory, 13th August

5 Polish Army Groups

18 Polish Infantry Divisions, initial position
BC BC-Brigade of Cavalry, SB-Siberian Brigade, B-Brigade,
DV-Division of Volunteers, DL-Legionary Division

Polish Supreme H.Q.

Initial Polish counterattacks, 13th–17th August
Polish lines of advance during the General Pursuit, 18th–25th August

XV, 53 Soviet Armies and Divisions, 13th August

Line of Red Army retreat

KK Kavkor

2
2DL
Vistula
KOCK
MACIEJOWICE
16 21
4BC
DEBLIN
(IVANOGRAD)
12B
14
1DL
LUBARTÓW
PUŁAWY
Wieprz
3DL
7
4
3

formation; dispersed in the mist across several hundred square miles, they could disguise their intentions right up to the moment of impact. Serious errors were made on both sides. Piłsudski was told at an early date that the Soviet XV and III Armies seemed to be moving north of Warsaw, but he mistook them for the IV Army. Tukhachevsky actually received the full text of Piłsudski's plan, found on the body of a Polish liaison officer killed near Chełm; he thought it too good to be true and dismissed it as a fraud or a local diversion.[17] Thus the two armies blundered into battle.

Piłsudski's frank admission of the 'absurdity' of his task leads one to suspect that his account of the Battle of Warsaw is nearest to the truth. In his book *Rok 1920* written some five years later, he resisted the temptation to describe the battle in standard military terms, or as a set piece contested by omniscient generals and decided by superior planning and tactics. He himself called it a '*bijatyka*' and a '*bagarre*' which in English one would call a 'scrap' or a 'brawl'. He talked of 'the nullity of forces available', 'the nonsense of the situation', 'the irrationality of feebleness', 'the excessive risk, contrary to all logic and sound military principles'.[18] Piłsudski's plans were dictated by circumstance. His concept of the counter-offensive was the natural outcome of repeated failure with defensive tactics throughout July. Indeed, his reluctance to commit the main reserves to the crumbling defensive lines in Byelorussia had in itself created a situation where a radical change to offensive strategy was unavoidable. He had little choice in the location of his counter-offensive. He could not have launched it on his left wing, where his positions were already outflanked by the Soviet cavalry; he did not consider launching it from the centre, where he expected the Soviet frontal attack to develop; he could not launch it from the southern front, where his armies were nearly 200 miles away from the main theatre of action. He was left with only one serious possibility—a counter-offensive to the right of centre, at a point where a strike-force could be assembled from both northern and southern fronts. He pondered and checked these considerations during the night of 5–6 August, ruminating alone in his study at Belweder in Warsaw. In the morning, he received Rozwadowski and together they worked out the details. Rozwadowski pointed out the value of the River Wieprz, sixty miles south of Warsaw as the base for the counter-offensive. By the evening, Order No. 8358/3 of 6 August 1920, published by the Supreme Command and signed by Rozwadowski, was ready and issued.[19]

The endless polemics which have surrounded the authorship of this famous order are irrelevant. Whether the details were drafted by Piłsudski, by Rozwadowski, by Weygand, by all of them, or even by somebody else, is immaterial. Any moderately competent strategist, familiar with war on the Borders, would have expressed the desirability of similar dispositions. The crucial decision did not concern the order's details; it was one of moral judgement, whether one could dare to transform an army's entire array in the space of a week, whether an army could risk the disruption of its battle order when the enemy was already knocking at the gates of the capital. This decision could only belong to the Commander-in-Chief, and it was Piłsudski who took it. He described the experience in the words of Napoleon, 'like that of a girl giving birth to a child, a prey to the pangs of labour.'[20]

The order of 6 August created three fronts out of the existing two, and redistributed the Polish armies out of all recognition. The Northern Front stretched from Pułtuck on the Narew to Dęblin on the Vistula, and was assigned to General Józef Haller. On its northern extremity, it included reserve formations defending the lower Vistula. Next came the new Fifth Army of General Sikorski, instructed to contain the mobile right wing of the enemy to the north of Warsaw. In the Warsaw sector, the First Army of General Latinik and the Second Army of General Roja were to hold the perimeter of the capital's defences with the support of a strategic reserve under General Żeligowski. The Central Front stretched from Dęblin to Brody in Galicia, and was assigned to Piłsudski in person. It included the principal strikeforce under General Śmigły-Rydz, which was to be assembled on the Wieprz at Kock and Lubartów, assisted on its left by the Fourth Army of General Skierski and covered on its right by the Third Army of General Zieliński. The Southern Front remained much as before, dispersed along the upper Bug and the Strypa right to the Dniester, and commanded by General Iwaszkiewicz. It consisted of the

Sixth Army of General Jędrzejewski, the independent Cavalry Division of Colonel Rómmel, and the Ukrainian Army of General Pavlenko. Its task was to defend Lwów and to prevent the Soviet forces in Galicia from joining Tukhachevsky in the north. Supreme Headquarters were to be located at Puławy on the Vistula. All units were to be in position by 12 August at the latest. (See map, p. 196).

This regrouping demanded an operation of staggering complexity. Piłsudski described it as 'beyond human capacity'.[21] At the time of receiving the order, many of the units were engaged in combat and exhausted after five weeks of retreat. Now, still under pressure from an enemy constantly pushing forward, they were required to disengage, to change their command, to traverse the forward areas laterally across all the lines of communication, and to arrive within five days at positions often 100 or 200 miles distant. It was an act of faith that Piłsudski could have considered this operation feasible; that in the main it was effected, was a miracle, a miracle moreover, in the very sphere of staff organization and administrative liaison where so many western observers considered the Polish army incompetent.

It would be wrong, of course, to imply that everything went to plan. On the Northern Front, Polish reorganization was disrupted by the irruption of the Kavkor, which decimated the Group of General Roja, deprived the Second Army of its prospective commander, and seized the very sector between the Narew and Bug where Sikorski's Fifth Army was supposed to assemble. On the Central Front, General Zieliński's covering force turned out to be composed of largely fictitious or absent units. Piłsudski himself admitted that dispositions on paper did not always tally with reality on the ground. The proliferation of 'groups, sub-groups, super-groups, advance groups, and rear groups' sometimes resulted in staffs without soldiers and at one point in a band of one hundred soldiers divided into three 'brigades' each commanded by a full general. At Maciejowice near Dęblin the red cockades of the 15th Regiment of Uhlans were mistaken for red stars and attracted the murderous fire of their own artillery.

The disposition of the Polish armies on 12 August matched in the main the functions which they were intended to fulfil.

The 156,000 men actually in position on the Northern and Central Fronts enjoyed a considerable superiority, even over Tukhachevsky's nominal strength of 116,000.[22] Fifteen of the twenty-one divisions were occupying defensive positions, which judging by World War standards, could expect to hold out against up to three times their own number. The Polish Southern Front with its 29,000 men was roughly equal to the two offensive armies of the Soviet South-Western Front, XII Army and the Konarmiya. Polish reserves and supply services were close at hand; the population was friendly; they were on their own ground. Though their exhaustion could not be less than the enemy's; their morale was raised by the hopes of the new plan. Once their regrouping was complete, their most vulnerable period had passed without challenge.

The Battle of Warsaw was fought in four distinct movements, on four separate sectors—the Vistula Bridgehead, the Wkra, the Wieprz, and the Prussian frontier. Each movement formed part of a harmonious whole—*Agitando, Maestoso, Presto*, and *Tutti*. (See map, p. 196).

The Vistula Bridgehead at Warsaw was well defended, and should not have caused the Polish command much trouble. Its triple lines of barbed wire and double trench system formed an even semi-circle, centred on the east bank suburb of Praga. Its deepest point was at Radzymin, thirteen miles from the river. Its left wing ran to the Bug opposite Serock and its right wing to the Vistula near Karczew; it could not be easily turned on the flanks. It possessed the strongest complement of all the Polish sectors—46,000 infantry and nearly 2,000 cavalry, 730 heavy machine-guns, 192 artillery batteries, and a company of tanks, concentrated along a perimeter seventy kilometres in length. With 690 men, ten machine-gun posts, and three artillery batteries per kilometre it was the only sector of the Polish-Soviet War which ever approached World War levels of concentration. It possessed only one division, the 4th Infantry Division of the Second Army, which had been imported from afar and which might have been disorganized by a lengthy journey. Its commanders were men of experience—Haller, once of 'Blue Army' fame now surrounded by the prestige of the volunteers; Latinik, the determined defender of Teschen in the previous year against the Czechs;

Raszewski, the Poznanian; Zieliński, who had once held a high Tsarist command.

The handling of the battle for the bridgehead, and the panic which occurred, is rather surprising. Contact with the enemy was made on the evening of 12 August, when units of Putna's 21st Division of the Soviet III Army reached the outer line before Radzymin, to be joined during the night by all five divisions of Sollogub's XVI Army. On the next morning, while the Polish batteries were still firing over their heads at 5–6,000 metres, the Soviets rushed the outer wire and stormed the first line of trenches. Radzymin was taken. The Polish 11th Division was broken, and retreated against orders. Haller took fright. He did not see Radzymin as a local setback. Without waiting for confirmation, he assumed that the full weight of the Soviet thrust was menacing the heart of Warsaw. Rozwadowski was with him, and together they telegraphed in all directions for aid. 14 August was a day of hand-to-hand fighting, with bayonets and grenades as much in use as the heaviest weapons. But no Soviet reinforcements arrived to exploit their early success. At last Haller comprehended that the Soviet assault had been undertaken not by four armies, but by one army and one division. On 15 August, he threw Żeligowski's reserves into the line. The tanks advanced until stopped by mechanical failure. Radzymin was recovered. On 16 August, the defenders sortied beyond their defences. On 17 August, the 15th Division progressed still further and at Minsk Mazowiecki met up with the forward units of the Central Front. On 18 August, the bridgehead was completely clear of Soviet intruders. The pursuit could begin.

Operations on the Wkra presented the toughest task, and Sikorski was given the least time to prepare them. His headquarters at Modlin and his assembly area were not chosen until 10 August. His troops were few in number, short of arms, motley in appearance, mixed in quality, and dispersed over a wide area. Of 45,000 'rationaires', he could field only 26,000 combatants, of which 4,000 were cavalry. His Fifth Army was composed of the most diverse elements. The garrison at Modlin consisted of local recruits who had not yet learned to shoot; they were armed with six Napoleonic cannon but had no powder and no shot. The Group of General Roja, which

had lost fifty per cent of its effectives in its recent encounter
with the Kavkor, had been escorted from the frontline under
guard. The 18th Infantry Brigade had lost thirty-five per cent
at Grodno. The 17th Infantry Division was reduced to 850
men. The Siberian Brigade of Colonel Rumsza, was splendidly
equipped with American and Japanese material, but in a
six-month voyage round the world had lost its edge for fighting.
The Volunteer Division was subject to ferocious discipline for
fear of waywardness among its priests and poets; yet it turned
out to be a first-rate unit, in Sikorski's words, 'la terreur de la
Russie'.[23] The core of the Fifth Army was formed from the
crack 18th Infantry Division and General Karnicki's cavalry
division. In the course of the next week, the Group of Colonel
Habicht at Działdowo, the Reserve Group of the Lower
Vistula, and the civilians behind the barricades at Płock, all
passed under Sikorski's command. The fifth Army's positions
were not the worst. Modlin itself had six separate forts, all in
disrepair, but covering a splendidly flooded valley. The Bug
at this point was 300 metres wide; the Vistula, which provided
a line of last retreat, was even broader; the Wkra was little
more than a stream, but clear and well defined. These were
the surroundings in which, on 13 August with most of the
units still in the process of reinforcement, provisionment, and
briefing, Sikorski received the order from Haller to advance
his operations by twenty-four hours. On the morning of
14 August, the Fifth Army took the offensive. The 18th
Infantry Division, still without its tanks, crossed the Wkra.
The Volunteer Division, waded across the Vistula, holding
their heavy English rifles above their heads, to take up positions
beside the Siberian Brigade. The start was indecisive, for Soviet
resistance was stiffer than expected. The next day, General
Karnicki executed a daring raid on Ciechanów, twenty miles
to the north-east. He charged into the town, which, despite the
presence of the command post of the Soviet IV Army, had
received no warning. The Soviet commander replacing the
wounded Sergeyev, panicked. He burned his own radio
station. Karnicki carried off the Soviet plans and cyphers.
The raid on Ciechanów was of enormous psychological
importance. Ciechanów, once the home of the Princes of
Mazowsze, figuring in the novels of Sienkiewicz and in the

epic wars with the Teutonic Order, was a marcher castle, steeped in Polish history and romance. Its capture, even for a few hours, caused jubilation in the Polish ranks and dismay among the Soviets. 15 August was the day, moreover, when both sides were for the first time getting a clear view of the overall situation. Sikorski now knew for certain that he had attacked, not just the Soviet right wing, but the main body of the enemy's centre. His three divisions of infantry and one of cavalry had challenged twelve infantry and two cavalry divisions of the Soviet IV, XV, and III Armies, all converging on the Wkra. Rozwadowski recognized his misplaced alarm for the Vistula Bridgehead, and, leaving Haller in Warsaw, drove to Modlin with Sosnkowski and Weygand. The performance of the Fifth Army in the next days would be decisive for the whole battle. There were spectres of 1831, when the Russian army of Paskevich had swerved to the right, swept through Ciechanów and taken Warsaw in the rear. Sikorski did not flinch. Fully aware of the odds against him and of the threat of a manoeuvre on his open left flank, he persevered with the attack. On 16 August, he pressed forward and entered Nasielsk. His tanks and his eight small armoured cars, probing the enemy's soft spots achieved a quite disproportionate effect; his two armoured trains, steaming back and forth on the Modlin—Ciechanów line, spraying the enemy's positions with bursts of shell fire, gave the impression of twenty heavy batteries. On 17 August, he advanced again, and on 18 August yet again, drawing near to his objectives on the Orzyc and Narew. By this time the Soviet command was on the horns of a dilemma. By rallying their XV and III Armies, and accelerating the recall of the IV, they could easily bring their vastly superior numbers to bear on Sikorski and reverse his advance; but in so doing, they would leave themselves exposed to total encirclement by Polish forces from the other sectors. Sikorski, at the risk of his own annihilation, had ensured the clearance of the Vistula bridgehead and the success of the counter-offensive from the Wieprz. To escape from their dilemma, the Soviet XV and III armies were obliged to withdraw, to leave Sikorski unpunished, and to cut their own IV Army adrift.

The counterattack from the Wieprz was the most dramatic

event in the Battle of Warsaw; yet its success depended on the actions which preceded it. If the Vistula bridgehead had collapsed or the Fifth Army been overrun, Piłsudski's daring manoeuvre would have been irrelevant. Its execution proved far simpler than anyone dreamed. Most of the hard fighting had been done before it set out. But Piłsudski at Puławy knew none of this. He intended to wait until the battle on the Northern Front was well and truly raging, before driving his strike-force through the enemy's lines of communications. He knew the value of such a move, if successful, but he expected complications. He thought that the strike-force's 20,000 men—two divisions of infantry, two brigades of cavalry— were being pitted against four whole armies, the XV, III, XVI, and the Mozyr Group whose numbers might well redeem their tactical disadvantage. He knew that he would raise chaos, but that chaos could envelop him as well as the enemy. He knew that the price of failure was almost certain encirclement, with its attendant choice between capture and a fight to the death. He must have winced at the prospect of capture, with visions of a reunion with his old schoolmate Dzierżyński or of a journey in chains to a Bolshevik triumph in Warsaw. It was all possible. His fears cannot have been calmed by Haller's telegrams, which suggested that the Northern Front was crumbling. He did not have news of Sikorski's success. He did not have word that Tukhachevsky's centre was in front of Sikorski and not in front of himself. He delayed as long as he dared, but finally advanced his departure by one day. At dawn on 16 August, he released the strike-force of Śmigły-Rydz with Skierski's divisions in lateral support. He watched his legions move off from the Wkra into circumstances as murky as the morning. His anxieties were not relieved, when the patrols reported no sign of the enemy. He suspected a trap. He was, he says, 'menaced by mysteries'.[24] He spent 17 August motoring round the forward areas, 'looking for traces of a phantom enemy'. On 18 August, he drove back to Warsaw, only beginning to guess the measure of his success. In Warsaw, he met further trouble. The Northern Front command was dispirited by its poor performance, and only his personal insistence persuaded it to join in an energetic and general pursuit. His orders were ignored by General Latinik, who preferred to lend a hand to the hard-pressed Sikorski. In Warsaw, at least, he learned how matters stood. He learned that the 1st Legionary Division and Jaworski's cavalry stood at Drohiczyn, more than half way to Białystok, having covered seventy miles in three days, that the 3rd Legionary Division and its accompanying cavalry brigade were on the outskirts of Brest-Litowsk. The strike-force had brushed through the lines of the Soviet Mozyr Group capturing the siege artillery destined for Warsaw, but had not collided with the mass of XVI, III, or XV Armies. During that night Tukhachevsky ordered a general retreat.

The net result of the actions between 12 and 18 August was to transfer the focus of conflict away from the environs of Warsaw to the area near the Prussian frontier. The eastward retreat of the Soviet armies contending with the northerly thrust of the Polish strike-force combined to cause a rapid movement of operations in a north-easterly direction. By August it was evident that the final round of the battle would take place in the quadrilateral bounded by Myszyniec—Wyszków—Białystok—Grajewo. The four northerly Soviet armies, IV, XV, III, and XVI, and fragments of the Mozyr Group were all bound to pass through this area, where elements of five Polish armies, the Fifth, First, Second, Fourth, and Third, would all be within striking distance. Piłsudski's total victory depended on the closing of the ring, Tukhachevsky's survival on his immediate escape. Tukhachevsky, however, moved fast. His XV Army, still at Ciechanów on 19 August, was at Ostrołęka on the 20th, and Łomża by the 22nd, making for Lipsk and Grodno; it completely outpaced Sikorski, who was still engaged with the IV Army. The III Army, at Wyszków on the 19th, at Zambrów on the 20th and at Tukocin by the 22nd, was not chased by Latinik and struggled past the fingertips of the strike-force into safety. The XVI Army ran hard and fast into trouble; at Węgrów on the 19th, Bielsk on the 20th, and Białystok by the 22nd, it had to carve a path first through the 21st Division of Fourth Army, then through Jaworski's cavalry and finally through the 1st Legionary Division; it was badly splintered but managed to keep some remnants together on the road to Grodno. These three armies, fighting rearguard actions as they marched, covered fifteen miles a day. Although it did not compare with the winged onset of the Polish strike-force, it was double the average speed of their earlier advance and sufficed to save them from encirclement. In the instant before the stable door was shut, these three horses had bolted. It was otherwise with the fourth.

The Soviet IV Army was condemned from the moment the retreat was announced. On that day, 18 August, the IV Army's 18th Division was ordered to proceed with the siege of Płock; its 53rd and 54th Divisions continued to engage Sikorski's flank; its 12th Division was still in Działdowo; Ghai's Kavkor was roaming on the lower Vistula. That Tukhachevsky did nothing to rectify this situation, but on the contrary for four days actually encouraged it, can only be explained by the contention that he still regarded the retreat as a temporary measure. At the end of those four days, the IV Army's isolation was complete. Hopelessly late it began to withdraw. Most of the infantry was soon overtaken and overpowered. Only Ghai had the means and the will to break out. The Kavkor was undefeated in seven weeks of campaigning; its morale was high; by marching in the hours of darkness, it aimed to pass unnoticed through the Dobrzyn lakeland and Kurpie forests and still make thirty miles a day; it was helped by rainy weather and night fog. The first obstacle was the Polish Fifth Army, whose elements were streaming north to cut them off; and after the Fifth, there would be the Fourth and eventually the strike-force of Śmigły-Rydz. Notwithstanding, Ghai set out. On 21 August, just before dawn, he collided with the cavalry of Colonel Orlicz-Dreszer in the woods near Żuromin. Dreszer held off, not seeking combat in the darkness. He would have done better to risk an engagement. When daylight came, the Kavkor had gone. The next day, Ghai found himself caught in a ring of four divisions near Mława. He waited till well after midnight, then opened up a barrage of extravagant fury on the station at Konopniki. He charged into the nocturnal chaos, sabred the defenders, and broke clear. On 23 August, he sliced through the Volunteer Division at Grabowo, like a Cossack knife through student butter, and later fought through the Siberian Brigade in Chorzele. On 24 August he caught up with the Soviet 53rd Division whose road to Kolno was blocked by two divisions of the Fourth Army. He decided to assist them. A two-day battle ensued, in which the Kavkor vainly sought to protect its weaker partner. It was a hopeless point of honour. Behind the Fourth Army, the legionaries of Śmigły-Rydz waited to take up the fight. The 53rd Division was driven across the frontier. The Kavkor with no cartridges left, no food and no choice, followed them at dawn on the 26th, taking with them into Germany 600 wounded, 2,000 prisoners and eleven captured guns.[25] The Kavkor, which in its brief career had accounted for four provincial cities, five major rivers, six tanks, seven aeroplanes, eight fortresses and 21,000 Polish casualties, ceased to exist.[26] Ghai was taken to a German camp at Salzwedel near Berlin, his men to a camp at Altdam near Stettin. By their own admission they were the avant-garde of the Revolution in Germany; they were the only part of the Red Army to reach their destination. They crossed the Prussian frontier singing the 'Internationale'. Their singing formed the terminal cadence of the Battle of Warsaw.

The immediate effects of the battle were evident to all. The Soviet invasion of Poland had been repulsed. The fighting was now far removed from Warsaw. The life of the Polish Republic no longer hung in the balance. Tukhachevsky's armies were in full flight. Of his five armies which set out for the west on 4 July, one had ceased to exist, two were decimated, two were severely mutilated. If the Polish estimates of 66,000 Soviet prisoners in Poland and 44,000 interned in Germany were only half correct, and allowing for Soviet dead and wounded to be roughly equal to the 40,000 Polish casualties, one arrives at the conclusion that two-thirds of Tukhachevsky's invading force was eliminated. At least 100,000 Red Army men were lost in one way or another, although many of these were stragglers, waggoners, service staff, and camp followers from the rear. There is no doubt of the scale of the defeat. Within a fortnight of the first encounter at Radzymin, the Red Army's retreat had become a rout.

Most accounts of the Battle of Warsaw may be divided between those which eulogize Piłsudski's victory and those which apologize for Tukhachevsky's defeat. Although they seem to be discussing the same events, they have little in common. They offer little more to the serious historian than the once fashionable talk in Poland of a 'miracle on the Vistula' or the continuing Soviet fashion of not talking at all when inconvenient. It is pointless to speak of 'long lines of communications' or Tukhachevsky's 'contempt for space'. These are not explanations. The lines of communication between Russia and Poland cannot be shortened. The vast space of the Borders is a well-known fact, which every general must first accept then ignore; a strategist who treated the expanse of the Borders with due respect would never fight at all.

It is very revealing to find that the main concept of Tukhachevsky's strategy was repeatedly praised by Piłsudski. Despite their endless polemics on matters of secondary importance, both commanders continued to believe that the plan of marching into Poland at full speed was fundamentally correct. Piłsudski said 'it was not a bad plan, not a bad plan at all, which I might have adopted myself.'[27] Tukhachevsky remained unrepentant: 'The Red front,' he said in 1923, '*was* capable of achieving its mission, although in the event it did not accomplish it . . . Neither the politics nor the strategy were faulty.'[28] These two men, who knew more of the subject than anyone else, differed in their opinion from many of the Polish generals and from almost all the Western observers, who have always held the view that Tukhachevsky's undoing was the natural consequence, to use the words of Sir Henry Wilson, 'of Gadarene swine' galloping fast to their own destruction.[29] Piłsudski's sympathy is surprising, for Tukhachevsky's advance from the Bug, leaving 200 miles of unprotected flank, seems to have invited the counter-attack which indeed destroyed him. The real problem, however, was one of calculated risk, and in particular of timing. Tukhachevsky knew perfectly well that his flank was wide open, but he did not intend to leave it that way for more than a few days. He did not believe that the Polish army could regroup with sufficient energy. He was happy enough to see Polish divisions being drawn from the line in preparation for a counterattack which could only be delivered when Warsaw had fallen. His original date for the fall of Warsaw was 12 August, which implied an assault on the city launched perhaps two or three days before. He was quite right in his belief that the defenders of Warsaw could not be in position by 9 or 10 August; they were not. Unfortunately for him, *he* was not in position by 9 or 10 August either, a fact which explains his late decision to avoid a frontal attack and his manoeuvre to the north of Warsaw. This decision extended his flank still further, and gave Piłsudski's counterattack a target of terrible simplicity. Thus one arrives at the conclusion that Tukhachevsky's failure was due, not to the haste of his advance, but to its tardiness. He deliberately risked a transiently weak position, in the expectation that the Poles would be powerless to exploit it. He was foiled, not so much by the counterattack, which by the time it was launched was almost certain to succeed, but by the astonishing feat of Polish regrouping between 6 and 12 August and by the series of successful delaying tactics, on the Bug and the Narew, at Biała, on the Vistula bridgehead, and on the Wkra. Despite its extraordinary pace, Tukhachevsky's advance was just too slow. He missed his goal by three or four days at the most. Speed, which had virtually ceased to exist as a strategic factor in Western Europe, was still the essence of warfare in the East.

One has only to look at the alternatives. Tukhachevsky's supply system was inadequate; his support services were far behind; his numbers were dwindling; the resistance of the local population was growing every day; the further the fighting moved away from the Russian bases in Vyazma, Smolensk, and Polotsk, the nearer it came to the Polish bases in Poland. Tukhachevsky knew all this better than anyone. To have tarried on the Niemen or the Bug would certainly have improved his condition; but it would have improved the condition of the Polish army even more. Every day's delay served the Polish advantage. Tukhachevsky had no real alternative but to ride for Warsaw at breakneck speed.

The psychological aspect was also important. In campaigns where fortunes swing to and fro in quick succession, the question of morale is paramount. It is far harder for commanders to keep the confidence of their men than in the wars where action moves slowly and where regular habits and safe precautions are easily established. In July, Tukhachevsky's lightning offensive quickly demoralized the Polish troops, and there was every reason to believe that its further prosecution in August would have the same effect, indeed that it would have a greater, cumulative effect. That it did not, was due to the superior leadership of the Polish commanders, and to the will to resist, which lodged in the breast of the Polish soldier defending his native soil.

Political considerations complemented the psychology. The political purpose of the Red Army's advance was not to conquer Europe directly. The Red Army of 1920 could hardly be sent with thirty-six divisions to achieve what the Tsarist army of 1914–17 had failed to achieve with 150. Its purpose was to provoke a social revolution. Tukhachevsky was undoubtedly told, and probably believed, that if only he could reach Warsaw on time, the civilian population would do the rest. Speed was the essence of Bolshevik politics as well as of Soviet strategy.

The one element in the Battle of Warsaw which no one would query is the absence of co-ordination between the Soviet Western and South-Western Commands. Despite an order of 13 August to join the Western Front, the South-Western Command played no significant part in the battle whatsoever. Its XII Army launched an attack on Hrubieszów with one division, which threatened nobody; the Konarmiya's manoeuvre towards Zamość, begun on 20 August, coincided not with the attack on Warsaw but with the general retreat; the XIV Army, now facing the Dniester, did not attempt to engage. The consequences were undoubtedly serious. The assembly of Piłsudski's strike-force, only sixty miles from the XII Army and eighty miles from the Konarmiya, was allowed to proceed undisturbed for ten days. The Polish army's fear of fighting on two fronts was removed. The Polish High Command was presented with the golden opportunity of dealing with Tukhachevsky and Budyonny separately, and of defeating each in turn.

The behaviour of the South-Western Command has never been satisfactorily explained. The most frequent explanation is the one put about by Trotsky, who blamed the private ambitions and petty jealousies of its political officer, Joseph Stalin. According to Trotsky, Stalin could neither bear to watch Tukhachevsky's triumph at Warsaw, nor to be over-shadowed by the success of Tukhachevsky's political officer, Smilga; Stalin wanted at any cost to enter Lwów at the same time that Smilga and Tukhachevsky were to enter Warsaw . . . 'Stalin was waging his own war':

When the danger to Tukhachevsky's army became clearly evident and the Commander-in-Chief ordered the South-Western Front to shift its direction sharply towards Zamość-Tomaszew . . . the command of the South-Western Front, encouraged by Stalin, continued to move to the west. For three or four days our General Staff could not secure the execution of this order. Only after repeated demands reinforced by threats did the South-Western Command change direction, but by then the delay had already played its fatal role. On 16 August, the Poles took the counter-offensive and forced our troops to roll back. . . . If Stalin and Voroshilov and the illiterate Budyonny had not had their own war in Galicia and the Red Cavalry had been at Lublin in time, the Red Army would not have suffered the disaster . . . [30]

It is unfortunate that Trotsky's allegations can only be checked against the counter-allegations of the Stalinists, whose sole purpose in later years was to shift the blame back onto Trotsky. Stalin's remarks before the closed hearing at the Tenth Party Congress in March 1921, the accounts of Yegorov and Voroshilov published in 1929 and of Rabinovich's *History of the Civil War* published in 1935, were directed towards a political and not a historical audience. They contrived to blame Trotsky not only for Tukhachevsky's failure to take Warsaw but also for Budyonny's failure to take Lwów.

One can best hope to approach the truth by returning to the position as it stood in the second week of August 1920, starting from the realities of the military situation. The intended direction of the Red Army's movements can be exactly established and measured. Yegorov's directive of 22 July stated Lublin as the objective for his XII Army, Rawa Ruska for the Konarmiya, Mikolajów for the XIV Army.[31] Tukhachevsky's directive of 10 August stated Włocławek as the objective for his IV Army, Wyszogród for the XV, Modlin for the III, Warsaw for the XVI, Dęblin for the Mozyr Group.[32] To be exact, Yegorov's line of march was to the west-south-west, Tukhachevsky's to the west-north-west. They were divided by a deliberate divergence of forty-five degrees. This meant that for every four miles they marched, they grew three miles further apart. One can safely conclude that the Soviet Supreme Command had no immediate intention of using the Western and South-Western Fronts in unison.

Then there is the vital matter of timing. Yegorov's directive was dated 22 July. The South-Western Front had been moving away for over three weeks before anyone thought of calling it back. Tukhachevsky's directive was dated 10 August. In direct anticipation of the Battle of Warsaw, he deliberately shifted his centre of gravity northwards, thus making liaison with Yegorov even more difficult than before. The two fronts were both behind schedule. Tukhachevsky, who aimed to reach Warsaw on 12 August had been delayed by the battles on the Narew and Bug; Yegorov, who aimed to reach Rawa Ruska on 29 July had been delayed by an even greater margin by the battle of Brody. Both fronts were only approaching their objectives at the time when they should have won them. Each was too preoccupied with its own problems to spare any thought for the problems of the other. (See maps, pp. 196, 228)

The 'separatism' of the South-Western Command is not hard to understand. It had emerged during the Civil War in the Ukraine and had little interest in an invasion of Poland. Its leaders, Yegorov and Stalin, based at Alexandrovsk, were both of the opinion that the defence of Russia should have priority over an adventure into Europe. They were responsible for the operations against Wrangel in the Crimea and for defending the Rumanian frontier. They were increasingly embarrassed by the Galician campaign whose constant westward progress threatened their overall cohesion. They were busy enough elsewhere without having to join in the Battle of Warsaw. They had received little consideration from the Supreme Command for months past, especially with regard to requests for reinforcements, all of which seemed to be earmarked for Tukhachevsky. Stalin's intercessions at the highest level, with Trotsky and Sklyansky, aroused no response.[33] They were rapidly approaching a genuine crisis, which would soon oblige them to resign from the Galician campaign altogether. At the beginning of August, they resolved that as soon as Lwów was taken, the Konarmiya should be withdrawn and sent to the Crimea.[34]

This was the background to the catastrophic attempt of the Bolshevik leadership to harmonize the conflicting interests of the Western and South-Western Fronts. On 2 August, the Politburo decided to divide the South-Western Front in two.[35] The XII Army and the Konarmiya were to pass under the orders of the Western Command, making a unified offensive front against Poland, whilst the XIII Army and the XIV Army were to pass under the orders of a new Southern command, making a unified defensive front in the Ukraine. Stalin was to supervise the operation. The Politburo's decision was prompted by the earlier undertaking to unify the Western Front when the Bug was reached, and was passed to the Commander-in-Chief, Sergey Kamenev, on 5 August. No date was set for its execution.

Kamenev's vacillation during the next ten days turned a straight-forward problem into a major crisis. He was torn between the demands of Tukhachevsky and the difficulties of Yegorov and Stalin. On 8 August, he told Tukhachevsky that the immediate transfer of the XII Army and Konarmiya was 'out of the question.'[36] He was encouraged to procrastinate by Smilga's entirely erroneous estimate that the Western Front enjoyed a superiority of three to two over the Polish forces.[37] On 11 August he consulted the South-Western Command, about the feasibility of the proposed transfer on the 15th, but his cable took two days to arrive.[38] On 12 August, he ordered the transfer of the XII Army but said nothing of the Konarmiya.[39] On 13 August he received the inevitable protest from Tukhachevsky. Speaking on the direct line,[40] he told Tukhachevsky that it was 'just as important to liquidate Wrangel as to settle your problem.' He agreed, however, that 'the Konarmiya should be held in readiness, to be used as a battering-ram in the event that our plan miscarries and your own fist proves too weak'. He finally accepted Tukhachevsky's point that 'further delay could prove troublesome'. Kamenev's Order No. 4774/1052 to the South-Western Command repeated word for word what Tukhachevsky had dictated on the telephone.[41] It ordered that by noon on 14 August both the XII Army and the Konarmiya should pass to the Western

Front. It sparked off a chain reaction of misunderstandings which nicely paralysed the entire Soviet command during the whole period of the Battle of Warsaw.

The genesis and progress of Order 4774/1052 deserve to be followed. It was issued as a precautionary measure, not as a matter of urgency. It was *not* issued as a countermove to Piłsudski's concentration on the Wieprz, which at that time was not known either to Kamenev or to Tukhachevsky. It brought the disgruntlement of the South-Western Command to boiling point.[42] It was the third cable which Yegorov and Stalin had received that day from Kamenev. In the morning they had received his 'consultative cable' of 11 August, closely followed by his instructions of 12 August relating to the XII Army. They had replied to the former in the negative, explaining that 'in the present conditions, a radical change of assignments is impossible'. Now in the afternoon they were presented with an order which made a mockery of the previous consultations. They must have noted its administrative arrangements with dismay. The XII Army and the Konarmiya were to be transferred to the Western front but their supply services and reinforcements were to remain the responsibility of the South-Western Front. Stalin sent an angry rebuff to Kamenev:

> Your order needlessly frustrates the operations of the South-Western Front, which has already commenced its advance. This order should either have been issued three days ago when the Konarmiya was in reserve or else should have been postponed until Lwów had fallen.[43]

Meanwhile, Yegorov had to obey. Orders from the Supreme Command were orders for him, if not for his political officer. He prepared instructions for transmission to the armies concerned, and signed them. But Stalin remained adamant. The instructions were countersigned by Stalin's deputy, R. I. Berzin, and transmitted late that night. By 14 August, Order No. 4774/1052 was, in theory, in operation. The XII Army and the Konarmiya were now Tukhachevsky's concern, and they awaited Tukhachevsky's further favour. Yegorov and Stalin washed their hands, and turned their thoughts to the Crimea.

Tukhachevsky's efforts to give practical effect to his theoretical control of the XII Army and Konarmiya have an air of total unreality.[44] He was near Warsaw, and they were in Galicia. He could only communicate through a lengthy radio chain and an 'operational point' in Kiev. In the absence of any specific prohibition, they continued with the operations in which they were already engaged. On 15 August he despatched Order No. 0361 which made provision for the Konarmiya to move by four daily marches to the region of Ustiług-Włodzimierz, He received a reply two days later:

Directive 0361. received 16 August 21.14 hours. Konarmiya unable to break off engagement. Line of Bug overrun. Our units approaching outskirts of Lwów, ten miles from the city. Orders already given to occupy Lwów. After concluding this operation, Konarmiya will proceed in accordance with your directive.

Tukhachevsky then repeated his order, and soon after midnight on the third day, he received another reply:

Directive received 19 August 23.30 hrs.... In two to three days, Lwów should be taken by Konarmiya. 45th and 47th Infantry Divisions not strong enough to hold sector without us. We beg your further orders.

He repeated his order a third time, and for some reason, the ether and the Konarmiya obliged almost immediately. His message reached Budyonny at 6 a.m. on 20 August, and the Konarmiya moved off. Nothing in this operation makes sense. Tukhachevsky's original order would have brought the Konarmiya into position near the Wieprz on 19 August, three days *after* the Polish strikeforce had left. His first repetition of the order, late on 17 August was made when he himself was contemplating a general retreat. His second repetition of the order on 20 August sent the Konarmiya to certain encirclement in an area which the other Soviet armies had completely abandoned. The operation was as incomprehensible to the people involved as it must be to the historian. Whatever its exact significance, it had less to do with the Battle of Warsaw than with the quarrel within the Soviet command.

The immediate victim of the quarrel was Budyonny. Budyonny's recent memoirs provided full documentation of the episode, which, as he frankly admits, 'during the era of the personality cult of J. V. Stalin was explored in a one-sided manner'.[45] He also provides a colourful picture of the resultant tribulations of the field commander. On 11 August, the Konarmiya was resting, awaiting orders. The Red cavalry men were sharpening their sabres in the sunshine, feeding their horses, patching their uniforms, bathing in the river, dancing to the 'Don Cossack'. Budyonny left his command post at Werba in his open Fiat and toured his divisions. He was prepared to go anywhere. On 12 August, orders arrived:

> The Konarmiya is to destroy the enemy on the right bank of the Bug in the shortest possible time and, having forced the river, to follow on the heels of retreating Third and Sixth Polish Armies and seize the city of Lwów.[46]

He made his dispositions for a three-pronged attack. On 13 August he signalled the start of the engagement. In the morning, he reminded Voroshilov that it was the 13th, the unlucky day of the month. 'Yes,' replied Voroshilov, 'but we are Godless men, and on a devils' wake the devils ought to work for *us*.' Radziechów was stormed. On 14 August, Budyonny was at Łopatyn. He was woken in the morning by fighting in the streets. Leaning out of the window of his billet, he drew his Mauser and killed a Pole who was crawling up on the command post's sentry. During the night, the town had been infiltrated in the fog by General Szymanowski at the head of 2,500 men armed with automatic rifles. The fighting lasted all day. In the evening, at nine o'clock, Budyonny returned to his command post, and was handed new instructions:

> In accordance with the Supreme Commander's Order 4774/1052 of 13 Aug. 1920:
> 1. XII Army and First Cavalry Army, but without 8th Division of Red Cossacks, to pass by 12.00 hours 14 August under orders of Western Front...
> 2. War Council of First Cavalry Army to put 8th Division of Red Cossacks at the disposition of XIV Army...
> Signed in name of War Council, South-Western Front. Yegorov. Berzin.[47]

He found these instructions hard to understand, but there was nothing in them to indicate any new operational procedure. On 15 August, the battle raged still more fiercely. The bridges on the Bug were down. The Poles had twenty planes in constant use. The 6th Cavalry Division swam the river under fire, climbed the high western bank, and pressed to within nine miles of Lwów. On the 16th the Poles counterattacked. Budyonny yielded his forward positions but dug in on the bridgehead. He was in a critical predicament. To advance was costly; to stand still was to present an easy target for the Polish aircraft and heavy batteries; to retreat was to invite a rout. At 9.30 p.m. he received his first order from the Western Command, Order 0361 of the previous day. It made no mention of the present situation, but ordered him to march to Ustiług-Włodzimierz eighty miles distant. The countersignature of the political officer was missing. Tukhachevsky was clearly unaware of the Konarmiya's plight. Budyonny cabled for clarification. At the same time he decided to advance, deeming it the only way to free himself for a change of direction. He cabled his decision to Tukhachevsky. On 17 and 18 August, the Konarmiya battled on. On 19 August, Lwów was surrounded on three sides at a radius of four to six miles. Budyonny and Voroshilov had slept in a haystack and were woken accidentally by a stray Polish soldier, also looking for a billet, who might easily have captured them instead of being captured himself:

'Iesus Maria,' exclaimed the Pole, 'Who are you? Don't shoot me, I'm the only one left.'
'This is Budyonny, and I am Voroshilov.'
The soldier was dumbfounded. Rolling his eyes, he could only glance at people about whom he had heard such terrible things.[48]

In the evening Budyonny received Tukhachevsky's repeated order, which contained news of the Polish counter-offensive. Budyonny was still of the same mind. He could only free himself by defeating the forces with which he was engaged. He begged Tukhachevsky for new orders. But at six o'clock in the morning, Tukhachevsky's order, repeated a second time, arrived unchanged. There could be no doubt now. Budyonny's new superior did not care for the Konarmiya's present situation. There was no point in remonstrating. On 20 August at midday, the Konarmiya abandoned the siege of Lwów, whose spires were in view and whose defenders would now sortie with a vengeance. It set off for the unknown delights of Ustiług-Włodzimierz. Voroshilov's 'devils' wake' had turned into a Polish fiesta. (See map, p. 228)

Stalin's part in the quarrel is difficult to determine. He was not a man to expatiate on his motives, and was sufficiently devious to cover all his moves with plausible arguments. His previous record of insubordination in 1918 and 1919 undoubtedly made him suspect, and there is definite proof that he accepted the Politburo's plan with bad grace. On 4 August, when Lenin informed him of the proposed division of the South-Western Front, he cabled back: 'The Politburo ought not to bother with such trifles' and evoked a curt request by return 'to explain your motives'.[49] His main motive clearly was to keep his friends together. He insisted that the proposed Southern Command should inherit the staff of South-Western Command *en bloc*, yet that also made for administrative simplicity. He raised a series of technical objections to the immediate transfer of the armies, yet these objections proved only too accurate. He refused to countersign Kamenev's Order 4774/1052 of 13 August, yet he did not countermand it, as he did on the famous occasion at Tsaritsyn in 1918 with an order of Trotsky's. He did nothing to prevent the execution of the order once it was made, nor to influence the behaviour of Budyonny. The real puzzle is to decide why Stalin ordered the Konarmiya to besiege Lwów on 12 August, knowing full well that it was due to be transferred to the west. He was perfectly within his rights as the political officer of the front command, but it was hardly a gesture of harmony. Was it to spite Tukhachevsky, as Trotsky said and as several Soviet commentators have repeated more recently?[50] Was it to win glory? Was it to enmesh the Konarmiya in an engagement from which no order of Kamenev's could extract it? Was it a simple operational command? The answer depends entirely on one's view of the man. All one can say for certain is that Stalin was profoundly suspicious of the regrouping, and that his suspicions were supported by very cogent military reasons; he certainly did nothing to help, but he was not guilty of insubordination.

At the closed hearing of the affair in March 1921, Stalin apparently exculpated himself from Trotsky's charges by a very curious remark. He said that Smilga, his opposite number on the Western Front, had 'promised' to take Warsaw by a certain date, and had failed, and had thereby upset the plans for co-operation between the fronts.[51] He obviously overstated his case; there was no such 'promise'. But there *was* a target date for the fall of Warsaw; it was 12 August. It is perfectly possible that on 12 August Stalin sent the Konarmiya against Lwów because he knew that by then it could not conceivably contribute to the Warsaw operation. Certainly his argument about dates and schedules touched the core of the quarrel. In the second week of August, the Red Army was behind schedule on both fronts; it had no premonition of the disaster which its tardiness had invited. When disaster struck, everyone blamed everyone else. Trotsky blamed Stalin, and Stalin blamed Smilga; Tukhachevsky blamed Budyonny, and Voroshilov blamed Tukhachevsky. All could have blamed Kamenev, who as Commander-in-Chief was chiefly responsible. Lenin recognized the weakness of the Supreme Command. On 14 August, he made the following note:

> The Supreme Commander does not dare to get angry with anyone.... Warsaw must be taken.... To talk of speeding peace talks when the enemy is advancing is an idiotism. If the Poles have taken the offensive, it is necessary to act boldly and not to snivel. It is necessary to think up a countermove.[52]

Lenin knew the truth, but like everyone else was too late to put things right.

The dissensions in the Soviet command provide a classic illustration of Clausewitz's principle of 'friction':

> Everything is very simple in War, but the simplest thing is difficult.... Imagine a traveller who at the end of his day's journey expects to complete two more stages on the post-road, four or five leagues. It is nothing. But at the last stage but one he finds no horses, or very bad ones, then hilly country, bad roads, a dark night...So in War through an infinity of petty circumstances, difficulties accumulate, and we fall short of the mark.... An Army is in fact simple but it is composed entirely of individuals, each of which keeps up its own friction in all directions.[53]

Tukhachevsky was such a traveller. He fell short at the last stage but one. His radio link jammed; his cyphers got muddled;

his orders were lost; his baggage went astray; his ammunition ran out; his timetable was ruined. He lost contact with Ghai; he spent days arguing with Kamenev; he failed to communicate with Budyonny; he angered Yegorov and Stalin. This cumulative friction is the real explanation of his failure before Warsaw.

As for the Polish success, one must look to Clausewitz's other maxim. 'Friction', he said, 'can be overcome', but only by 'a powerful iron will'. Between 5 and 12 August, the Polish army successfully undertook a regrouping plan of even greater complexity than that attempted by the Soviets. There was plenty of cause for friction, between Sikorski and Haller, between Rozwadowski and Weygand. But confusion and dissension was kept to a minimum. This was due to the 'iron will' of Piłsudski, the architect and the executor of victory.

In spite of persistent rumours to the contrary, the Allied governments and their senior representatives played no part in the Battle of Warsaw. The Allied diplomats in Poland passed the week of the battle in total and utter disarray, at odds with themselves, with their governments at home and with the government to which they were accredited. The British Ambassador, Rumbold, whose private opinion had long held that 'the Entente has been flouted by the Bolsheviks, has eaten more dirt than is good for anybody and ought to declare war',[54] had dutifully fulfilled Lloyd George's opposite instructions to the point where on 10 August they were flatly rejected. Three paragraphs of Lloyd George's crucial telegram recommending Lev Kamenev's preview of the armistice terms reached Warsaw wrongly cyphered, and it was eight days before they were made intelligible.[55] During this period Rumbold received a second, different preview of Kamenev's terms from Tommassini, the Italian ambassador, which proved inaccurate, and an assurance from Panafieu, the French ambassador, that Millerand was in agreement with Lloyd George, which proved to be untrue. One can sympathize with his undiplomatic but frank outburst to his wife: 'I don't know which I dislike the most, Poles, Bolsheviks, or Lloyd George.'[56] The situation was not clarified till 18 August when the diplomats learned for certain that Kamenev's preview had been false, that Lloyd George could no longer recommend it, that the Polish government was no longer interested in Allied advice, and that Paris and London were no longer in harmony. The Interallied Mission fared little better. The civilian members, D'Abernon and Jusserand, sent a stream of appeals for assistance to Poland. On 4 August, D'Abernon recommended that the Allies should declare war; on 6 August, he insisted that an expeditionary force of six infantry and two cavalry divisions was the minimum contribution consistent with Allied interests, honour, and promises.[57] All the appeals went unheeded. The military members were helpless. They had nothing to do but tour the front. General Carton de Wiart and General Radcliffe were in the citadel at Brest-Litovsk when it was stormed by surprise on 1 August, and escaped at the last moment. On another occasion, having taken a trip by automobile into No-Man's Land near Modlin and passed a band of Cossacks busily cutting telegraph wires, they were fired on by a Polish sentry who mistook them for Bolshevik commissars.

General Weygand's position was particularly galling. He had travelled to Warsaw in the expectation of assuming command of the Polish army. He was the chief of staff of Marshal Foch, the Supreme Commander of the victorious Entente. He could be forgiven for expecting homage and respect. Yet he met nothing but humiliation and insults. His first meeting with Piłsudski on 24 July was disastrous. He had no answer to Piłsudski's opening question, 'Combien de divisions m'apportez-vous?' He had no divisions to offer. He had the misfortune to praise two generals whom Piłsudski regarded with the utmost suspicion—Józef Haller, who had made his name in France, and Dowbór-Muśnicki, who had recently refused to serve. On 27 July, he was installed as 'adviser' to the Polish Chief of Staff. But his relations with Rozwadowski were worse than with Piłsudski. He was surrounded by officers who regarded him as an interloper and who deliberately spoke in Polish, depriving him not only of a part in their discussions but even of the news from the front. His suggestions for the organization of Poland's defence were systematically rejected. At the end of July he proposed that the Poles hold the line of the Bug; a week later he proposed a

purely defensive posture along the Vistula. Neither plan was
accepted. He has admitted in his memoirs that 'la victoire
était polonaise, le plan polonais, l'armée polonaise'.[58] One of
his few contributions was to insist that a system of written
staff orders should replace the existing haphazard system of
orders passed by word of mouth. He was of special assistance
to General Sikorski, to whom he expounded the advantages
of the River Wkra. But on the whole he was quite out of his
element, a man trained to give orders yet placed among people
without the inclination to obey, a proponent of defence in the
company of enthusiasts for the attack. On 18 August, when he
met Piłsudski again he was told nothing of the great victory,
but was 'regaled instead with a Jewish tale'. The snub offended
his dignity as 'représentant de la France' and he threatened to
leave. Indeed there was nothing to do but leave. The battle
was won; armistice negotiations were beginning; the crisis
had passed. He urged D'Abernon and Jusserand to pack their
bags and make as decent an exit as possible. He was depressed
by his failure and dismayed by Poland's disregard for the
Entente. On the station at Warsaw on 25 August he was
consoled by the award of a medal, the Virtuti Militari; at
Cracow on the 26th he was dined by the mayor and corporation;
at Paris on the 28th he was cheered by crowds lining the
platform of the Gare de l'Est, kissed on both cheeks by Premier
Millerand and presented with the Grand Order of the Legion
of Honour. He could not understand what had happened. He
was the first uncomprehending victim, as well as the chief
beneficiary, of a legend already in circulation that *he*, Weygand,
was the victor of Warsaw.

The legend of Weygand's victory is an excellant instance of
the principle that what really happens in history is less important than what people believe to have happened. It has
suited the prejudices of people in Western Europe, who always
enjoy an Allied victory, and has flattered the prejudices of
communists, who demand that every tale should have its
imperialist villain. It has been believed by almost everyone
outside Poland from that day to this. It thrived for forty years
even in academic circles until the lie was nailed.[59]

In Poland, on the morrow of the battle, Piłsudski's enemies
canvassed the names of two candidates for the title of victor;

these were Weygand and God, the latter for home consumption, the former for abroad. The press of the National Democratic Party, led by the Warsaw daily *Rzeczpospolita*, first launched a phrase which was destined for a long and notorious career— *Cud nad Wisłą*, (the Miracle on the Vistula). In a Catholic country, the phrase was irresistible. It introduced a theme which resounded from every pulpit in the land; it suggested what every pious Catholic wanted to believe—that the chosen land had been delivered by Divine Intervention; it inspired a whole series of visions whereby the Black Madonna of Częstochowa, Holy Mother of Poland, had been seen to descend from a fiery cloud above the trenches at Radzymin and smite the Bolshevik hosts with confusion. But there remained a corollary. If God had worked the miracle, he must have had an agent. This could hardly be Piłsudski, an associate of revolutionaries and socialists, a friend of Jews and atheists. The definitive solution was given by Count Zamoyski, Polish ambassador in Paris, a National Democrat and member of Dmowski's wartime National Committee, who officially thanked the French government for the services of General Weygand. The legend became official.

In France, Weygand's triumph was never questioned. It came as a tonic to the nation as a whole and a godsend to the government. It flattered the nation's pride and swelled the rising influence of Catholicism. The 'Miracle on the Vistula' coincided not only with the canonization of Joan of Arc, whose efficiency as heavenly patroness of French arms it clearly confirmed, but also with the presidential election campaign, which the government was fighting on the platform of 'the defence of Christendom'. The government's Bloc National had recently returned a majority of Catholic deputies to the National Assembly for the first time in the history of the Third Republic, and was now seeking to promote their leader, Millerand, from the premiership to the presidency. In the early stages, its slogans had met with little response; Millerand's record as champion of Christendom was not impressive. He had lost control of Allied policy to a Welsh Methodist; he had agreed to abandon intervention; he had allowed French interests on the continent to be dominated by those of Great Britain; he had not saved Russia from Bolshevism; he had not raised his hand to protect Poland—or so it seemed until news of the Red Army's defeat at Warsaw filled the headlines. His managers did not miss a chance like that. Now it was said that Millerand had had the situation in hand all along; Millerand had not panicked when the Red Peril was afield; Millerand had beaten the Bolsheviks in his own good time; Millerand had sent Weygand to Warsaw, and Weygand had triumphed. No wonder Millerand kissed the astonished general on both cheeks. Millerand was elected President of France.

A still more astonishing feat of political dexterity was performed on the other side of the Channel. Millerand's clumsy electioneering pales in comparison with the effortless sleight-of-hand of Lloyd George. Lloyd George's performance was a piece of pure conjuring. On 15 August he left for a holiday in Lucerne. On 20 August he received definite news of the Polish victory, and on the 22nd, in conjunction with Italian Premier Giolitti, whom he was entertaining at Lucerne, he issued a communique.[60] He condemned the Bolsheviks for attacking the independence of Poland, but did not congratulate the Poles for defending it. He made no mention of Piłsudski, and confined his personal remarks to D'Abernon and Weygand, whose skill he implied to have tipped the balance. By commending the Interallied Mission, he channelled the applause of the Western world back to that far-sighted Welshman who thought of sending D'Abernon and Weygand to Warsaw in the first place. His trick was hardly noticed. The illusion was complete. Lloyd George shared the laurels of a battle which he had done everything in his power to prevent.

One cannot avoid reflecting on what might have happened if Warsaw had actually fallen. This is not merely an unanswerable 'if' of history; it is a prospect which Lloyd George was seriously considering during those first newsless days in Lucerne. The fall of Warsaw would inevitably have produced a call for renewed intervention and for an end to trade with Russia; Curzon and Churchill would surely have had their say. Lloyd George would either have had to resign, as he was eventually obliged to do in 1922 in parallel circumstances, or contrive to keep his position by a humiliating admission of failure and a complete reversal of policy. In the event, he was spared the choice. In 1920, Lloyd George did not save Poland; Poland saved Lloyd George.

The generally accepted version of the Battle of Warsaw is so far from the truth that one is tempted to attribute it to deliberate and conscious falsification. Yet calculated lies could hardly have been so effective. One is faced in fact with a classic case of universal self-delusion. It is essential to recognize that popular opinion throughout Europe was preconditioned to discount Piłsudski's success. For as long as his name was known, Piłsudski had been associated with failure and treachery. In 1920, he had none of the prestige which later accrued to him. As a prewar revolutionary, he led his party into faction and strife; as a World War general, he led his Legions into internment and proscription; as a self-appointed marshal, he led his army into Kiev and Wilno, both of which had now been lost. He had abandoned the Polish Socialist Party; he had deserted Germany; he had defied the Entente. In England and France, he was seen as a treacherous ally leading Poland to ruin, in Russia, as a false servant of the Allies, leading imperialism to destruction. No one outside Poland saw him as a single-minded patriot battling with changing circumstance. Everyone, from Lenin to Lloyd George, from *Pravda* to the *Morning Post*, regarded him as a military incompetent and a political disgrace. In August 1920, the overwhelming weight of opinion had predicted that Piłsudski's career of disaster would be crowned by the fall of Warsaw. When the opposite happened, when in the course of a couple of days the Red Army was defeated and repulsed, it was inconceivable that Piłsudski could be responsible. Previous experience made the truth unbearable. As Voltaire might have said, if Weygand had not existed, Weygand would have had to be invented.

CHAPTER SIX

THE DECISIVE CAMPAIGN

THE Battle of Warsaw did not end the Polish-Soviet War. It was not a Waterloo or a Sedan which at a stroke could overturn an empire or initiate immediate peace. It still left Poland in grave peril, estranged from her Allies and at war with a giant neighbour. It did not destroy Soviet Russia. Its immediate effect was to sting the Bolshevik leadership into mobilizing their immensely superior resources for a second attempt. As Lloyd George remarked on 22 August, 'if Russia wants to crush Poland, she can do so whenever she likes.'[1] Russia could afford to lose a battle; Poland could not afford to lose the campaign. In the long run, the exploitation of victory would be more decisive than the victory itself.

The first encounter was already developing in the south. For five days following its departure from Lwów, the Konarmiya wandered aimlessly on the upper Bug, its objectives varying from day to day to suit the vacillating plans of its distant superiors. But on 25 August it began to move more purposefully. At the end of the month it provoked the engagement which in Soviet writing is known as 'the Raid on Zamość' or the 'Zamość Ring' and which in Polish military history is frequently referred to as the 'Battle of Komarów'.

Although the general situation before Zamość is clear enough, the emphasis which should be given to its component parts is hard to establish. Polish historians often regard the charge of the uhlan regiments at Komarów on 31 August as the consummate engagement of the war. A recent claim describes it as 'the greatest cavalry battle since 1813 and the only one in the 20th century'.[2] Budyonny's detailed memoirs make no mention of the action at all. Colonel Przybylski's standard account states inexplicably that 'L'Armée de Cheval, demoralisée, n'accepta pas le combat et se retira'.[3]

Polish precautions were swift and sound. General Sikorski arrived to take command. As the Konarmiya progressed in two columns from the South-east, he gradually enveloped it on either side, on the north with the elements of his reconstituted Third Army—the 7th Infantry Division on the Bug, the 2nd Legionary Division at Hrubieszów, the 6th (Ukrainian) Division and the Kuban Cavalry Brigade—on the south with the Group of General Stanisław Haller—13th Infantry Division, and 1st Cavalry Division, drawn from the Sixth Army. Zamość itself was garrisoned by three local battalions hurriedly reinforced by the 10th Infantry Division from Krasnystaw. Sikorski drew Budyonny on. Every day the envelope grew smaller and tighter. When, on 30 August, the Konarmiya ran up against the defences of Zamość, Haller was able to seal it in, first along its southern flank by the capture of Komarów and Tyszowce, then across its rear by the occupation of the River Huczwa. The Konarmiya was caught in a corridor some eight to ten miles long. Its four divisions were ranged like the carriages of an intruding train in a terminal station, its engine fast on the buffers, its tail trapped by an obstacle on the track, its sides surrounded by a hostile crowd on the platforms. Its only hope was to back out, before the Poles could uncouple the carriages and dismantle them piece by piece. (See map, p. 228)

Budyonny's account shows how perilous life in the 'Zamość Ring' became. He spent the three days, 30 August, 31 August, and 1 September, galloping up and down with Voroshilov, encouraging the divisions to fight off attacks which fell upon them from all sides. His command post at Stara Antoniówka was demolished by Haller's artillery on the 30th; his signalling equipment, his command staff, his personal waggons and horses were annihilated, fortunately during his absence. He moved his base first to the village of Miączyn, then into a wood outside the village. On 31 August, the 11th Division was spiked by a sortie from Zamość; the 14th Division was grappled by a multiple attack from Grabowiec; the 4th Division was pinned down before Choryszów. The 6th Division was in the most hazardous state. Two of its brigades were stranded

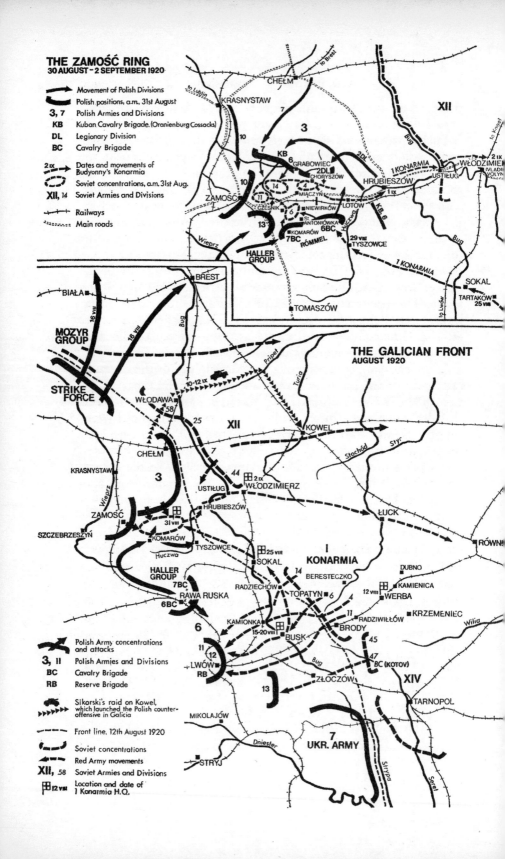

THE ZAMOŚĆ RING
30 AUGUST – 2 SEPTEMBER 1920

⌐	Movement of Polish Divisions
⌐	Polish positions, a.m., 31st August
3, 7	Polish Armies and Divisions
KB	Kuban Cavalry Brigade. (Oranienburg Cossacks)
DL	Legionary Division
BC	Cavalry Brigade
2 ıx	Dates and movements of Budyonny's Konarmia
⌐⌐⌐	Soviet concentrations, a.m. 31st Aug.
XII, 14	Soviet Armies and Divisions
╫╫╫	Railways
═══	Main roads

THE GALICIAN FRONT
AUGUST 1920

⌐	Polish Army concentrations and attacks
3, II	Polish Armies and Divisions
BC	Cavalry Brigade
RB	Reserve Brigade
▶▶▶▶	Sikorski's raid on Kowel, which launched the Polish counter-offensive in Galicia
╍╍╍	Front line, 12th August 1920
⌐⌐⌐	Soviet concentrations
◀╍╍	Red Army movements
XII, 58	Soviet Armies and Divisions
⊞ 12 vııı	Location and date of 1 Konarmia H.Q.

near Zamość; the others were surrounded near Komarów. They fought all day. At 4 p.m. they charged the Kuban Brigade at Czesniki;* they retired to Hill 255 whence they were dislodged by artillery; from 6 p.m., they were repeatedly charged by the Polish uhlan regiments in turn; late in the evening at the third attempt they crashed through Niewirków to rejoin the centre of the ring. The Konarmiya was helped by the day-long downpour of rain. Visibility was bad; offensive ardour was damped; confusion was rampant. Budyonny describes how in the midst of the fighting he came across a group of carts in the middle of an open meadow. Some of the horses were dead in their traces; the others were stuck in the mire. The occupants were huddled underneath, hiding from the double deluge of rain and shells. They were the actresses of the Konarmiya's field theatre. 'Ah, our cultural forces!' said Budyonny, 'How do you like *this* concert?'[4]

The cavalry engagement of 31 August deserves more attention than Budyonny allows. It was an engagement for which the Polish command had been spoiling for two months past. Though not in itself decisive, it was an important event in the demise of the dreaded Konarmiya. It was the only occasion in the war when two major cavalry forces confronted each other in mass formation. It was perhaps the last pure cavalry battle of European history. The Polish cavalry division of Colonel Juliusz Rómmel, with its two brigades, could not equal Budyonny's four divisions. But it was not called on to challenge the Konarmiya as a whole; it was required to contain one sector of the southern flank of the Ring. It was engaged in two separate rounds of fighting, in the morning and then in the evening, against units of the 6th and 11th Soviet Divisions. Its 7th Brigade attacked at 7.45 a.m. from overnight positions in Komarów. It was led by a charge of the 2nd Hussars, a mere 200 men, followed by the more numerous 8th Regiment of Uhlans. The arrival of the 9th (Galician) Uhlans sustained the line until a charge of the 6th Brigade near Niewirków cleared the field of battle. Their adversaries, the Soviet 6th Division, withdrew out of reach across the marshy valley. Polish losses had been heavy, especially among

* See Babel's description. p. 36.

the officers. The 9th Uhlans lost all their squadron leaders; the 6th Brigade had many wounded, among them Lieutenant Komorowski; every regiment sustained scores of casualties. The evening battle resulted from the unexpected return of the Soviet 6th Division from Czesniki. Rómmel did not realize what was happening until the Soviets re-emerged from the woods in front and prepared to attack. It was a tense moment. The Red cavalry men were yelling and whistling and banging their sabres in true Cossack style. The Poles were still binding their wounds. The 9th Uhlans, the most severely injured unit in the field, steeled themselves to win the race for the charge. They plunged into the oncoming ranks, raising a close mêlée in which revolvers, daggers, and even bare hands were used to dismount the enemy. Shouts of 'Urrah!' announced the arrival on their right and at the gallop of the 8th Uhlans of Krzeczuno-wicz followed by the 1st (Krechowiecki) Regiment with Rómmel himself at their head. Somehow, the 9th Uhlans found the strength to extricate themselves and charge again. The 6th Division fell back leaving a field strewn with human and equine debris, and a spectacle which Europe has never seen since.[5]

Sikorski should not have permitted the Konarmiya to escape. Although he did not match the punch of Budyonny's cavalry, he had great superiority in artillery and infantry. He was too slow and too cautious. During the night of 31 August he failed to disturb the Konarmiya's regrouping; he failed to strengthen the guard on the Huczwa, the Konarmiya's only line of retreat, or to blow the bridges. He decided that an erosive action should precede the final challenge, where the Konarmiya's brute strength might still outweigh his own better placed but individually weaker formations. On the morning of 1 September, the Konarmiya was already moving east. At Lotów, Tyulenev's 2nd Brigade of the 4th Division, riding over the dyke which surrounded the marshy environs of the village, burst through the Polish lines, and raced on to seize the Huczwa bridges. This action was watched in ap-preciation by Budyonny, and in amazement by Stanisław Haller, from opposite ridges of the valley. The rest of the Konarmiya followed. On 2 September it rode into Włodzimierz and met up with Soviet XII Army. The Konarmiya lived to fight again. Sikorski's bull had bolted. The Polish matador missed his kill. Savaged by Haller's pike and bloodied by the barbs in his back, Budyonny nonetheless contrived to find the tunnel of the ring and with a last mighty gasp to rush headlong to freedom.

Although Budyonny's extraordinary energy kept the main body of the Konarmiya intact, many of the troopers were left to fend for themselves. Babel was one of them. On the night of 30 August, he had slept under the stars. He was in sight of the walls of Zamość which enclosed the magnificent Renaissance palace of the Counts Zamoyski and a large Jewish ghetto with many synagogues. He talked about the Jews with a local peasant. 'How many are there in this part of the world,' he was asked. 'Ten million or so.' 'Well, by the way this war is going, there won't be more than a couple of hundred thousand left.' Babel, himself a Jew, was apt to agree. On the 31st, he fought all day with the 6th Division. Then he was on his own:

We reached Sitanets in the morning. I was with Volkov, the quartermaster. He found us a hut on the edge of the village. 'Wine,' I said to the old woman, 'wine, meat and bread.' 'There ain't none here,' she said, 'and I don't remember the time when there was.' I took some matches from my pocket and set fire to the rushes on the floor. The flames blazed up. The old woman rolled on the fire and put it out. 'What are you doing, sir,' she cried, recoiling in horror. 'I'll burn you, old hag,' I growled, 'and that calf of yours which you've obviously stolen.' 'Wait!' she said. She ran into the passage and brought a jug of milk and some bread. We had not eaten half of it, when outside bullets began to fly. Volkov went to see what was happening. He put his head through the window. 'I've saddled your horse,' he said; 'mine has been shot. The Poles are setting up a machine-gun post only one hundred paces away.' There remained only one horse for the two of us. I mounted in the saddle, and Volkov clung on behind. 'We've lost the campaign,' Volkov muttered. 'Yes,' I replied.[6]

The Konarmiya retreated in a state of material and moral exhaustion.[7] Its 11th Division was reduced to 1,180 men and 462 mounts out of its original complement of 3,500; the 6th Division lost all but four of its twenty squadron leaders; the 4th and 14th Divisions were in no better condition.

Although 400 political workers from Moscow, 500 reinforcements, and 1,000 horses reached them at Włodzimierz, they were still without adequate clothing. Despairing of the regular channels of supply, they sent a private appeal to their 'respected friend and comrade', Grigory Ordzhonikidze in the Caucasus to despatch 20,000 pairs of *burki* (felt boots).[8] The commander of the XII Army, N. N. Kuzmin, came over to discuss the substitution of relief formations, but explained that his two nearest divisions, the 7th and the 44th, had no rifles. On 13 September, the Konarmiya was driven out of Wlodzimierz, salvaging such stores as it could. Its retreat was harassed by Polish aviation and by the ever more confident Polish cavalry. It was making for Zhitomir, 250 miles away, which was designated as a rest area. It had to fight by day and march by night. At 3 a.m. on 18 September, the Polish cavalry broke into Równe and trapped Tyulenev's brigade. Two days later, Budyonny spoke with Tukhachevsky on the direct line and received permission to retire completely. Only then was he relieved by the XII Army. He was at Novograd on 26 September when ordered to prepare for transfer to the front against Wrangel. Even so, his troubles were not yet over. On the march to the Dnieper his beloved troopers perpetrated a series of pogroms.[9] He arrested two brigadiers of the 6th Division whose chief of staff was held responsible. A purge was carried out. Severe punishments were awarded. The Konarmiya failed to keep to its schedule of twenty-five miles a day, which on the outward march it had maintained for weeks on end. The Galician campaign had strained the discipline and morale of the Red Army's proudest formation to the limit. As Babel's companions turned their backs on Poland for good, they were reverting to the primitive and lawless instincts of the Cossack bands from which they were first recruited.

In the north, operations developed more slowly. After the turmoil on the Prussian frontier, the main bodies of the armies had lost contact. Both sides needed time to regroup, yet both sought a new engagement. Tukhachevsky's orders were still to take Warsaw: Piłsudski's aim was to destroy the enemy which he had already repulsed. The advantages were evenly shared. Tukhachevsky enjoyed a fixed base along the Niemen, where his armies dug in at the end of August. He also enjoyed a favourable surplus of services and supplies, having retreated towards the stores and reinforcements originally intended for the advance on Warsaw. By 1 September, his effectives, stood at 113,491; they were less than 3,000 men below the total for 1 August and growing daily.[10] Losses had been offset by reinforcements and by the transfer of the XII Army and the Konarmiya. The Mozyr Group had perished; Chuvayev's IV Army, now convalescing east of Brest-Litovsk was reduced to one third; Sollogub's XVI at Różana was 5,000 below strength. But Lazarevich's III at Grodno and Kork's XV at Wołkowysk had actually increased. Piłsudski, in contrast, could rely on first-class morale, on possession of the initiative, on the momentum of his advancing army, and on the luxury of attacking a stationary target. (See map, p. 234)

For those who think of battles in terms of aesthetic composition, the Battle of the Niemen provides the prettiest ensemble of the war. Piłsudski conceived a plan of classic simplicity. The Red Army's frontal sector was to be engaged and held round Grodno and Wołkowysk; its flanks were to be turned by cavalry leading a strike force round the rear; its centre could then be sandwiched and munched at leisure. He exploited a couple of factors reminiscent of Tukhachevsky's own advance in July—the proximity of the Lithuanian frontier on the north and the threat of intervention from the neighbouring front in the south. The Second Army was assembled in Białystok, and entrusted to General Śmigły-Rydz; its Attack Group was hidden in the woods of the Suwałki lakeland, which first had to be cleared of Lithuanian troops infiltrated there in the summer. The Fourth Army of General Skierski was transported *en masse* from Łomża to Brest–Litovsk. The first action occurred on 20 September.

The execution of the Battle of the Niemen proved less perfect than its conception. Although Piłsudski did not misinterpret the enemy's intentions as he did at Warsaw, he overestimated the capacity of his own troops. The central attack met fierce resistance from the start. The 21st (Alpine) Division attacking Grodno, with the Volunteer Division and 3rd Legionary Division on either side, made no appreciable progress for nearly a week. The four divisions of the Fourth Army found themselves fairly matched. For three days, 23 to 25 September, the issue

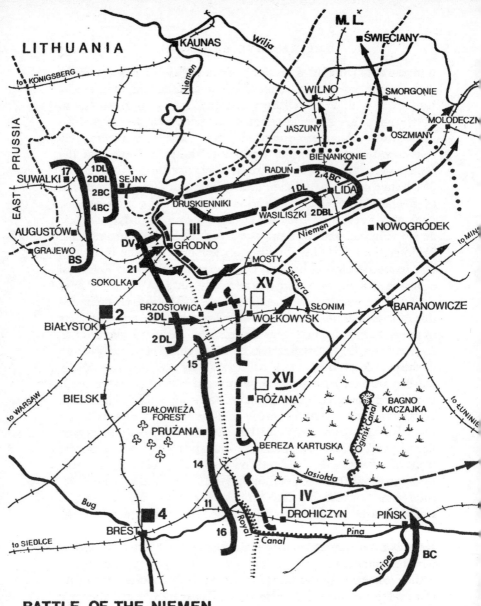

BATTLE OF THE NIEMEN

⌐	Polish Army concentrations	ˏˏˏˏˏ	Soviet front line 20th September 1920	•••• Polish front line 1st October 1920
➤	Polish attacks	⇠⇢	Red Army concentrations	↑ Polish attacks October 1920
■	Polish Army H.Q.	⇐	Soviet counterattack	
2, 17	Polish Armies and Divs.	➡	Soviet line of retreat	**Z** Zeligowski Group October
BS	Siberian Brigade	⊓	Soviet Army H.Q.	
DL	Legionary Division			
DBL	Byelorussian-Lith. Div.	**XV**	Soviet Army numeration	
BC	Cavalry Brigade	**M.L.**	Area ceded to Lithuania by the Soviet-Lithuanian Treaty of 15th July 1920, reoccupied by the Poles in October 1920 and included in the Independent State of MIDDLE LITHUANIA	
DV	Div. of Volunteers			

hung in the balance; it was only decided by the success of the attack group. Co-operating with the Suwałki Group of General Osiński, the 1st Legionary Division and 1st Lithuanian-Byelorussian Division emerged from Sejny and descended on the Niemen from Lithuanian territory. On 23 September they took Druskienniki and cut the Grodno-Wilno railway, the III Army's main lifeline. The cavalry reached Raduń. In two more stages they approached Lida, blocking the second line of retreat. On 26 September, on the opposite wing, General Krajowski's cavalry took Pińsk in Polesie, severing the IV Army's lifeline. Tukhachevsky ordered the retreat. Fortunately for him, the crust of the Polish sandwich was too thin to hold firm. The III Army, pushed from its positions in Grodno and elbowed on its southern side by the XV Army's equally precipitate withdrawal, collided on 27 September with the Polish attack group; it overwhelmed the Lithuanian-Byelorussian Division at Lida by sheer weight of numbers only to run into the 1st Legionary Division on the following morning; it contrived to pass them at the third attempt but in the manner of a boiled egg passing through a slicer—fragmented, crumbling, incapable of further cohesive movement. The XV, XVI, and IV Armies were luckier. They retreated on Oszmiany, Molodeczno, and Kojdanów, damaged but intact. The Polish victory was clear but not complete. Once again, the hope of corralling the enemy was frustrated.

The combined effect of the Zamość Ring and the Battle of the Niemen was to facilitate a general Polish advance on all sectors of the front. Sikorski led the way, using a column of armoured vehicles and motorized infantry, which occupied Kowel on 13 September. He was followed by Stanisław Haller, who occupied Łuck on 16 September, by General Żeligowski, who recovered the battlegrounds of Sokal and Brody, by General Jędrzejewski who took Równe on 18 September, by General Latinik who reached Zasław on 23 September, and by Pavlenko's Ukrainians, who, having forced the Dniester, began to operate along the banks of the Zbrucz. By the end of September, Galicia was cleared; the XII and XIV Armies were in full flight; the Konarmiya had been withdrawn. General Krajowski's traverse of Polesie on to Pińsk linked the Galician advance to the aftermath of the Niemen. In the first weeks of October the pursuit turned into a hunt. On 10 October the 3rd Legionary Division took Święciany, Ghai's old prize, only fifty miles from the Dvina. Molodeczno fell on 12 October and Minsk on 18 October. Colonel Rómmel's cavalry in the south raided Korosten, only ninety miles from Kiev. The first snow fell.

Piłsudski recognized that military operations were reaching their natural term. The Polish army was almost back to the situation of the previous winter. It held all the areas of consolidated Polish settlement, with one exception; it held the vital lateral railway network of the Borders; it had repelled the Red Army far from its objectives in central Poland; it had driven a wedge between the Red Army and the Lithuanians; it had destroyed Trotsky's idea, mooted in September, of assembling a new western strike force drawn from Siberia and the Caucasus, and Sergey Kamenev's illusions of retaking the offensive.[11] The pursuit could not continue indefinitely. The autumn was well advanced. Military caution supported the diplomatic arguments which had already made an armistice possible.

Piłsudski's one reservation concerned Wilno. Everyone knew that he would never rest till his native city was Polish once more. The military problem was of no consequence. At the beginning of October, a new Third Army—the third 'Third' in two months—had been added to the Northern Front. It was commanded by General Sikorski. It manned the north-western sector, whose nearest point at Bienankonie was only twenty-five miles from Wilno. Its battle-hardened veterans could cross that gap whenever the signal was given. The obstacle was not military, but political. Wilno was occupied by the Lithuanians, and was recognized as Lithuanian, formally by the Soviets and provisionally by the Entente, who had referred the matter for final settlement to the League of Nations. For Piłsudski to occupy Wilno with the Polish army was to risk a breakdown of the armistice negotiations with the Soviets and to defy the specific instructions of the Entente; to leave it in the hands of the Lithuanians or at the mercy of the Soviets was unthinkable. He could point to several anomalies in the Lithuanian occupation. There were virtually no native Lithuanians in the city. The wishes of the local population had not been consulted either by the Lithuanian government, or by the Soviets, or by the Entente. If a plebiscite were held, the contest would be between the Poles, who would probably vote for incorporation into Poland, and the Jews, who would probably prefer to claim federal status within the Polish Republic, the outcome Piłsudski himself preferred. Piłsudski's solution was inimitable. He staged a fictitious mutiny. He stationed the 1st Lithuanian-Byelorussian Division at Bienankonie, and put General Lucjan Żeligowski, a native of Wilno, in command. On 8 October the division 'mutinied'; Żeligowski formally resigned his subordination to Sikorski's Third Army command, and led his men forward. In addition to his own division he took a battalion of the 201st Infantry Regiment, two squadrons of cavalry, and a battalion of scouts. There was a skirmish at Jaszuny, before Wilno was entered to popular rejoicing. A new state of 'Middle Lithuania' was declared. A Provisional Ruling Commission was appointed, pending the calling of a plebiscite. The tricky theorem of how to square self-determination with military conquest had been ably demonstrated. In later years, Piłsudski recounted the story with gusto.

Tukhachevsky, in these days, was striving in desperation to rally a demoralized army. His theory of revolutionary warfare had misfired; his machine for the permanent offensive was out of control in reverse: he lost faith in all but the staunchest communists. On 12 October he issued the following order:

...Commanders, Commissars, Communists! Your socialist fatherland demands new exploits in the front ranks. Conquer or perish! Death or Victory! Forward! This order to be read in all regiments, battalions, companies, squadrons, batteries, staffs and departments.[12]

Before the order could be read, the armistice was signed. Tukhachevsky was as much out of touch with political developments as he was with his own army.

Piłsudski was reluctant to abandon war for diplomacy, especially with the Bolsheviks suing for peace. But now personal feelings were cast aside. On 12 October he permitted the Polish delegation to sign the armistice. At midnight on 18 October the fighting between Poland and Soviet Russia ceased. For the first time in twenty months all was quiet.

With one or two exceptions in the next weeks, it was to remain quiet for nineteen years.

Piłsudski's order of the day for 18 October 1920 was intensely emotional and personal:

> Soldiers! You have passed two long years amidst heavy toil and bloody strife. You are ending the war with a magnificent victory....
>
> Soldiers! It is not in vain that you have laboured.... From the first moments of its existence, envious hands were stretched towards the New Poland. There were numberless attempts to reduce Poland to a state of impotence, and to make it a toy for others. It was onto my shoulders as Commander-in-Chief, and into your hands, as defenders of the homeland, that the nation placed the heavy burden of protecting Poland's existence, of establishing general respect, of giving her freedom to dispose of her destiny in all its plenitude.
>
> Soldiers! You have made Poland strong, confident, and free. You can be content with the fulfilment of your duty. A country, which in two years has produced soldiers such as you, can regard its future with tranquility.[13]

It was his farewell to arms.

The end of the fighting brought a welcome term to the suffering of the civilian population; it also brought a series of investigations and attempts to apportion the blame. The Polish army was charged with repressive and brutal police measures, the Red Army with wanton anarchy and classicide; both armies were charged with anti-semitism, though in an area with a large Jewish population it is hard to say where common violence ends and anti-semitism begins. The Warsaw and Moscow press competed with each other over their stories of the enemy's frightfulness. Every pulpit in Poland reverberated weekly to tales of the 'Bolshevik horrors', of Soviet cannibalism, of the nationalization of women, and of the murder of priests. *Pravda* ran a daily column called *Zhertva Panov* ('Victims of the Polish Lords'). Despite the propaganda, there are well documented instances of atrocity. In April 1919 at Holszany near Wilno, among the communist prisoners executed was a girl whose naked, lifeless, and limbless body was dragged round the streets tied to a horse's tail.[14] At Leman near Kolno, Polish hostages were turned loose with their hands tied behind their backs and used for live sabre practice.[15] The agonies of innocent civilians is an unsavoury subject which politicians and generals are not eager to air. It is not really surprising that Budyonny disowned Babel's *Konarmiya* stories and denounced their author for 'rooting around in the garbage of the army's backyard'. Regrettably, most armies do have a 'back-yard' where 'garbage' invariably collects.

Babel recorded the entry of the Red Army into the towns of the Borders in his own sardonic style:

We rode past the Cossack graveyards, past the ancient watch-tower of Bogdan Chmielnitsky, and then, unfurling our banners, burst into Beresteczko to the sound of a thunderous march... The citizens had put iron bars across their shutters, and an almighty silence had ascended its small town throne....I washed off the grime of the march and went into the street. Some Cossacks were trying to shoot an old Jew for spying. But Kudrya of the machine-gun section seized the old man's head, drew a knife, and, without splashing himself at all, cut his throat...From my window I could see the sacked castle of the Counts Raciborski, late proprietors of Beresteczko. It was surrounded by meadows and hopfields and obscured by a watery ribbon of twilight. In the square below a meeting was being held. Peasants, Jews, and Russian tanners from the suburbs had been assembled. Above them rang the voice of Commander Vinogradov, fired with enthusiasm, and the clank of his spurs. He was talking of the Second Congress of Comintern, passionately pleading with the bewildered townsfolk and plundered Jews. 'You are the government,' he said, 'Everything here is yours. The gentry have gone. I now proceed to the election of the revolutionary committee...'[16]

The Polish forces invariably attempted to undo whatever the Soviets had undertaken. Polish commanders had strict instructions 'to seek out and arrest all inhabitants who during the [Bolshevik] invasion acted contrary to the interests of the Polish army and state'. Such individuals were to be sent to the nearest court-martial, 'or, in the event of insufficient evidence for legal proceedings, to internment'. The effect of such primitive instructions does not need to be imagined. Military police moved through the towns and countryside on a circuit of terror. 'Random arrests, investigations invariably accompanied by beatings and sadism, mass executions' served the very cause they were intended to crush. Many Ukrainian and Byelorussian peasants who had served the Red Army, now paid the penalty.[17]

The numerous Jewish community of the Borders suffered doubly. The Jews provided at once the main commercial class as well as the only cohesive, radical intelligentsia. The Red Army persecuted the former and courted the latter. Bolshevik propaganda exploited the situation cleverly. There is hardly an issue of *Red Star* or *Standard of Communism*, without its report of 'Jewess raped' or 'Holy books burned by the White Poles'.[18] The Polish army had the obverse preferences. They tended to tolerate the Jewish traders, who had traditional links with the Polish gentry and middle class, whilst persecuting the Jewish intellegentsia. The Jewish community, concentrated in the urban centres, the *shtetln*, was the first to suffer from the looting and brutality of both sides, and from suspicions of harbouring, trading with, or spying for, the enemy.

The pattern was far from regular, however. In Węgrów, the Soviet occupation, in July 1920, was peaceful. The Polish mayor retained his office. The town's revolutionary committee included two Jews. Between fifty and sixty young Jews joined the Red Army. The return of the Poles in August caused more trouble. The shops, mainly Jewish, were forcibly requisitioned for five days. A riot followed in which Polish civilians caused damage estimated at 50,000 marks. On market day, Polish officers prevented Jewish stalls from opening and forced suspected 'collaborators' to clean the public lavatories.[19] In Łuków, a township between Lublin and Brest-Litovsk, the revolutionary committee consisted of three Poles and two Jews, even though the Jewish community represented seventy per cent of the population. The return of the Poles was accompanied by looting, and the local rabbi was injured whilst remonstrating with a Polish officer.[20] In Grodno, the Red Army 'shot a few rich Jews', whilst at Lida, before evacuating the town, they massacred and mutilated their Polish prisoners.[21]

Political reprisals were harshest in Wilno. The Polish occupation of April 1919 caused sixty-five deaths, mainly Jewish. The Soviet occupation of July 1920 caused 2,000 deaths, mainly Polish, for which the local Cheka committee consisting of a Jew, a Pole, and two Lithuanians was largely responsible. General Żeligowski's coup in October 1920 caused no deaths at all.[22]

In the autumn of 1920, a Polish government commission under Vice-Premier Daszyński heard evidence from the Parliamentary Club of Jewish Deputies. Most of the blatant grievances were promptly settled. The internees were released; the political charges were dropped; the camps disbanded. By the end of 1920, the Jewish question in Poland, which earlier in the year had shown signs of developing into a national feud, relapsed into parliamentary rhetoric. The leaders of the Jewish communities, alienated by the Soviet suppression of traditional Jewish organizations, accepted the Polish administration as the better of two evils. In December 1920, the Jewish Conference in East Galicia voted for incorporation into Poland.[23] In Wilno in 1921, the Jewish community abstained from the elections, assuring thereby a Polish majority and the eventual union of 'Middle Lithuania' with the Polish Republic.[24]

The Polish-Soviet War did not offer any positive solution to the social problems of the Borders. Although the Soviets aimed to destroy the old order, it was not clear in 1920 what they intended to put in its place. The peasantry welcomed the removal of the great feodaries; but they had no love for collectivist agrarian theories. The Poles, despite their identification with the landlords in certain areas, were acclaimed as the guardians of law and order by the majority of a population for whom the class struggle was a senseless piece of jargon. Their return was welcomed by church authorities, Orthodox, Uniate, and Catholic, by the minority communities, Jewish, Tartar, and German; they were tolerated by the various nationalist organizations with the exception of the Lithuanians. The Soviets were universally associated with anarchy and appealed mainly to the small-time traders and poor smallholders who benefited from the disruption of 'business as usual'; their permanent programme had not been established and would not have been intelligible; their departure was not widely mourned.

The defeat of the Red Army and its repulse into the heart of Russia undoubtedly served the interests of the Entente powers. The capitalist system in Eastern Europe was saved from embarrassment; the Versailles settlement was reprieved; the punishment of Germany could proceed undisturbed; the full attention of the European powers could be turned to their colonial empires. Much of this was due to Piłsudski and the Polish army.

Piłsudski, however, was not regarded as the servant of the Entente either by himself or by the Allied governments. He had defended Poland for Poland's sake, and with Polish blood. He cared little for France and less for Great Britain and nothing for 'the Allied cause'. The Allied governments knew it, and it heightened their exasperation.

The British government's conduct towards Poland was even more severe after the Battle of Warsaw than before it. Lloyd George restored control of Polish policy to the hands of Lord Curzon, and Curzon was furious. Curzon had suffered the double humiliation of abdicating the responsibilities of his office, and of watching the Prime Minister's quite undeserved triumph. Now he was asked to clear up the mess. Anglo-Polish relations, which were in a very depressed state, sank still lower with the departure of D'Abernon to Berlin and the transfer of Rumbold to Istanbul. British officials continued to browbeat the Polish representatives for the faults of Piłsudski. When the Polish Minister in London, Jan Ciechanowski, sought an interview at the Foreign Office in order to complain of the British government's lack of sympathy for Polish problems, he was treated to the following tirade from the head of the Northern Department, J. D. Gregory:

You charge Great Britain with being consistently anti-Polish. The very reverse is the case. But we are more far-seeing than you and are alive to the danger, which you apparently are not, that a fresh partition is by no means out of the question. Russia and Germany are being antagonised all the time, and in the long-run History will repeat itself, and we shall not only be powerless but unwilling to help if disaster overtakes Poland as a result of her rejecting our advice...'[25]

Gregory's words were strangely prophetic, and in the long-run, perfectly accurate; in the short-term, they were offensively patronizing. At the end of the year, Curzon went still further. On 6 December, he received a memorandum which predicted

Poland's imminent collapse from economic chaos. His experts recommended that the Cabinet be asked to extend British credit to stave off disaster. He refused:

The Poles have completely alienated the sympathies of the Cabinet by their levity, incompetence and folly...The patient must have confidence in the doctor, be loyal, helpful and obedient. Poland has none of these qualities, and the attempt to resuscitate her would be a European parallel of the experience we are now going through in Persia.[26]

As far as Curzon or the British government cared, Poland could perish. Curzon's mood arose from his frustrated desire to control Piłsudski. As he noted in the margin of a document on the Wilno crisis in October, 'We are beating the air and attempting to hide our impotence'.[27]

The French government was less bitter, but far from cheerful. Millerand, like Lloyd George, was content to rest on his undeserved laurels, and relinquish Polish policy to his subordinates. Among these subordinates, a pretty quarrel was brewing.[28] On its return to Paris, the Interallied Mission to Poland had engineered the recall from Warsaw of General Henrys, head of the French Military Mission, who was generally considered too subservient to Piłsudski. The French Ministry of War chose to interpret his recall in the spirit of a domestic vendetta with the Quai d'Orsay, which in February had borne the indignity of removing its own minister in Warsaw, Eugène Pralon, following a disagreement with General Henrys. Henrys was replaced by General Niessel, whose open championing of Wrangel proved extremely tactless. Niessel neutralized the painstaking efforts of the French Ambassador, Hector de Panafieu, to restore normal relations. While it lasted, the Wrangel affair generated considerable friction between Warsaw and Paris. Having officially recognized Wrangel, the French government expected its Polish client to co-operate. But Piłsudski was no more interested in Wrangel than he had been in Denikin; he ignored the intercessions of Prince Sapieha to extend assistance to Wrangel or at least to time his own military operations to Wrangel's advantage.[29] The storming of Perekop by the Soviet XIII Army on 7 November 1920 and the consequent annihilation of Wrangel was directly facilitated by the cessation of hostilities on the Polish front. Yet it also removed the cause of friction with the French. At the end of the year, relations improved sharply. On 3 February 1921, Piłsudski travelled to Paris, was warmly received by President Millerand, and prepared the Franco-Polish Treaty. It cannot have escaped the Marshal's notice that the accompanying military convention was established at a time when aid was no longer urgently needed and when the French policy of encouraging anti-Bolshevik operations had been completely abandoned.

The disharmony between British and French policies in Eastern Europe was never greater than during the autumn of 1920. From August to November, France's unilateral recognition of Wrangel as *de facto* ruler of Russia was regarded in London as a betrayal of trust and as a flagrant violation of the agreement of 16 January. It represented a definite regression to the former policy of intervention and ran diametrically counter to Lloyd George's policy of trade with Russia. The first attempt to heal the rift occurred in October. Britain and France were both in despair about Piłsudski, the former on account of his presumed designs on Wilno, the latter in consequence of his disregard for Wrangel. On 5 October Curzon proposed 'common action against the extreme military party in Poland'; on 10 October, when Żeligowski's coup at Wilno was an accomplished fact, Curzon proposed that diplomatic relations with Poland should be severed.[30] His intentions were defeated by the 'fiction' of the mutiny. When M. Panafieu made representations on behalf of the Allied powers, Piłsudski told him that 'he would rather resign his offices . . . and live in Wilno as a private citizen than abandon his soldiers and compatriots.'[31] The Polish government officially disavowed Żeligowski's action and disclaimed responsibility. Curzon's proposals brought no result beyond an affirmation by his counterpart, M. Leygues, that henceforth the British and French legations in Warsaw should act in concert.[32] Concerted action, however, was obstructed by the crisis in Upper Silesia, where French officers of the Interallied Commission appeared to be conspiring with the Polish insurgents and British officers colluding with the Germans. In September, Curzon threatened to withdraw all British personnel from the Interallied Commission unless its French president,

General Le Rond, were removed.[33] Le Rond stayed. In October the British Legation in Warsaw alleged that General Niessel had advised the transfer of Polish divisions from the Soviet front to Upper Silesia.[34] In December, the British representative in Upper Silesia, Colonel Percival, demanded that the Silesian leader Wojciech Korfanty should be expelled.[35] The French refused. The British government set great store on the idea that European prosperity depended on the economic integrity of Germany. The French dissented. Lloyd George was unwilling to cede Upper Silesia to Poland without a plebiscite. The plebiscite was not held till 20 March 1921; the Allied Supreme Council did not discuss the matter till August 1921; the division of Upper Silesia did not take place till 12 October 1921. Anglo-French disunity with regard to Poland was thus prolonged for more than a year.

The realities of relations between Poland and the Entente during the Polish-Soviet War continue to be misunderstood by historians who insist on a logical analysis. It is logical, for instance, to expect that the French government with its paramount continental interests and its stronger antipathy to Bolshevism, should have prevailed over the British government in the formulation of Allied policy to Poland. It is logical to expect that the Entente should have championed Poland against Soviet Russia. One must admit that if Warsaw had actually fallen, these logicalities would probably have asserted themselves. But in the event they did *not*. Whatever may have happened later, in 1919 and 1920 the personal dominance of Lloyd George, the succession of weak ministries in Paris, the stubborn waywardness of Piłsudski, the multifarious disputes over Wilno, over Wrangel, over Upper Silesia, denied France her rightful position in Warsaw and denied Poland the assistance she could reasonably have expected. This was fully recognized, and lamented, by Prince Sapieha.[36] Despite persistent statements to the contrary, the Entente did *not* play the role of Poland's protector; the Entente did *not* support Poland either politically, morally, or, to any massive extent, materially. In the period of the war before July 1920, the policy of the Entente was one, not of neutrality, but of official disinterest; French military aid was only matched to Poland's defensive purposes. In the period after July 1920, the Entente expressed continual and uninterrupted disapproval of Piłsudski, of the Polish government, and of Polish aspirations, to the extent that they sought to remove the first, repudiate the second, and sabotage the third. French military aid was reduced to less than one eighth of its former, defensive, level. The Entente's 'junior', 'weaker', and 'dependent' partner contrived to fight the war and to negotiate the peace *alone*. At that point, early in 1921, the French government began to support Poland; later in 1921 the British government concurred. One can only conclude that the world is sometimes out of joint.

The best expression of Poland's anomalous position with regard to the Entente is to be found in Paderewski's speech to the founding assembly of the League of Nations on 4 December 1920. The League had been founded by the victorious Allied powers, and its activities were dominated by them. Hostility to Bolshevism was, at that stage, a unifying sentiment. In December 1920, the Polish-Soviet War was drawing to its close; the Red peril had been averted; the interests of the Entente had been served. Yet the League's agenda was packed with complaints against Poland—against her invasion of the Ukraine, her occupation of Wilno, her supposed offences in Silesia. In an atmosphere brimming with contempt, Paderewski rose to speak:

La Pologne remplira sa mission jusqu'au bout et fera son devoir, tout son devoir. Elle défendra son indépendence. Elle n'acceptera jamais des conditions incompatibles avec son honneur. En agissant autrement, elle serait indigne de la Société des Nations.[37]

His speech defied the basis of the League's very existence—the peaceful settlement of disputes under the aegis of the Entente. Absurdly, it was applauded to the echo.

'War weariness' was an undoubted factor in the ending of hostilities, as it was in the discussions during the armistice period as to whether hostilities could or ought to be restarted. Personal privation, social disruption, economic chaos, and political discontent reached a high level in both Poland and Russia.

The war weariness of the Polish-Soviet War, however, is inseparable from the effects of the five years of World War and

Civil War preceding it. When the Polish-Soviet War started, Poles and Russians were already mourning their 'lost generations', already floundering in the aftermath of fallen empires, already living amidst austerity and anarchy. It is impossible to analyse the effects of the War on the existing order, when order had been destroyed. In the economic sphere in 1919–20 there were very few developments. War industries hardly existed. Poland in 1920 was unable to produce anything more sophisticated than hand-grenades; Soviet Russia could not even satisfy her armies' demand for rifles. Financial systems hardly existed. Tsarist roubles still circulated in both countries, not to mention Austrian marks or Kerensky notes or gold rings or sugar. The growth of the state is attributable, not to the war, but to the administrative vacuum. Instances of state enterprise arising directly out of the war are extremely few. The building of the railway from Gdynia to Hel in Pomerania to avoid Danzig, and the building of the port of Gdynia, a project conceived by General Sosnkowski, are isolated cases. The Agrarian Reform Law, passed in the Polish Sejm on 15 August 1920, was enacted in the spirit of Lenin's 'Decree on Land' of 1917—to give the peasants land since they were already taking it for themselves; it was a frank admission of the government's lack of control rather than a forceful example of economic policy. In the main, a subsistence economy in Poland and 'war communism' in Soviet Russia persisted throughout 1919 and 1920. The Polish-Soviet War did no more than perpetuate the existing misery. It was fought off people's nerves, off the remnants of inherited resources, off foreign relief, and with surplus weapons. The effects of its termination were far more definable than the effects of its prosecution.

In Poland, miserable conditions were mitigated by the belief that 'victory' would bring improvement. Conditions did not suddenly improve, however, and for a time actually deteriorated. The winter of 1920–1 saw hard times indeed. Demobilization started in January 1921. Casualties totalled a quarter of a million; the number of dead stood at nearly 48,000. Material destruction was estimated at ten milliard gold francs. Soldiers returned to homes which they could not support. In the countryside, parcelling of land proceeded at snail's pace; landowners concerned themselves with their own business; peasants in the eastern provinces watched helplessly as the *ancien régime* was reinstated. In the towns, employment was impossible to obtain. Industry could not be restarted. There was no coal, pending the plebiscite in Silesia; there was no private investment; there was no bank credit. Inflation was rampant. The rate of the Polish mark against the US dollar rose from 9 on 31 December 1918 to 110 in 1919, 590 in 1920, and 2922 in 1921. Prices were rising. The purchasing power of a Warsaw metalworker's wage in 1921 stood at twenty-five per cent of the 1914 level. Political dissensions appeared. The Coalition Ministry began to disintegrate. Grabski resigned in November 1920, Daszyński in December. Strikes broke out. In February 1921 the railwaymen stopped work; in March, the agricultural labourers, in April, the coal miners. In March 1921 Poland was paralysed by a general strike, by the militarization of the railways, by a state of emergency, and by rival demonstrations over the nature of the proposed constitution. In a sense, these manifestations were the luxuries of peace. Thanks to the American Relief Administration and to a reasonable harvest, no one was starving; no one doubted that the first harvest of peace would be still better; no one seriously suggested in the spring of 1921 that the Republic should be replaced. Post-war disillusionment did not reach a head in Poland till 1923.

In Soviet Russia, the situation was more grave. Although the Red Army's defeat on the Western Front was offset by news of the victory over Wrangel in the Crimea, conditions in the western regions gave cause for alarm. The emotional impact of threatened disaster in the winter of 1920–21 was all the greater for having followed a summer of relative relaxation. Budyonny recalls that his men were losing heart for the Polish campaign at the end of August. 'Once again, nothing but bad news from home,' one Soviet soldier said; 'Here we are battling for the Soviet power in Galicia . . . whilst there in the land of the Soviets our old folk, wives and children are battling with starvation.'[38] Whilst Tukhachevsky was still advancing on Warsaw, the minutes of a meeting of the party provincial committee in Smolensk revealed 'a serious deterioration in the supply situation':

1. Disrepair of corn mills and poor bread supply. It is necessary to make the population repair the mills.
2. The peasants are not grinding all their corn. It is necessary to strengthen the *prodotrady* [supply detachments]
3. Shortage of sacks. It is necessary to mobilize women for sewing.
4. Shortage of sacking. It is necessary to strengthen the work of certain factories.
5. Absence of responsible party workers to lead the supply campaign in the towns.
6. Bad state of roads and bridges. It is necessary to rouse the population for roadworks.
7. Lack of co-operation between supply agencies and other Soviet officials.

Comrade Perno stressed the need to collect more potatoes, as there was no grain left from last year.

Comrade Vladimirov stated that the Smolensk garrison alone consumed 1,382 tons of flour monthly, and that at present there were no stocks available.

Uniforms—Although there is enough cloth to make 50–60,000 uniforms monthly, the working day in the workshops has had to be increased from eight to ten hours...

Resolved: to repair the corn mills, to mend roads and bridges, to find fuel, to form potato squads, to give priority to army supplies, to divert workers into supply, to improve propaganda.[39]

One wonders what effect such resolutions could possibly have had. 'It was necessary' to dragoon the population in every detail. The Western Front was clearly struggling to feed its men even at the height of its success when the soldiers received priority. During its retreat conditions must have been considerably worse.

In the autumn, open mutinies spread like a rash. On 3 September, only a fortnight after the Battle of Warsaw, the Smolensk party committee was discussing the position in the province's garrisons:

Comrade Milov: It is reported that the reserve units are uneasy. Strong agitation against the Soviet power is being carried on, and was started by the arrival of certain Red army men from Dorogobuzh. Withdrawal of all these units is being prepared.

Comrade Ivanov: The recent mutiny of the garrison at Roslavl is the result of extreme economic conditions. The position of the Smolensk units is no better. The economic basis for dissatisfaction is strong, and the White Guard incitement at Roslavl is not unconnected with it. Counter-revolutionary appeals find fertile ground. . .

Comrade Vashkeyvich: The position has been aggravated by a non-party meeting held under counter-revolutionary slogans. This is to be dealt with by the Special Section [of the Cheka]. Normal political work has stopped.

Comrade Andreyev: There is great dissatisfaction in Yelnya and Dorogobuzh, with desertion on a large scale, especially of the 1901 class. In Yelnya it was decided to distribute the food reserves of the cooperatives to prevent an open mutiny. If the abnormal situation is not overcome, we can expect worse events than in Autumn 1918.

Garrison Commander Sokolov: The situation has a purely economic cause, and only an improvement in supply will help it.

Comrade Petrayev: There are 250,000 people quartered in our district. The Red Army men live in quarters unfit for habitation. They must either be sent to the front, or be discharged into the country, which would disperse the army altogether. They can only be clothed by taking clothing from the people by force. . .

Comrade Milov: At all events, we must put the 'Special Section' into a state of readiness.⁴⁰

The trouble had started in Vyazma some 150 miles west of Moscow. Vyazma was a small provincial town which served as the supply centre for the whole Western Front. It enjoyed excellent communications with Petrograd and Kiev as well as with Moscow, whence supplies and reinforcements from all ends of Russia were collected for forwarding to Smolensk, Polotsk, and Minsk. It was a natural focus for bad news and discontented men. In August 1920, Vyazma's warehouses, containing the main stocks for Tukhachevsky's armies, were burned to the ground. When no explanation for the fire was forthcoming, the central government in Moscow turned on the local party officials and held them responsible. A number of communists were summarily tried on charges of negligence. Several were shot and others were given long sentences of hard labour. Political work in the area came to a halt. Disaffection spread to the neighbouring garrisons, especially at Roslavl, where the open mutiny had to be suppressed by armed force. For the rest of the autumn, the party secretary of the province, Ivanov, spent his time travelling back and forth from Moscow, vainly urging leniency and mercy on his intransigent superiors.[41]

By January 1921, the condition of the western regions was desperate. Gangs of bandits roamed unchecked in ever increasing numbers. The amnesty for deserters, announced by the central army authorities on 7 November 1920, had little effect. The Cheka could not cope.[42] They were turning their attentions in the Smolensk province to the remaining Red Army garrisons and to other easy targets like speculators, illegal printers, and 'suspicious foreigners, especially Polish nationals'. The numbers of arrested persons in their temporary 'house of detention' reached a peak at the end of February. They ran a concentration camp for the benefit of internees who were not shot. Their 'justice' was extremely haphazard. They sentenced a 'speculator' to six months in the camp, another man charged with 'counter-revolution and drunkenness' to a similar term, and an 'agitator' to two years. A thief was shot for stealing some sugar, as were two of their own Chekists for stealing meat. With starvation, anarchy, and Red Terror afoot, the western regions were plunged into a crisis as bad as that of the blackest days of the Civil War. In such a situation, it is unthinkable that the Soviet government could have used the area for re-starting the war against Poland, even had they so wished. The 'Power of the Soviets' on the Western Front had reached the end of its tether.

If, in the classic phrase, war is the province of uncertainty, peace-making is the sister province of double uncertainty. The peace talks, which opened at Minsk on 17 August were as unpredictable as the fighting, and continued to be unpredictable long after the fighting had stopped. Their outcome, at the end of seven months of negotiations, was the opposite of the purpose for which they were originally convened.

The Minsk conference was convened to quantify the fruits of Soviet victory. It was arranged when Tukhachevsky's forces were approaching Warsaw. The first plenary session met on 17 August when the result of the battle was still not known. Credentials were exchanged, and confusion was caused by the fact that the Poles had not realized that they were at war with a state they had never thought of as a separate entity, the Ukrainian SSR, as well as with the Russian Federative SSR. On 19 August, the chairman of the Soviet delegation, K. Danishevsky, presented the Soviet terms.[43] He described a generous frontier settlement, leaving Chełm in Poland as well as all territory west of the Curzon Line, with harsh conditions for Poland's internal organization. Point 4 limited Polish forces to 50,000 men plus 10,000 staff, to be supplemented by a Citizens' Militia organized from the workers. Point 6 concerned the disarmament of the Polish forces to a level consistent with point 4, and the transfer of military equipment under Soviet supervision to the Citizens Militia. Dąbski, the Polish chairman asked for time to consider the terms, which on the questions of disarmament and the militia exceeded his instructions and made important additions to Kamenev's original preview. On 20 August, a manifesto signed by Tukhachevsky was posted in the streets of Minsk charging the Polish delegation with a disturbance of the peace and with attempts to indulge in espionage. The commandant of the local Cheka called on Dąbski to warn him that he was containing the indignation of the populace with difficulty. All this time the Polish delegation was confined to its quarters. Its radio set was constantly jammed by 'atmospherics'.[44] As Danishevsky explained, there were independent Red Army radio stations in the area whose activities he could not control; he suggested that Dąbski communicate with Warsaw by telegram via Moscow.[45] A debate took place on the origin of hostilities, which in the Polish view were caused by the Soviet 'Target Vistula' operation of 1918–19, and which in the Soviet view were caused by 'the war policy of the Polish government of landlords'.[46] Dąbski claimed that 'Russian soil', (meaning Great Russian ethnic territory) had never been touched by the foot of any Polish soldier, and that the Ukraine had been occupied for the sole purpose of protecting its right to self-determination. Danishevsky claimed that Polish soil had been occupied by the Red Army as an act of self-defence. There is an element of truth in all these contentions. At this point, the Polish delegation's radio operator caught a fragment of a war communiqué broadcast from Warsaw. He learned that Tukhachevsky was in full retreat having lost hundreds of guns and thousands of prisoners. At the next plenary session on 23 August, Dąbski stated that the Soviet terms were unacceptable and that further discussion was pointless.[47] On 25 August, he was still more belligerent, comparing the Soviets' treatment of Poland to the policy of Catherine the Great. Danishevsky reminded him that 'a battle lost is not a lost campaign, nor even a campaign lost the end of the war.'[48] Radek arrived to prevent complete breakdown. It was clear to all that the former basis for negotiation had been altered. To facilitate a new atmosphere concordant with the new situation, it was decided to transfer the conference to neutral territory, to one of the cities of the Baltic states.

In between conferences, in September, the Poles played the same game as the Soviets had played in July. They combined sweet reasonableness on the diplomatic front with a relentless offensive on the battlefield. Just like Lenin, they aimed to pursue peace talks to the point where a treaty could be signed quickly whenever the need arose. It was now their turn to prevaricate, to quibble, to taunt. The Soviets waited desperately for a change in the military situation. As Lenin said, it was 'idiocy' to negotiate when one's army was retreating.[49] On the other hand, it was better to negotiate than to see one's army destroyed and the heart of one's territory invaded. For these reasons, nearly a month passed before the talks reopened.

The choice of venue reflected the state of play. Chicherin would have preferred a city in Estonia, in a country which had already signed a peace treaty with the Soviets. Prince Sapieha, however, preferred Riga, the capital of a country from which Polish forces had helped to expel the Red Army. When Chicherin hesitated, Sapieha imperiously announced on 30 August that the Latvian government had agreed to host the Polish-Soviet conference in Riga.[50] The next session was to start on 21 September.

Preparations for the Riga talks reflected the condition of the opposing parties. The Polish government laid their plans in ample time. The Rada Obrony Panstwa meeting on 11 September, drew up a set of instructions which expressed a cautious confidence.[51] They insisted that agreement should be reached on the principle of self-determination before details could be discussed, and that the delineation of the future border should precede any debate on legal recognition. They entrusted the talks to a team headed again by Jan Dąbski and including the forceful National Democrat, Stanisław Grabski. In contrast, the Soviet government experienced enormous trouble laying their plans. Throughout September an argument raged in the Central Committee. Judging by the articles Trotsky wrote at this time—'Another lesson is necessary', 'We are stronger than ever', 'The lords do not want peace'— he was now in favour of the strong line against Poland which earlier he had studiously avoided.[52] Bukharin considered negotiations with Poland as a retreat to the mentality of Brest-Litovsk. Radek, however, newly returned from Germany and Minsk, still contended that peace on the Western Front was essential and that hopes for a European revolution were unfounded. Lenin was now inclined to agree. When the Soviet delegation left for Riga on 16 September, its leader Adolf Joffe, an experienced negotiator who had served at Brest-Litovsk, still possessed no precise instructions. A firm decision was not taken for another week and then only in panic at the news from the Niemen. On 23 September, Lenin sent Joffe the following cable:

> The crux for us is firstly that we should have an armistice in a short time and secondly and most importantly that we should have a real guarantee of effective peace within ten days...If you can ensure this, you are to make the maximum territorial concessions up to the rivers Szczara,...and Styr...If in spite of all our efforts and concessions, this proves impossible your task must be to unmask the prevarications of the Poles and to convince them of the inevitability of a winter campaign.[53]

It was a tall order. By then, the conference at Riga was already in session.

The State chamber of Riga's Schwarzhaupterhaus provided a fitting arena for the clash of two worlds—the old world of Europe, symbolized by the glittering uniforms and immaculate etiquette of the Polish officers, and the new world of the Bolsheviks, represented incongruously by Joffe's squat figure, his seedy suit, his pince-nez, his Havana cigars, and his appearance of some tired colonial governor. Appearances were deceptive, perhaps deliberately so. The Polish officers were the least active part of their delegation, and Joffe's wits were considerably sharper than the cut of his clothes. The negotiations turned out to be a fascinating contest between Dąbski's stubborn defence of a superior bargaining position and Joffe's superior skill. The first week provided a number of sensations but no real progress. During the first session on 21 September, Joffe took the initiative by asking for recognition of the representatives of the Ukrainian SSR. It was a shrewd knock. For the Poles to refuse, on a point already conceded for the purposes of the Minsk talks, was to make an exhibition of wanton obstinacy; to accept was to sow dissension among themselves and to abdicate from the future settlement of the Ukraine. Dąbski accepted. At the second meeting on 24 September, having just received the instructions of the Central Committee, Joffe made the dramatic announcement that if agreement was not reached within ten days the Soviet delegation 'reserved the right to change its conditions'. This also was a bold move, but a risky one. In the first instance, it gave the Poles the impression of being trifled with and encouraged Dąbski to make objections and to delay proceedings. Delay was the last thing Joffe wanted. After a day or two, however, an atmosphere of mutual nervousness was created from which compromise and agreement were born. On 1 October, Joffe and Dąbski met privately, having reached virtual stalemate in the stab and bludgeon of public debate. In a night-long tête-a-tête conducted in German they discussed each other's problems instead of their governments' proposals. Joffe said he feared the 'war party' in Moscow and stressed he had more to lose from Lenin's ten-day ultimatum than the Poles had. He was worried by the confirmation of Tukhachevsky's latest defeat. Dąbski, too, was concerned for his personal position. He knew that the poor start to the conference would encourage Sapieha to replace him and might encourage Piłsudski to abandon diplomacy altogether. Both negotiators saw that failure was at hand, yet intolerable. Their private meetings were renewed, and on 5 October the bargain was struck. Joffe offered to meet Dąbski's territorial demands in toto, provided that matters already agreed like the Soviet Ukraine and Polish East Galicia were not disturbed, that Soviet right of transit to

Lithuania and Germany was guaranteed, that the wording of the treaty did not appear as a diktat, that an armistice would be followed by a general financial settlement, and that agreement on the preliminaries would be finalized by 8 October. Dąbski assented. He signed a protocol listing Joffe's provisions and formalizing the bargain.[54] Here was the act of will which in due course ended the Polish-Soviet War.

The protocol of 5 October was received in Moscow as a statute of saving grace. It gave Lenin his 'real guarantee of an effective peace' within the stated term. It removed the threat of a winter campaign which the Red Army was incapable of fighting. It completely overshadowed the news of Żeligowski's attack on Wilno, which went almost unnoticed. But in Warsaw, it was received with horror. It was described as 'Dąbski's coup d'état'. It was criticised by Sapieha for ignoring the interests of the Entente.[55] It was repudiated by the Army High Command, who ordered their representative to dissociate them from it. It shocked Piłsudski, whose possession of Wilno was not yet effected and whose federalist schemes were nonchalantly nullified. It rode roughshod over Dąbski's instructions of 11 September. But it could not be easily reversed. Poland and Russia were committed to make peace.

It was not humanly possible to prepare the instruments of agreement in the three days mentioned by the protocol. But seven days of constant work by the staff of the two delegations forged the legal text which made up the peace preliminaries, the armistice convention, and the supplementary economic agreement. All was signed and sealed on the evening of 12 October.

The peace preliminaries consisted of seventeen articles,[56] of which the first was by far the most important. The haste with which it was drafted may explain its inconsistencies. In its preamble it recognized the independence of Byelorussia, although the provisional frontier described thereafter neatly partitioned Byelorussia in two. There was no representative of Byelorussia on either the Polish or the Soviet delegations. The frontier roughly coincided with the frontline at the moment of signature. In the north it ran from the Dvina to the Wilja and thence southwards. It gave Poland a common frontier with Latvia, but separated Russia from Lithuania. It left the lateral railway Lida-Baranowicze-Łuniniec and the Radziwiłł estate at Nieśwież on the Polish side, and Minsk on the Soviet side. In the centre, it divided Polesie cleanly in two, halfway between Pińsk and Mozyr. In the south, it was tucked in somewhat westwards to reach the old Galician boundary on the Zbrucz. Its formulation can be attributed to Stanisław Grabski. As a leading 'incorporationist', one might have expected him to press Joffe's bargain to the uttermost. In later years, he claimed that a Drissa-Berdichev frontier, a hundred kilometres further east could easily have been obtained. In the event he moderated the Polish demands. The empty acres of the Borders were not at stake. The Soviets were separated from Lithuania by a solid wedge of territory and specifically excluded from the future assignation of Wilno. The whole of East Galicia, including Lwów, was in Poland. (See endpaper map.)

Article II, which was concerned with non-interference in internal affairs, included the phrase, 'mutual and entire respect for state sovereignty'.[57] Without actually saying so, it could only be interpreted to mean that the Polish Republic and Soviet Russia recognized each other *de facto* and *de jure*.

The armistice convention fixed the details and conditions of the ceasefire.[58] The ceasefire was timed for midnight, 18 October 1920, when the Soviet forces were to withdraw some fifteen kilometres further east to open up a neutral zone. After the ratification of the preliminaries not later than 2 November, both armies were to move towards their new positions at a rate of not less than twenty kilometres a day. A Mixed Commission was to control withdrawals, settle disputes, and ensure the security of property and installations in the neutral zone. The armistice was to last in the first instance for twenty-one days unless renounced by either side at forty-eight hours notice, after which time it would be automatically extended until the signature of a peace treaty unless renounced by either side at fourteen days notice. These details reflect Polish insistence on maintaining their military advantage whilst negotiations continued.

The supplementary economic agreement took the form of a secret protocol.[59] It exempted Poland from any liability deriving from her participation in the economic life of the former Russian Empire, whilst at the same time entitling her to a share in the reserves of the former Tsarist State Bank. It ruled that an unspecified advance on this share was to be paid in gold, raw materials, and forestry concessions. Soviet Russia undertook to return all movable state property, art treasures, libraries, archives, trophies, removed or confiscated from Poland between 1772 and 1914, and all industrial equipment and railway stock requisitioned between 1914 and 1918. Poland undertook to guarantee the free transit of goods between the Soviet republics and Germany and Austria.

It is important to note that many influential people in Poland and Soviet Russia regarded these agreements of 12 October 1920 not just as provisional but as purely temporary measures, which were bound to be replaced by a different, 'more realistic' settlement. Prince Sapieha was sceptical of agreements reached in defiance of the Entente, of the Russian Whites, and of the Ukrainian and Byelorussian nationalists. As he told Dąbski, 'We are the victors.' He expected that the imminent collapse of the Bolshevik régime would invalidate all the agreements they had signed.[60] There were people in Russia who agreed with his conclusions though not, of course, with his reasoning. Dmitri Manuilsky, the Ukrainian signatory of the agreements, described them as 'senseless'. Julian Marchlewski thought they had turned the Polish Republic into another multinational Empire, whose undertakings would last no longer than those of the Kaiser and the Emperor-King at Brest-Litovsk.[61] Even Lenin was still hoping that his change of course might soon be reversed. On 9 October, he stated that henceforth Poland could only maintain its authority in the Borders by force, that Tsarist gold could only be used to repay Poland's debts to the Entente, and that the military situation could only improve.[62] Lenin was buying time. Notwithstanding these powerful doubts, the agreements were duly ratified, by the Polish Sejm on 22 October, and by the Bolshevik Central Committee one day later. The documents of ratification were exchanged according to plan at the Latvian port of Liepaja (Libau) on 2 November.

Despite the armistice, the Polish High Command continued to support their former allies. In the north, they supported the 'Army of Byelorussia of General Bulak-Balakhovich, now some 12,000 strong. This army which was originally formed in 1918 in the region of Novgorod to fight for the Bolsheviks, had defected to Yudyonich before passing into Polish service in 1919. In mid-November 1920, Bulak-Balakhovich moved out of his Polish refuge, captured Mozyr and proclaimed a 'Free Byelorussia'. He was soon defeated by the Soviet XII Army. By the end of the year, the remnants of his army had struggled back to the Polish lines where they were disarmed and interned. In the south, there were two formations—the so-called 'Third Army' of General Peremykin and the Petlurist 'Ukrainian Army' of General Pavlenko. Peremykin's two divisions—Boboshko's infantry and Trusov's cavalry—consisted of recruits raised in Poland by Russian exiles. An agreement of 3 October 1920, subjecting them to Polish command until they could be transferred to the Crimea, represented one of the few gestures of co-operation between Piłsudski and Wrangel.[63] On 11 November the news from Perekop forced them into a premature raid into the Ukraine. They did not get very far. They met Primakov's 'Red Cossacks' of Uborevich's XIV Army, who took no more than a fortnight from their terminal campaign against Makhno to drive both Peremykin and Petlura back across the Zbrucz.

At last, on 7 January 1921, the Polish army was put onto a peace footing for the first time in its existence. It was the first moment when one can safely say that a renewal of hostilities between Poland and Soviet Russia was not seriously likely.

When Dąbski and Joffe met again at Riga on 14 November, Joffe had much to complain of. The Polish army was continuing to support armed action against Soviet Russia. All the Polish troops had not yet been pulled back to the ceasefire line, particularly in Volhynia. Dąbski did not deny the substance of the charges, but taunted his opponent with the arguments Joffe had himself used in October. He had a 'war party' to contend with at home and anything which provoked Piłsudski too strongly could only result in a winter campaign. Joffe was not too insistent, especially as Wrangel had by that time been eliminated. A military protocol was signed, enjoining all Polish troops to observe the armistice requirements but making no mention of the Russian White detachments.[64] As a make-weight, Dąbski consented to keep expenditure on the sugar mills at Shepetovka and six other places in the Ukraine at current levels and to receive in return seventy per cent of the 1920–21 production.[65] This very strange arrangement only makes sense when one realizes that the sugar mills were in the area east of the Zbrucz occupied by Petlura. By consenting to receive part of the 1921 production, from the Soviet authorities Dąbski tacitly and tactfully consented to the elimination of Petlura from the Ukraine.

As on the Polish side, the Soviet military was less disposed to accept peace than the political leadership. Once Wrangel had been eliminated, the Soviet Southern Command was sorely tempted to punish all those whom they believed to have collaborated with him. They included in this category both the Rumanians, who subsequently gave sanctuary to Makhno, and the Poles who were already harbouring Peremykin and Petlura. Their anxieties were greatly increased by the Franco-Polish Military Convention of 18 February 1921 and the Polish-Rumanian Military Convention of 3 March. Although these conventions were purely defensive in nature, the Soviets could not reasonably have been expected, in the light of past experience, to believe so. If exclusively military considerations could have prevailed in isolation, a preventive campaign on the Dniester might well have been launched by the Soviet Southern Command in the early spring of 1921.

In such an atmosphere the peace talks could not make rapid progress. They were attended now by Colonel Matus-zewski of the Polish High Command and Julian Leński of the Polish Communist Workers' Party, each of whom seemed to play the part of delayer and *éminence grise* to their respective delegations. As in September the public debates quickly reached deadlock. Dąbski and Joffe met in private on 29 November to prevent a breakdown. Yet no visible progress was made till mid-February, when the Polish Finance Minister, Steczkowski, and Leonid Krasin, both appeared in Riga. For the first time, a definite figure, thirty million roubles, was discussed in relation to the agreed Soviet payments of Tsarist gold. On 24 February, a series of protocols was concluded concerning repatriation, the extension of the notice for denouncing the armistice from twenty-one to forty-two days, and the Mixed Border Commission.

The Repatriation Protocol deserves to be reproduced

in extenso, if only as a reminder of how complicated the normalization of relations had become.[66] Unfortunately, its forty-two clauses are rather longer than all the previous armistice agreements put together. It presents a picture of officialdom suddenly confronted with the detailed supervision of millions of people whose very existence had been all but ignored for half a decade.

The weeks which followed the signing of the protocols were filled with feverish excitement and with feverish activity. In Soviet Russia, manifold discontent came to a head with the outbreak on 2 March of the Kronstadt Rising. The disaffection of the Baltic Fleet, which boasted the reddest sons of the Revolution and which had hitherto been a bulwark of the Bolshevik régime, threatened to unhinge the entire Soviet system. Tukhachevsky was recalled from idleness on the Western Front to lead the assault across the ice on the forts of the island garrison. In Poland, preparations were being made for the plebiscite in Upper Silesia, scheduled for 20 March. The Polish army was put in a state of readiness and General Szeptycki set up his staff in Cracow to prepare for the eventuality of civil war or operations against Germany. The vote in the Sejm on the controversial new constitution was due on 21 March. In Riga, the Soviet and Polish diplomats worked fast and furiously to draft a treaty which could be signed and sealed whilst the signatory governments were still in control. After months of dallying, the Treaty was a rushed job.

The Treaty of Riga was concluded at seven o'clock on the evening of 18 March 1921.[67] It ended the state of war. It established a final frontier, confirming the line of 12 October 1920 with only one or two minor adjustments in Poland's favour. It corrected the earlier ambiguities about Byelorussia. It outlined the principles for deciding matters of citizenship, political crimes, treatment of minorities, commercial and railway communications, and the settlement of accounts. It envisaged the immediate establishment of diplomatic relations. The crucial details which had delayed proceedings so long were those related to the settlement of accounts. They filled ten amendments. Seen in retrospect, they tried to calculate the incalculable. To quantify the wrongs done to Poland over 144 years of Tsarist rule, was powerfully emotive for the

Bolsheviks as well as for the Poles, yet it was clearly impossible, as would have been shown by a glance at the contemporary chaos of German reparations, which sought to quantify the wrongs of only four years. In the five months between the armistice in October and the treaty in March, some of the estimates had to be multiplied tenfold to allow for the effects of inflation. Nonetheless, the emotions were there and the attempt had to be made. After the initial Soviet undertaking to set aside a fund of thirty million gold roubles from which future payments were to be made, the treaty strays into ever more complex and unintelligible details of quantification and costing. If applied conscientiously, the financial provisions of the Treaty would have occupied all the algebrists and quantity surveyors in Poland and Russia for decades. They had this one virtue, that algebrists and quantity surveyors were likely to prove less lethal guardians of Polish-Soviet relations than the generals.

In Soviet Russia, the prevailing view was that of Lenin, who regarded the war with Poland as 'an extremely heavy defeat' but the peace as an outstanding victory.[68] It stemmed from a deep belief that Poland had acted as the gendarme of the Entente, whose principal aim was to arrest the progress of Bolshevism. The Bolsheviks continued to believe that the Entente was trying to hunt them down even when the Entente under Lloyd George was trying desperately to open trade with Russia. For them, to have avoided arrest, even imaginary arrest, was a famous victory indeed.

In Poland, the prevailing view was, oddly enough, somewhat similar. Many Poles repeated the story of how they won the war but lost the peace. Piłsudski said the 'moral weakness of the nation' prevented him from pushing his victory to its logical conclusion. The federalists were dismayed at the abandonment of their plans. The incorporationists were disappointed by the abandonment of the frontiers of 1772. The Catholics were disgusted by the recognition of the atheist Bolshevik régime. It is true that many party politicians, whose profession is compromise, resigned themselves to what they saw as a compromise peace. The populist parties accepted it, although they would have liked more land for peasant colonization. The socialists accepted it, although one or two influential men like Tadeusz Hołówko, violently dissented. But on the two wings of the political spectrum, conservative and communist, opinion was united. Both the National Democrats and the Polish Communist Workers' Party denounced the Treaty of Riga. Both agreed that the war of 1919–21 was the product of Piłsudski's insane ambitions, that better terms could have been obtained and that the peace could not last.[69] On that happy but bizarre note of harmony, the Polish-Soviet War ended.

In objective terms, it is hard to recognize any victory. None of the contestants' war aims had been achieved. The Soviets had not broken out of isolation, had not provoked the longed-for revolution in Europe, and had failed to preserve the Lit-Byel. The Poles neither established the Federation of the Borders nor revived their ancient commonwealth from the Black Sea to the Baltic. The result of the Polish-Soviet War was not compromise, but stalemate. There was no solution.

CHAPTER SEVEN

REPERCUSSIONS

One cannot escape from the fact that the most sensational effects of the Polish-Soviet War are the ones which did not happen. It was one of those tantalizing historical events which promised more than was actually fulfilled. Historians are understandably unnerved when their subject, which might so easily have been the major crisis of the epoch turns out to be little more than a nine days' wonder. Their judgements have tended to be rather unbalanced, either magnifying the Polish-Soviet War into a drama of incalculable consequence or minimizing it as a mere triviality.

No one was better aware of the paradox than Piłsudski, who looked with Olympian disdain on a war which lesser mortals claimed to have confirmed his genius. It was, he said, 'a bizarre concourse of circumstances strewn with crass errors producing an impression of high comedy...an unreal war, a half-war, a quarter-war even, a sort of childish tussle, a brawl from which grand military theory was contemptuously excluded . . . a brawl, nonetheless, which launched the destinies of two states and of 150 million people and which all but shook the fate of the entire civilized world.'[1]

The classic account of the immediate Western reaction is to be found in Lord D'Abernon's diary, written on the spot in 1920 and published in book form eleven years later. The title of the book, *The Eighteenth Decisive Battle of World History*, betrays the theme, namely that the Battle of Warsaw was the latest in a series of epic conflicts which have protected 'civilization' from 'barbarity'. D'Abernon quoted a famous passage from Gibbon and added his own gloss:

If Charles Martel had not checked the Saracen conquest at the Battle of Tours, the interpretation of the Koran would be taught at the schools of Oxford, and her pupils might demonstrate to a circumcised people the sanctity and truth of the revelation of Mahomet.

Had Piłsudski and Weygand failed to arrest the triumphant advance of the Soviet Army at the Battle of Warsaw, not only would Christianity have experienced a dangerous reverse, but the very existence of Western civilisation would have been imperilled. The Battle of Tours saved our ancestors from the Yoke of the Koran; it is probable that the Battle of Warsaw saved Central and parts of Western Europe from a more subversive danger–the fanatical tyranny of the Soviet.

On the essential point, there can be little room for doubt; had the Soviet forces overcome Polish resistance...Bolshevism would have spread throughout Central Europe and might well have penetrated the whole continent.[2]

D'Abernon's final reflection, penned in 1931 was less confident:

It may be that communist doctrine repelled by force of arms in 1920 will later achieve the disruption it seeks. But should this come to pass, it will be due less to the military strength of the Soviet, less to propaganda, however lavish and persistent, than to disunion among its adversaries and to the strange incapacity to deal with the economic crisis which is today so grave a reproach to the intelligence of the Western world.[3]

Fourteen years after this book was published, the Red Army overran Central Europe and invalidated all D'Abernon had written. Under Soviet auspices, a new social order has been introduced into eight of Europe's twenty-four sovereign states. To paraphrase Gibbon, the interpretation of dialectical materialism is now taught at the schools of Cracow, Prague, and Berlin, whose pupils demonstrate to a classless society the sanctity and truth of the revelations of Marx, Engels, and Lenin. The Battle of Warsaw, far from redeeming an era, did not so much as save a generation.

Lenin soon regretted the events of 1920 and admitted his mistake. His regrets are enshrined in the record of his conversation with the German communist Clara Zetkin soon after the Riga armistice:

The early frost of the Red Army's retreat from Poland blighted the growth of the revolutionary flower...I described to Lenin how it had affected the revolutionary vanguard of the German working class...when the comrades with the Soviet star on their caps, in impossibly old scraps of uniform and civilian clothes, in bast shoes or torn boots, spurred their small, brisk horses right up to the German frontier...

Lenin sat silently for a few minutes, sunk in reflection. 'Yes,' he said at last, 'so it happened in Poland as perhaps it had to happen. You know all the circumstances which were at work, that our recklessly brave, confident vanguard had no reserves, and never once got enough dry bread to eat. They had to requisition bread from the Polish peasants and middle classes. And in the Red Army the Poles saw enemies, not brothers and liberators. The Poles thought, and acted, not in a social, revolutionary way but as nationalists, as imperialists. The revolution in Poland which we counted on, did not take place. The workers and peasants, deceived by Piłsudski and Daszyński, defended their class enemy and let our brave Red soldiers starve, ambushed them, and beat them to death.

'Our Budyonny is the most brilliant cavalry leader in the world. A young peasant—you know that? Like the soldiers in the French revolutionary army, he carried the marshal's baton in his knapsack...But all the excellence of Budyonny could not make up for our...political miscalculation. Radek predicted how it would turn out. He warned us. I was very angry and accused him of 'defeatism'....But he was right in his main contention. He knows affairs outside Russia better than we do. We were reconciled a short time ago.

'I myself believe,' Lenin resumed, 'that our position did not force us to make peace at any price. We could have held out over the winter. But I thought it wiser to come to terms with the enemy; the temporary sacrifice of a hard peace appeared to me to be preferable to a continuation of the war...We shall use the peace with Poland to throw all our forces against Wrangel...Soviet Russia can only win if it shows that it only carries on war to defend the Revolution..., that it has no intention to seize land, suppress nations, or embark on an imperialist adventure. But ought we above all, unless absolutely compelled, to have exposed the Russian people to the terror and suffering of another winter of war.... No, the thought of the agonies of another winter war were unbearable. We had to make peace.'

While Lenin was speaking...an expression of unutterable suffering was on his face...In my mind, I saw the picture of a crucified Christ of the medieval master Grunewald...And as such 'a man of sorrows' Lenin appeared to me, burdened, pierced, oppressed with all the suffering of the Russian working people.[4]

The message was clear; the use of the Red Army to provoke social revolution in Europe was counter-productive. There is evidence to suggest that Lenin issued an order at this time specifically forbidding the involvement of Soviet troops in attempts to implement revolution in the future.[5] This was the policy followed on the only relevant occasions of his remaining lifetime, in the German crisis of 1923 and in the Chinese crisis of 1923-4. But it has not prevailed. Despite Lenin's reservations, the new social order in Eastern Europe was established between 1944 and 1948 with the direct involvement of the Soviet Army, and has been maintained by the Soviet Army's continuous presence ever since.

Both D'Abernon and Lenin, like everyone else in 1920, vastly underrated the Red Army's potential. The former thought it could not be used as a revolutionary force, the latter that it should not be used. If either of them could have dreamed that the ragged heroes of Tukhachevsky and Budyonny could be transformed within a generation into the world's most powerful army, their views might have been different.

The repercussions of the Polish-Soviet War form a subject of endless fascination. Echoes and effects of the events of 1919-21 can be traced right through to our own day.

In terms of individuals alone the war provided a rich experience which influenced the lives of several participants who were to occupy positions of world responsibility. It would be most instructive to know how far the adventures of Monsignor Achille Ratti conditioned his performance during the seventeen years (1922-39) when as Pius XI he pontificated in Rome. It is not too much to say that his encyclical *Divini Redemptoris*, anathematizing atheist communism, was the universal application of his own personal defiance of the Bolshevik armies at Radzymin. It would be most instructive to know for certain how deeply the humiliations and accusations arising out of the 1920 campaign affected the feelings and actions of Joseph Stalin.

In the sphere of military theory and practice, the operations of the Polish-Soviet War brought mobility and offensive strategy to the notice of a continent whose major armies had just completed a four years' course in trench warfare. For the purposes of comparison, they displayed a rich mixture of ancient and modern features, of cavalry and tanks, of provincial guards and national conscript armies, of enterprising offensives and concentrated defence. Some observers, like the representatives of the Interallied Mission, dismissed the fighting in Poland as insignificant. General Radcliffe noticed the mobility, but thought it was the product of medieval conditions, which could not be applied to the activities of modern armies.[6] Lord D'Abernon thought the fighting had 'an eighteenth century air'.[7] Weygand thought that the Poles had triumphed by 'breaking all the rules'.[8] In the years after 1920, the majority of military experts made provision for the Second World War by perfecting the techniques of the First. Only a few pondered seriously on the contrast between the experience of 1914–18 and that of 1919–20, and sought to profit by it. Most frequently the actions of the Polish-Soviet war were invoked by reactionary tacticians seeking to revive support for horse cavalry. They pointed to the dramatic impact of Budyonny and Ghai, and to the later successes of the Polish cavalry. They argued that a war of movement had demonstrated the limitations in speed and reliability of armoured vehicles. They concluded that tanks were suitable enough for use in the trenches or perhaps for patrolling the city streets, as was done at Warsaw, but far inferior to the horse in a prolonged and mobile offensive. In Soviet Russia, the cavalry leaders perpetuated their supremacy throughout the inter-war period. In Poland, the cavalry enjoyed unchallenged prestige. Even in England and France and America, cavalrymen took heart from what they believed to be the lesson of the Polish campaigns.[9]

Among the soldiers who dissented, it is curious to find that three outstanding names all belong to veterans of the Polish-Soviet War. Charles de Gaulle, Władysław Sikorski, and Mikhail Tukhachevsky all participated in the campaigns of 1919–20, and one cannot doubt that their active service in Poland provided an important stimulus to their thinking. They all suffered the disparagement which the *avant-garde* of military theorists generally evokes. De Gaulle was distinguished from his contemporaries for retaining the offensive spirit which until 1914 had been the French army's watchword,

partly perhaps because of his service in a foreign army where the
Napoleonic ideals were still alive. His lectures at Rembertów
provided the first occasion when the concepts of *Le Fil de
l'Epée* took seed. His mind was original enough to grasp the
truth, which nowadays seems obvious, that technological
deficiencies presented the only serious impediment to a
marriage between the highly desirable mobility of the Polish
campaigns and the firepower of the First World War. His
interest in tank warfare was as eccentric among French generals
as his familiarity with Eastern Europe was among Western
politicians. Sikorski thought along similar lines. Already in
1920 he had experimented successfully with tanks and armoured
cars on the Wkra. His raid on Kowel with columns of motorized
infantry has been described by his devotees as the first exposition
of blitzkrieg. In the years of his forced retirement between
1928 and 1939, he committed his thoughts to paper. He published a book *Przyszła Wojna* ('The Future War') which was
made available in 1935 in a French translation with the
innocuous title of *La Guerre Moderne*. In it, he advocated the
exploitation of tanks for offensive purposes, and correctly
forecast that their use would first be developed by Hitler's
Wehrmacht, the only European army freed from the old
traditions. Unlike de Gaulle or Sikorski, Tukhachevsky did
not live to see his justification, humiliating though it proved
to be. He never recanted from his strategy in Siberia and
Poland, and despite the opposition of older generals pressed
on with his theory of revolutionary warfare. As director of the
Soviet Military Academy from 1921 to 1925, and as deputy
president of the Revolutionary War Council of the USSR from
1931 to 1937, he wielded considerable influence. He had the
misfortune to be championed by Trotsky, whose downfall
was the cause of the period of disfavour and ultimately of his
death. His experimentation with parachute troops, airborne
divisions, and heavy tanks during the early 1930s was shared
by the German Luftwaffe and Panzer Corps secretly training
in Russia. The ultimate irony of the story was revealed in
1939–41 when Heinz Guderian, pupil of Tukhachevsky and
self-confessed admirer of de Gaulle, realized Sikorski's forecast
by destroying first the Polish army, from which Sikorski had
been excluded, secondly Weygand's French army, in which
de Gaulle was the only commander to achieve even a local

success, and thirdly the entire strategic reserve of the Red Army, which in Tukhachevsky's absence had assumed a static, defensive posture. Any doubts concerning the conclusions which ought to have been drawn from the inter-war cavalry debate were quickly resolved on 9 September 1939 when on the Prussian frontier the Polish uhlans charged into Guderian's tanks in exactly the same heroic manner that they had charged into the Konarmiya at the Battle of Komarów nineteen years before. This time the result was catastrophic. The ideas of de Gaulle and Sikorski were only given credence when the armies for which they were intended had been annihilated. Tukhachevsky's reflections on the 'New Problems of War', composed in 1931–2, were not published for thirty years, by which time they were neither new nor problematical.[10]

In the political sphere, the war of 1919–20 had the greatest effect in Poland. It was the major formative influence in the period of the Republic's rebirth. It determined the dominating personalities, institutions and ideology of the next two decades. It confirmed the personal supremacy of Marshal Piłsudski. He emerged from the war indisputably the leader of the nation, yet disgruntled by the political settlement and disgusted by the treatment Poland received from its 'allies'. In peacetime, he was a fish out of water. He lay on the promised shore of national independence gasping for the danger and conspiracy on which he thrived. His personality quickly deteriorated. His imperious manner declined into sheer bad temper, his inimitable aphorisms into vulgar and public abuse. At first, he retired from politics, sickened by the wrangling of the parties, by the continued attacks of the National Democrats, by the 'ingratitude' of the democratic process. He refused to run as a candidate in the presidential election of 1922, and resigned his office as Commander-in-Chief. But on 12 May 1926, aided by that incomparable mutineer, General Żeligowski, now Minister for Military Affairs, he appeared in the eastern suburbs of Warsaw at the head of his rebellious uhlans. After three days of civil war, he fought his way across the Vistula bridges, forcing both government and president to resign. Until his death nine years later, he was the real ruler of Poland. By the 'May Coup' he completed the last stage of Tukhachevsky's intended 'March on the Vistula' in more senses than one. His was a revolt of the Left, mounted by the army but supported by the socialists and by the communists. His avowed purpose was to prevent the spread of fascism. His chief target was Wincenty Witos, who had just formed a third Coalition Ministry. But Piłsudski's regime quickly degenerated into the private dictatorship of his own circle, progressively eliminating opponents of whatever persuasion. The very day of the coup, a communist meeting celebrating the victory was dispersed by the sabres of his mounted police. In 1930, most of the opposition leaders, including Witos, were arrested, and charged with treasonable conspiracy. Many who failed to escape abroad were incarcerated in the notorious camp at Bereza Kartuska, whose name became the symbol, not of the period of national unity during the Soviet war which started there in 1919, but of national disunity and degradation.

Piłsudski's supremacy was closely bound up with the dominant position of the Polish army, which the war of 1919–21 firmly established as the official saviour of the nation. Army officers occupied the pinnacle of social respectability and in due course the seat of political power. Their influence was such that they eventually monopolized not only the government but the opposition as well. In the first, constitutional period, control of the army was a political nettle which none of the transient ministries dared to grasp. Sikorski's demission from the premiership in July 1923 and Sosnkowski's resignation from the Ministry of Military Affairs in 1924 were both occasioned by the insoluble problem of who, other than Piłsudski, might receive the appointment of Inspector-General of the Armed Forces. The 'May Coup' split the army in two. Piłsudski's following consisted in the main of a group of relatively minor officers like General Sławój-Składkowski, General Orlicz-Dreszer, Colonel Józef Beck; the forces loyal to the Government were headed by men of greater stature— Malczewski, Rozwadowski, Zagórski, Stanisław Haller, Szeptycki, Anders, Kukiel, and Sikorski himself. The conflict was so acute that on 13 May 1926 Sosnkowski tried to kill himself. Rozwadowski and Malczewski were arrested; Rozwadowski and Zagórski died mysteriously some time later. Henceforth the loyalists were retired. They were excluded from both army and state. Their hour was still to come. The militarization of Polish politics proceeded apace. After Piłsudski's death, General Sławój-Składkowski was Premier from May 1936 to September 1939; Colonel Beck was Foreign Minister from 1932 onwards; General Śmigły-Rydz stepped into the Marshal's mantle as Inspector-General and guiding spirit. The only active opposition to the government-sponsored *Ozon* Party (Camp of National Unification) was conducted by Piłsudski's closest henchman, Walery Sławek. At last one could speak of the 'Government of Colonels' with some reason.

The collapse of the Polish government in September 1939 brought the 'loyalists' back into prominence. Sikorski, whose offer to serve in any capacity against the German invasion had been turned down, re-emerged in Paris as Commander-in-Chief and Premier of the Government-in-Exile. Sosnkowski, who had commanded the gallant defence of Lwów, re-emerged as his deputy. Józef Haller and Marian Kukiel appeared as Ministers of Defence. Władysław Anders marched out of internment in Russia to take command of the famous Second Corps of the British Eighth Army. Bór-Komorowski took command of the Warsaw Rising. These men and their colleagues had one thing in common. They were the paladins of the Soviet war. They were by definition professional anti-communists, anti-Soviet crusaders. They were the sworn enemies of the only Allied army which could liberate their country. They aroused the implacable hatred of Stalin who systematically exterminated any of them on whom he could lay his hands. They aroused the suspicions of their Western protectors, who blandly urged them to reconcile their differences. Sikorski died in uncertain circumstances in 1943; Sosnkowski, who succeeded him, ended the war interned in Canada. They had no place in the post-war settlement. Poland's eastern frontier, for which they had battled twenty-five years before, was not an issue on which Stalin was prepared to compromise. They could not return in safety to homes in Vilnius (Wilno) now capital of the Lithuanian SSR or to Lviv (Lwów), now a city of the Western Ukraine. They were not welcome in People's Poland. The war-horses of 1919–20, and many thousands of Polish soldiers of a younger generation who shared their ideals, were put out to grass in honourable but unavoidable exile.

Among the Poles in exile, the ideology of pre-war Poland, conceived during the Soviet war, the so-called 'Sanacja', has survived. 'Sanacja', which literally means 'sanitation', can only be translated into English as 'ablutionism'. It was entirely military in spirit, and was motivated by the Catholic crusade against Bolshevism. It sought to wash all traces of corruption and dishonour out of the national life. Its annual rally was held, predictably enough, on 16 August, on the anniversary of the Battle of Warsaw. Like many other movements for moral rearmament, it was born in a barrack room of the belief that spit and polish can scrub the evil from men's souls. It served to deepen Poland's spiritual isolation, as much from the Western democracies as from her great atheist neighbour to the east. The Polish emigré communities in the West were the only people to celebrate the recent fiftieth anniversary of their 'Miracle on the Vistula'.

In Soviet Russia, the Polish War rarely gets special mention. In Bolshevik policy, it was just a small part of a greater design. At its beginning, it was seen as a mere interruption in the future Soviet development of the Borders; at its height, it was seen as a step on the road to European revolution; at its end, it was seen as an embarrassment to be liquidated as swiftly as possible. The Bolshevik leaders, though they gave spasmodic thought to Poland, tended to squeeze it into the framework of their wider policies and, like Lloyd George, to get extremely irate when they found it did not fit. They overlooked the fact that, because of its geographical implications and because of the crucial moment at which it was concluded, the Polish War could influence the development of the Soviet state in a manner out of all proportion to its intrinsic importance.

The end of the Polish War was the specific occasion on which Soviet Russia's western frontier was firmly closed. It was the specific event which perpetuated her isolation from Germany and from the rest of Europe. Hence, it may be argued, it was a prime factor, and perhaps the most important external factor in the economic, diplomatic, and political attempts to adapt to that isolation. It stemmed the high tide of internationalism in Soviet political practice. It started a trend which has never been reversed, to distinguish the interests of Soviet Russia from those of the World Revolution and to give overriding priority to the self-sufficiency of the Soviet state. It marked the decline of Comintern, of Trotsky, of the Bolshevik intellectuals. Its far-reaching reverberations are all the more surprising since Lenin's surrender of the revolutionary programme at the end of 1920 was only intended, like the introduction of British income tax in 1842, as a temporary measure.

The Polish War made a definite contribution to the crisis of War Communism and to the subsequent introduction of Lenin's 'New Economic Policy' (NEP). In the summer of 1920, eight of Soviet Russia's sixteen armies were in action against Poland. The Polish War was the Red Army's major and only foreign commitment, and was principally responsible for the strains put on the system of 'War Communism' by the militarisation of the railways, the intensification of requisitioning, the increased consumption of supplies and armaments. As the Smolensk evidence shows, the system never responded to the new demands made upon it. It is also true to say that the sudden collapse of the Polish campaign in the autumn of 1920 produced a shock no less damaging than the chaos which already existed. So long as the Red Army could be seen to be defending Russia from the 'Polish lords', the agonies of War Communism could be justified and tolerated. But when the Riga Armistice was signed, and the consequent 'coup de grace' delivered against Wrangel in November, the whole system lost its purpose. On 25 November 1920, the bloated complement of the Red Army was drastically reduced; two-and-a-half million men, who could not be used and who could not be fed, were sent home. War Communism had reached the end of its usefulness, and would have to be replaced. Whilst the Polish campaign was still being prosecuted and hopes of exporting the Revolution into Europe were still alive, the NEP was superfluous; as soon as the Polish campaign ended in failure, it became a logical necessity. Although Lenin resisted the introduction of the NEP for several months more, he was increasingly aware that his retreat from a revolutionary posture in foreign and political policy must necessarily be followed by a corresponding retreat in home and economic policy. It is no mere accident that the signing of the Peace with Poland in March 1921 coincided with the momentous debates at the Tenth Party Congress over the introduction of the NEP.

The Treaty of Rapallo of 1922 was a natural adjunct to the NEP. To ally with the German bourgeois republic abroad was theoretically as indefensible as to ally with the peasant proprietor at home. Yet both 'alliances' were expedient. It is often forgotten however, that until the Treaty of Riga was signed the need for Rapallo did not exist. So long as hopes were alive for a revolutionary bridge between Russia and Germany, there was no need for a formal, diplomatic bridge. The original hopes were dashed, not by the end of the Civil War, whose favourable conclusion gave the Bolshevik leadership its one and only chance to export revolution to Germany, but by the unfavourable territorial settlement of the Polish War.[11]

The Polish War inevitably affected the development of the Bolshevik Party and the Red Army. Until the end of 1920 the Bolsheviks who had been imported into Russia from foreign exile—Lenin, Trotsky, Zinovyev, Bukharin, entirely dominated the 'homegrown' men. Stalin and his henchmen, who were destined to assume complete control, were as yet of little significance. After the Polish War, when Soviet Russia was obliged to solve its problems in an exclusively Russian way, Russian experience, hitherto underrated, was at a premium. Under Stalin, foreign experience gradually became a stigma; western contacts became a sign of disloyalty. This reached its logical conclusion during the Great Purges of 1937 and 1938 when all the old Bolsheviks still surviving were ruthlessly eliminated, first from the party then from the army. Its most dramatic act occurred on 5 June 1937, when Voroshilov, Budyonny, and Yegorov signed the death warrants of Tukhachevsky, Yakir, Uborevich, Kork, Primakov, and three others. At the end of the Purges, the only Marshal to survive, along with Budyonny and Voroshilov, was Timoshenko, their Konarmiya comrade.

The chief victim of Soviet Russia's change of direction was the international communist movement. The second Congress of the Comintern, which in 1920 had been heralded as the house-warming party of World Revolution, proved to be something of a last supper. Henceforth, the communist parties of Germany, France, Italy, and Great Britain, which in 1920 had unified their various fractions in the expectation of power, were conspicuously ignored. Foreign communists who took refuge in Russia were treated with contempt. The Polish Communist Workers' Party reaped the full harvest of Stalin's gratitude. Unable to operate effectively in Poland, it gradually found itself cast into oblivion in Russia. Its cosmopolitan, Luksemburgist background obliged it to associate with the Trotskyist opposition. It was condemned to proscription. In 1939, it ceased to exist; its name was struck off the register of communist parties; its entire central committee, with one notable exception, was liquidated. In 1944 when the Red Army returned to Poland for the second time, the Comintern itself had ceased to exist.

Without in any way prejudicing the foregoing observations one must be careful not to exaggerate the *causative* nature of the Polish War's role in Soviet History. Although the Polish War was closely bound up with the introduction of the NEP, the Treaty of Rapallo, the transformation of the Bolshevik Party and so on, it obviously did not of itself cause these developments. What it did do—and here the choice of metaphor must be very precise—was to draw attention for the first time to the inadequacy of the Bolsheviks' revolutionary programme. It may best be described as the alarm bell which prompted the Soviets to look to their own preservation before attempting the salvation of others.

In this context, defeat in the Polish War appears as a fortunate event from the Soviet point of view. If Tukhachevsky had not been defeated, if Warsaw had fallen and Europe been successfully invaded, one cannot doubt that the vastly superior resources of the capitalist world would have been turned against Bolshevism in earnest. Although one cannot predict the outcome of a contest which never materialised, one may nonetheless be sure that Soviet Russia would not have enjoyed the two decades of respite which followed and which enabled her to change from an underdeveloped country into the second most powerful state in the world. The very helplessness of the infant Soviet Republic, as demonstrated by the feeble performance of its army in Poland, made the infanticidal designs of the Interventionists appear superfluous and thus contributed in no small measure to its survival.

The disgrace of defeat at the hands of Poland profoundly affected the Red Army. In the short term, it was a painful humiliation. In the long term, it was the spur to self-improvement. It initiated two decades of intensive rethinking, retraining and rearmament. It trimmed the political precocity of the marshals, and left the way open for the absolute rule of the Party. Tukhachevsky was destroyed, but he left behind him a fighting force with few illusions and with a resilience and professionalism which amazed the world. His comrades from 1920, notably Voroshilov, Zhukov, Timoshenko and Chuikov, distinguished themselves during the Second World War above all expectations.

The termination of the Polish-Soviet War provided the platform on which a new diplomatic system for Eastern Europe was constructed. French initiative, which had been noticeably absent on the field of battle, effervesced in the field of international relations. But none of the deficiencies which had made themselves evident in 1919–20 was remedied. The tendency of the Western democracies to support their Eastern European allies in word but not in deed remained. The possibility of Soviet Russia consorting with Germany was not anticipated. The 'Bolshevik Bogey' was allowed to obscure all other dangers. Poland was given a false sense of security and a false sense of her own importance. She was encouraged to shift for herself, then chastised for doing so. During the next European crisis of 1938–9 all these deficiencies recurred. Poland's 'Second Republic' was an early and total casualty.

Throughout the inter-war period, the memory of the Soviet invasion of Poland served to reinforce fears of the 'Bolshevik Bogey'. Anti-communists could always point to August 1920 as definite and tangible proof of the Red Peril, which at any moment might renew its march to the west. What the Bolsheviks had tried once, they could always try again. Anti-Fascists, in contrast, could invoke no similar precedent, and their warnings about Nazi designs appeared to be both exaggerated and hypocritical.

At the present-day, the Polish-Soviet War is still an embarrassment in the two countries where it is best remembered. The leaders of People's Poland and of the Soviet Union quite naturally recoil from memories which threaten to disturb the even tenor of their comradely relations. They are rightly concerned lest a headstrong nation such as the Poles should be misled into comparing their present condition with the supposedly golden independence of fifty years ago. The Soviet government does not want to be reminded of the time when a former Tsarist province refused to join the Soviet club and inflicted the only unredeemed defeat in the Red Army's history. Needless to say, the projection of the past into the present in this way is a purely emotional exercise. It has no rational basis. It is dangerous simply because it conjures up mirages and nightmares which cannot be contained by logical argument. In reality, the Poland of Gierek is as far from the Poland of Piłsudski as Brezhnev's USSR is from the Soviet Russia of Lenin. Polish-Soviet relations today are essentially different in all respects.

The generation which fought the Polish-Soviet War is now largely dead and gone. Many of those who survived the events of 1919–21 perished in the still more terrible happenings in Russia and Poland sixteen, eighteen, or twenty years later. Except for a few incorrigibles, the men who are still alive have outlived the passions which once drove them into battle. As with all wars, not much remains. The last word is with Isaak Babel, whose own valuable life was to be pointlessly squandered by the system he had bravely served:

During the night fighting at Khotin, my horse had been killed. Stars crept out from the cool belly of the night. Deserted villages blazed against the horizon. Carrying my saddle across my shoulders, I was stumbling along a rutted track, and stopped at a corner to attend to a call of nature. As I buttoned up my breeches, I felt something brush my hand. I lit my lantern, and there, lying on the ground at my feet, I saw the corpse of a Pole, doused in my urine. It was spilling out of his mouth, percolating through his teeth, collecting in the empty sockets of his eyes. Beside him lay a notebook containing a list of petty expenses, a programme of plays from the theatre in Cracow, a birthday reminder for a woman called Marie-Louise and a proclamation signed by Piłsudski. I took this Proclamation of the Marshal and Chief-of-State, and with it carefully wiped the brow of my unknown brother. Then I slung the saddle on my back once more, and passed on.[12]

BIBLIOGRAPHY

1. *Published Documents.*

'*Bor'ba za Sovetskuyu Vlast' v Litve, v 1918–20 g.g.*' Sbornik Dokumentov. Vilnius (1967).

'*Direktivy Glavnogo Komandovaniya Krasnoy Armii*'. Voenizdat. Moscow (1969).

'*Documents on British Foreign Policy, 1918–45*' (*First Series*) London (1947–   ).

'*Dokumenty i Materiały do Historii Stosunków Polsko-Radzieckich*' Vols. I, II, III. Warsaw, Moscow, (1962—66).

V. I. LENIN. '*Polnoe Sobranie sochinenii*'. 5th Edition. Moscow (1958).

V. I. LENIN. '*Korespondencja wojenna*', *1917–20*'. Warsaw (1958).

'*Leninskiy Sbornik*'. Moscow (1924).

'*Livre Rouge—Recueil des Documents Diplomatiques Relatifs aux Relations entre la Pologne et la Russie, 1918–20*'. Narkomindel. Moscow (1920).

J. PIŁSUDSKI, '*Pisma Zbiorowe*' Vols. I–X. Warsaw (1937–8).

S. POMARAŃSKI, '*Pierwsza Wojna Polska*', (Collection of War Communiqués, 1918–21). Warsaw (1920).

L. TROTSKY, '*Kak Vooruzhalas' Revolyutsiya*'. Vols. I–III in 5 parts. Moscow (1923–5).

'*The Trotsky Papers*': ed. J. MEIJER. The Hague (1964–   ).

2. *Memoirs, and Secondary Works.*

G. A. AIRAPETYAN. '*Legendarnyy Gay*'. Moscow (1965).

A. AJNENKIEL. '*Od rządów Ludowych do przewrotu majowego*'. Warsaw (1964).

ARSKI, KORTA, ET AL. '*Znowa grabieżców. Awantura Piłsudskiego w 1920 r*'. Warsaw (1950).

I. BABEL '*Konarmiya—Odesskie Rasskazy—P'esy*.' Letchworth, (1965).

H. BAGIŃSKI. '*Wojsko-polskie na Wschodzie 1914–20*'. Warsaw (1921).

S. M. BUDYONNY. '*Proidennyy Put*' Vol. II, Moscow (1965).

CAMON, Général. '*La Manoeuvre Libératrice du Maréchal Pilsudski contre les Bolcheviques. Août 1920.*' Paris (1929).

E. H. CARR. '*The Bolshevik Revolution*'. Vol. I—III. London (1950–3). Penguin Edition. London (1966).

A. CARTON DE WIART. '*Happy Odyssey*'. London (1950).

CHESTERTON, Mrs. C. '*The Chestertons*'. London (1947). Chapter III, 'In Poland'.

W. CHOCIANOWICZ. '*I pułk artylerii lekkiej Legionów im. J. Piłsudskiego*'. London (1967).

279

280   BIBLIOGRAPHY

I. COHEN. '*Vilna*' Philadelphia (1943).

Lord D'ABERNON. '*The Eighteenth Decisive Battle of World History*'.
London (1931).

J. DĄBSKI. '*Pokój Ryski*'. Warsaw (1931).

I. DASZYŃSKI '*Pamiętniki*.' Cracow (1925–6).

ALEKSY DERUGA. '*Polityka Wschodnia Polski wobec ziem Litwy, Bailorusi
i Ukrainy, 1918–19.*' Warsaw (1969).

ISAAC DEUTSCHER. '*The Prophet Armed*'. Oxford (1954).

R. DMOWSKI. '*Polityka Polska i odbudowanie państwa*'. Warsaw (1925).

J. DOWBÓR-MUŚNICKI. '*Moje Wspomnienia*'. Poznań, (1936).

J. ERICKSON. '*The Soviet High Command*'. New York (1962).

M. FAINSOD. '*Smolensk under Soviet Rule*'. London (1950).

G. D. GHAI. '*Na Varshavu*'. Moscow (1928).

S. GRABSKI. '*The Polish-Soviet Frontier*'. London (1943).

'*Grazhdanskaya Voyna*' '*1918–21*'. ed Bubnov, Kamenev, Eidemann.
Moscow, (1928–30).

M. GRINBERG. '*Z zagadnień wojny polsko-radzieckiej*'. Warsaw (1960).

L. GROSFELD. '*Polskie reakcyjne formacje wojskowe w Rosji, 1917–19*'.
Warsaw (1956).

W. GROVE. '*War's Aftermath—United States Relief Organisations in
Poland*'. New York (1940).

J. HALLER. '*Pamiętniki*'. London (1964).

A. F. HATSKYEVICH. '*Pol'skie Internatsionalisty v bor'be za vlast' sovetov v
Belorussii*'. Minsk (1967).

'*Historia Polski*' Vol. IV. part 1. Polish Academy of Sciences.
Warsaw (1966).

J. HOLZER, J. MOLENDA. '*Polska w Pierwszej Wojnie Swiatowej*'.
Warsaw (1967).

A. IDZIK. '*4 pułk piechoty*'. London (1963).

'*Istoriya Grazhdanskoy Voiny v SSSR*'. Vols. III, IV. Moscow 1957,
1959.

N. E. KAKURIN. '*Russko-Pol'skaya Kampaniya 1918–20 g.g.*' (Brochure).
Moscow (1922).

N. E. KAKURIN and V. A. MELIKOV. '*Voyna s Belopolyakami 1920 g.*'
Moscow (1925).

T. KAWALEC. '*Historia IV Dywizji Gen. Żeligowskiego w zarysie*'.
Wilno-Lwów (1921).

S. M. KLYATSKIN. '*Na Zashchite Oktyabrya*'. (The organisation of a
Regular Army...in the Soviet Republic 1917–20.) Moscow (1965).

'*Komandarm Uborevich—Vospominaniya Druzei i Soratnikov*'. Moscow
(1964).

T. KOMARNICKI. '*The Rebirth of the Polish Republic*'. London (1957).

V. KOROSTOVETZ. 'Seed and Harvest'. London (1931).
Księga Polaków Uczestników Rewolucji Październikowej 1917–20. Biografie.' Warsaw (1967).
T. KUTRZEBA. 'Wyprawa Kijowska'. Warsaw (1937).
N. F. KUZ'MIN. 'Krushenie poslednego pokhoda Antanty'. Moscow (1958).
A. LEINWAND. 'P.P.S. wobec wojny polsko-radzieckiej, 1919–20.' Warsaw (1964).
B. H. LIDDELL HART. 'The Red Army'. New York (1956).
P. ŁOSSOWSKI. 'Stosunki polsko-litewskie w latach 1918–20'. Warsaw (1966).
J. MARCHLEWSKI. 'Pol'sha i mirovaya revolyutsiya'. Moscow (1920).
'Marshal Tukhachevsky—Vospominaniya Druzei i Soratnikov'. Moscow (1965)
S. A. MEZHANINOV. 'Nachalo bor'by s belopolyakami na Ukraine v 1920 g.' Moscow (1926).
L. NIKULIN. 'Tukhachevskiy'. Moscow (1964).
I. PAWŁOWSKI. 'Polityka i Działalność wojskowa KPP 1918–28.' Warsaw (1964).
ALEKSANDRA PIŁSUDSKA. 'Piłsudski—A Biography by his Wife'. New York (1941).
J. PIŁSUDSKI. 'Rok 1920'. Fifth Impression, London (1941).
W. POBÓG-MALINOWSKI. 'Najnowsza Historia Polityczna Polski'. Vol. II. London (1967).
V. PRIMAKOV. 'Reyd Chervonnykh Kazakov'. Moscow (1925).
K. PUTNA. 'K Visle i obratno'. Moscow (1927).
PRZYBYLSKI ADAM. 'La Pologne en lutte pour ses frontières.' Paris (1931).
K. RADEK. 'Voyna pol'skikh belo-gvardeytsev protiv Sovetskoy Rossii'. Moscow (1920).
B. ROJA. 'Legendy i Fakty'. Warsaw (1931).
J. ROMER. 'Pamiętniki'. Lwów (1938).
A. ROZWADOWSKI. 'Generał Rozwadowski'. Cracow (1929).
J. RYBAK. 'Pamiętniki'. Warsaw (1954).
E. SERGEYEV. 'Ot Dviny k Visle'. Moscow (1928).
B. SHAPOSHNIKOV. 'Na Visle'. Moscow (1930).
LADISLAS SIKORSKI. 'La Campagne Polono-Russe de 1920'. Paris (1928). being a translation of Władystaw Sikorski, 'Nad Wisłą i Wkra', Lwów (1928).
W. SIKORSKI. 'Modern Warfare, its character, its problems.' London (1943). a translation of 'Przyszła Wojna', published as 'La Guerre Moderne', Paris (1935).
P. V. SUSLOV. 'Politicheskoe obespechenie sovetsko-pol'sko kampanii 1920 g.' Moscow (1930).
ST. SZEPTYCKI. 'Front Litewsko-Białoruski'. Cracow (1925).

T. TESLAR. 'Polityka Rosji Sowieckiej podczas wojny z Polska'. Warsaw (1937).
T. TESLAR. 'Propaganda bolszewicka podczas wojny...' Warsaw (1938).
A. I. TODORSKII. 'Marshal Tukhachevskiy'. Moscow (1964).
L. TROTSKY. 'My Life'. New York, 1931.
L. TROTSKY. 'Sovetskaya Rossiya i Burzhuaznaya Pol'sha'. Speech at Gomel, May 1920. Moscow (1920).
L. TROTSKY. 'Stalin'. London (1947).
M. N. TUKHACHEVSKIY. 'Pochód za Wisłę'. Polish Text in J. Piłsudski, op. cit. pp. 168–217. Russian Text, 'Pokhod za Vislu' in 'Izbrannie Proizvedeniya' op. cit. Vol. I.
M. N. TUKHACHEVSKIY. 'Izbrannye Proizvedeniya' Vols. I—II. Moscow (1964).
P. S. WANDYCZ. 'Soviet-Polish Relations 1917–21'. Cambridge. Mass. (1969).
MAXIME WEYGAND. 'Mémoires'. Vol. II. Paris (1957).
W. WEJTKO. 'Samoobrona Litwy i Białorusi'. Wilno (1930).
D. FEDOTOFF WHITE. 'The Growth of the Red Army'. Princeton (1944).
F. WILLIAMS. 'Ernest Bevin, Portrait of a Great Englishman'. London (1952).
W. WITOS. 'Moje Wspomnienia' Vols. I—III. Paris (1964–5).
E. WOLLENBERG. 'The Red Army'. London (1938).
R. WRAGA (ANDREUS). Polska a kapitalistyczna Interwencja u ZSSR. Rome (1945).
P. ZAREMBA. 'Dzieje 15 pułku uhlanów poznanskich'. London (1962).
FEDOR G. ZUEV. 'Mezhdunarodÿy imperializm organizator napadeniya panskoy Pol'shi na sovetskuyu Rossiyu, 1919–20'. Moscow (1954).

3. Articles

N. N. AZOVTSEV, V. R. NAUMOV. 'Izuchenie Istorii Voyennoy Interventsii i Grazhdanskoy Voiny v SSSR'. in 'Istoriya SSSR' Nr. 6. 1970.
ROLF BRANDT. 'With the Soviet Army' in 'Living Age' 307, 2 Oct 1920.
I. COHEN. 'My Mission to Poland, 1918–19' in 'Jewish Social Studies' London XIII Nr. 2 (1952).
M. K. DZIEWANOWSKI. 'Pilsudski's Federal Policy' in 'Journal of Central European Affairs' 1950.
H. J. ELCOCK. 'Britain and the Russo-Polish Frontier 1919–21'. 'Historical Journal, 1969.' Nr. 1.
WERONIKA GOSTYŃSKA. 'Materiały archiwalne o tajnych rokowaniach polsko-radzieckich w Baranowiczach i Białowieży'. in 'Z dziejów stosunków polsko-radzieckich', Warsaw (1969) Nr. IV.
H. JABŁONSKI. 'Wojna polsko-radziecka 1919–20'. in 'Przegląd Socjalistyczny' (1948) Nos. 7–8.

A. JUZWENKO. 'Misja Marchlewskiego w 1919 roku na tle stosunków polsko-radzieckich'. in '*Z badań nad wpływem i znaczeniem rewolucji rosyjskich dla ziem polskich.*' Ed. H. Zieliński. Wrocław (1968).

K. KRZECZUNOWICZ. 'Na 50-lecie bojów kawalerii i artylerii w 1920 roju'. in '*Katalog Wystawy—Kawalerii i Artyleria konna*'. London (1970) pp. 7–20.

M. KUKIEL. 'The Polish-Soviet Campaign of 1920' in '*The Slavonic Review*' London. 1928.

J. LEWANDOWSKI. 'Prometeizm—Koncepcja Polityki Wschodniej Piłsudszczyzny' in '*Biuletyn Wojskowej Akademii Politycznej*' Seria Historyczna, I. Nr. 2(12) 1958).

L. B. MACFARLANE. 'Hands off Russia'. '*Past and Present, 1967*'.

J. MARCHLEWSKI. 'Mir s Pol'shey' in '*Kommunisticheskiy Internatsional*' (1920). Nr. 14.

J. MARCHLEWSKI. 'Pol'sha i mirovaya revolyutsiya'. in '*Kommunisticheskiy Internatsional*' (1919) Nr. 7–8.

W. NAJDUS. 'Polacy we władzach Republiki Litewsko-Białoruskiej, 1919' in '*Kwartalnik Historyczny*' (1967) Nr. 3.

W. SWORAKOWSKI. 'An error regarding East Galicia in Curzon's Note to the Soviet Government, 11 July 1920'. in *Journal of Central European Affairs, 1944*'.

P. WANDYCZ. 'French Diplomats in Poland, 1919–26' in '*Journal of Central European Affairs, 1964*'.

P. WANDYCZ. 'General Weygand and the Battle of Warsaw' in '*Journal of Central European Affairs 1960*'.

S. ŻBIKOWSKI. 'Zarys historii Zachodniej Dywizji Strzelców' in '*Z Pola Walki*' Warsaw (1960) Nr. 2.

4. *Archival Sources.*
Archiwum Akt Nowych, Warsaw (AAN)
Archiwum I. J. Paderewskiego (AIJP)
Komitet Narodowy Polski (KNP)
Presidium Rady Ministrów (PRM)
Central Party Archive of the Marx-Lenin Institute (Ts.P.A.I.M.I.)
Central State Archive of the Soviet Army (Ts.G.A.S.A.);
in secondary reference only.

Cabinet Records   Cab
Foreign Office Papers   FO
Public Record Office, London   PRO
War Office Papers   WO
British Museum   BM
Churchill Papers.
Rumbold Papers.
Lloyd George Papers.

INTRODUCTION

1. Polska Akademia Nauk, Akademia Nauk ZSRR, '*Dokumenty i Materiały do Historii Stosunków Polsko-Radzieckich*'

Tom II, (1961) Tom III, (1964). Warsaw. Henceforth '*Dokumenty; Materiały...*'.

2. See Bibliography.

CHAPTER ONE

1. A. Deruga, '*Polityka Wschodnia Polski wobec ziem Litwy, Białorusi i Ukrainy, 1918.-19*' Warsaw (1969) Chapter V.
2. Historical Institute of the Academy of Sciences of the Lithuanian S.S.R., '*Bor'ba za sovetskuyu vlast' v Litve v 1918–20 g.*' Vilnius (1967). Documents. No. 1. 16 Dec. 1918.
3. '*Dokumenty i Materiały...*' II, No. 68.
4. e.g. T. Komarnicki, '*The Rebirth of the Polish Republic*' London (1956) p 443 ff.
5. '*Direktivy Glavnogo Komandovaniya Krasnoy Armii 1917–20*' Sbornik Dokumentov. Moscow (1969). No. 133. Henceforth '*Direktivy ...*'.
6. *Ibid*, Nos. 153, 311.
7. The first directive of 16 Nov. 1918, *Ibid*, No. 136. was confined to a reconnaissance as far as Polotsk, Borisov and Gomel; that of 10 Dec. 1918 (*Ibid* No. 147) as far as Wilno, Lida, Mozyr.
8. '*Dokumenty i Materiały...*' II p. 98 note 7.

9. Deruga *op. cit.* p. 144.
10. The opening lines of '*Pan Tadeusz*.'
11. '*Dokumenty i Materiały...*' I, No. 286 29 Oct. 1918.
12. *Ibid*, II No. 12, 26 Nov. 1918; No. 20, 4 Dec. 1918; No. 30. 22 Dec. 1918.
13. *Ibid*, II, No. 37, 30 Dec. 1918.
14. *Ibid*, II No. 49, 8 Jan. 1919.
15. *Ibid*, II, p. 172.
16. From Babel's story '*Posle Boya*'.
17. A letter of Kazimierz Karski of the 1st (Krechowiecki) Uhlans, 5 Aug. 1920, in '*Przeglad Kawalerii i Broni Pancernej*' London viii No. 59. (1970) p. 240.
18. Kakurin N. E. and Melikov V. A., '*Voyna z belopolyakami*' Moscow (1925) p. 7; '*Direktivy ...*' pp. 157–8.
19. '*Direktivy...*' Nos. 310, 311.
20. T. Sariusz-Bielski 'Wspomnienia z wymarszu I Dywizji Kawalerii Na Ukraine w 1920 r.' '*Przeglad Kawalerii i Broni Pancernej*' London VIII N. 59 (1970) pp 192–6.

21. W. Chocianowicz, '*1 Pułk Artylerii Lekkiej Legionow im. J. Piłsudskiego*' London (1967) Chapter 1.; J. Stachowicz, 'Pociągi Pancerne w wojnie 1918–20' '*Przegląd Kawalerii i Broni Pancernej*' London VIII N. 59 (1970) pp 177–80.

22. '*Direktivy...*' No. 336. note 74 p 802.

23. PRO-FO 417/8/64.

24. *Bor'ba za sovetskuyu vlast' v Litve...*' *op. cit.* Documents 53, 76, 79, 97, 98, 100, 140, 166, 167, 174, 177, 185, 204.; '*Documenty i Materiały...*' III, 217.

25. '*Historia Polski*' Vol. IV. pt 1. Warsaw (1966) p. 258.

26. '*Izvestiya*' Moscow 8 May 1919. '*Dokumenty i Materiały...*' II, Appendix VI. pp 771–3.

27. Deruga, *op. cit.* p. 125. Quoting V. I. Lenin, '*Korespondencja wojenna 1917–20*' Warsaw (1958) p. 158.

28. '*Direktivy...*' No. 316.

29. Isaac Cohen, '*Vilna*' Philadelphia (1943) pp. 358–88.

30. A. F. Hatskevich, '*Pol'skie Internatsionalisty v bor'be za vlast' sovetov v Byelorussii*' Minsk (1967) pp. 92–3.

31. W. Gostyńska, 'Materiały archiwalne o tajnych rokowaniach polskoradzieckich... czerwiec-lipiec 1919.' Document 9. in '*Z dziejów stosunków polsko-radzieckich*' IV. Warsaw (1969) p. 161.

32. '*Dokumenty i Materiały...*' II, p. 786.

33. *Ibid.* II Appendix XI.

CHAPTER TWO

1. A. Piłsudska—'*Piłsudski—a Biography by his wife.*' New York (1941), p. 191.

2. Rumbold to Philip Kerr, 29 Dec. 1919 Rumbold Papers; Rumbold to Curzon, 7 Nov. 1920, FO 371 3599/2524.

3. L. B. Trotsky, '*My Life*' New York (1931) p. 389.

4. A. Juzwenko, 'Misja Marchlewskiego w 1919 roku na tle stosunków polsko-radzieckich,' in '*Z badan nad wpływen i znaczeniem rewolucji rosyjskich 1917 roku dla ziem polskich*'. Edited by H. Zieliński, Wrocław (1968), p. 55.

5. '*Dokumenty i Materiały...*' II, No. 235.

6. *Ibid.*, II No. 240.

7. Juzwenko, *op. cit.*, p. 76.

8. '*Dokumenty i Materiały...*' II, No. 229.

9. Marchlewski to Trotsky, 28 Nov 1919, in '*The Trotsky Papers*' Vol. I, No. 426; I. Deutscher, '*The Prophet Armed*', p. 458.

10. Juzwenko, *op. cit.* p. 81.

11. '*Dokumenty i Materiały...*' II, No. 271.

12. Juzwenko, *op. cit.* pp 78–9.

13. PRO WO 106/967 G 1285.

14. '*Dokumenty i Materiały...*' II, No. 236.

15. *Ibid*, II, No. 254.

16. *Ibid*, II, No. 266.

17. *Ibid*, No. 246.

18. *Ibid*, No. 260.

19. *Ibid*, No. 322.

20. *Ibid*, No. 224.

21. *Ibid*, No. 212

22. *Ibid*, No. 222.

23. Churchill to Paderewski, 24 October 1919. AAN-AIJP 777. The inexplicable omission of this vital document makes nonsense of the rest of the the correspondence as published in '*Dokumenty i Materiały...*'

24. PRO- Cab 23/14 War Cabinet 634 (4) 16 Oct. 1919.

25. PRO- Cab 23/14 War Cabinet 633 (6) 22 Oct. 1919.

26. PRO- Cab 23/18 C 12 App II (6) 25 Nov. 1919; also PRO- Cab 24/99 CP 716, 23 Feb. 1920.

27. Juzwenko, *op. cit* pp. 84–5.

28. Kutrzeba, T., '*Wyprawa Kijowska*', Warsaw 1937, p. 45.

29. Kakurin *op. cit.* p. 71 ff.

30. J. V. Stalin, 'Noviy Pokhod Antanty ra Rossiyu', *Pravda*, *25 May 1920;* F. Zuyev, '*Mezhdunarodnÿy imperializm organizator napadeniya panskoy Pol'shi na Sovetskuyu Rossiyu, 1919–20.*' Moscow. (1954); The most recent discussion and affirmation of the concept is by N. N. Azovtsev and N. R. Naumov, 'Izuchenie Istorii Voennoy Interventsii i Grazhdanskoy Voiny, SSSR' in '*Istoriya SSSR*', (1970) Nr. 6. pp. 18–9.

31. Curzon to A. J. Balfour, 10 Feb. 1918. BM Add. MSS 49734/44.

32. PRO-Cab 23/20 6/20

33. '*New York Times*', 18 Jan. 1920.

34. '*Dokumenty i Materiały...*' II, p. 349.

35. *Ibid*, II, No. 269.

36. *Ibid*, II, p. 491.

37. Lloyd George Papers, F/201/1/9.

38. PRO- Cab 23/20 C 7 (1920) 29 Jan. 1920.

39. '*Dokumenty i Materiały...*' II No. 203.

40. Millerand expressed these fears at the Lympne Conference, 8 Aug. 1920 PRO-Cab 23/22 46 (20); Hankey repeated them, PRO- Cab 24 CP 1724.

41. '*Dokumenty i Materiały...*' II p. 504.

42. *Ibid*, II No. 331.

43. *Ibid*. II No. 279.

44. *Ibid*, II No. 311.

45. '*Le Petit Parisen*', 6 Mar. 1920. Interview 28 Feb. 1920. Quoted by Komarnicki, *op. cit.* pp 563–4.

46. '*Dokumenty i Materiały...*' II, No. 329, 341.

47. *Ibid*, II, No. 360.

48. *Ibid*, II No. 361.

49. *Ibid*, II Nos. 378, 380.

50. *Ibid*, II No. 341.

51. *Ibid*, II, No. 379.

52. *Ibid*, III, No. 14.

53. *Ibid*, II, No. 381.

CHAPTER THREE

1. *Documents on British Foreign Policy. (1st Series)* Vol. X, Nos. 505, 581.
2. E. H. Carr, '*The Bolshevik Revolution*' Vol. III, (Pelican Edition). London (1966) p. 170.
3. Kakurin *op. cit.* p. 413.
4. Quoted in '*Historia Polski,*' (1966) Vol IV, pt. 1. p. 331.
5. '*Dokumenty i Materialy . . .*' III, No. 9 Note 1.
6. PRO- WO/106/972 G 2001. 31 May 1920.
7. Polish text in Kutrzeba, *op. cit.* p. 107.
8. Rumbold to Curzon 30 April 1920 PRO- FO 371 3914/196783.
9. E. H. Carr, '*The Bolshevik Revolution*' Vol. III (Pelican Edition) London (1966) p. 309.
10. Quoted by Komarnicki, *op. cit.* p. 589.
11. Churchill to DMI 19 May 1920 Churchill Papers 16/52.
12. Cecil to Curzon, 3 May, 1920 PRO- FO 371 3914/197475.
13. Curzon to Cecil, 11 May 1920, *Ibid.*
14. AAN- AIJP 738.
15. '*Historia Polski*' Vol IV pt 1. (1966) p. 346.
16. '*Dokumenty i Materialy . . .*' III, No. 7.
17. *Ibid.*
18. '*Dokumenty i Materialy . . .*' III, No. 27. Kalinin's speech at Ivanovo Voznesensk, 16 May 1920.
19. Kakurin, *op. cit.* pp. 98–9
20. '*Dokumenty i Materialy . . .*' III, No. 9.
21. *Ibid.* No. 11.
22. *Ibid,* Nos. 30, 32.
23. S. M. Budyonny, '*Proidonnyy Put*' Moscow (1965) Vol. II p. 28.
24. K. M. Murray, '*Wings Over Poland*' London (1932) passim.
25. Kakurin *op. cit.* Vol. II pp. 116–7.
26. Budyonny, *op. cit.* Vol. II p. 72 ff.
27. *Ibid.* p. 76.
28. *Ibid,* p. 97.
29. See Rumbold to Curzon, 12 June 1920, PRO- FO 417/8/65.
30. Kutrzeba, *op. cit.* pp. 220–1.
31. From Babel's story, '*Perekhod cherez Zbruch*'
32. Kutrzeba. *op. cit.* p. 394.
33. K. M. Murray *op. cit.*
34. Kakurin *op. cit.* p. 425.
35. From Babel's story, '*Eskadronnyy Trunov*'.

CHAPTER FOUR

1. Quoted by E. Wollenberg, '*The Red Army*' London. 1938. p. 197.
2. J. Piłsudski, quoted by Wollenberg. *Ibid.* p. 196.
3. '*Borisov Taken*'—headline in '*Pravda*', 26 May 1920.
4. '*Pravda*', 7, 28 May 1920; '*Dokumenty i Materialy . . .*' III, p. 132.

5. G. Sokolnikov. 'Novyy Period v Grazhdanskoy Voyne,' 'Pol'skaya Kerenschina.'; articles in 'Pravda'. 8, 9 May 1920.

6. See Chapter 3, note 21.

7. 'Voennoe Delo' Nr. 13. June (1920), 'Pervyye boevye shagi Marshala Pilsudskogo'. Trotsky 'Kak vooruzhalas' Revolyutsiya' III, p. 165.

8. K. Radek. 'O Kharakter voyny s beloy Pol'shei' 'Pravda' 11, 12 May 1920.

9. Ibid.

10. This a precis of 'Pol'skiy Front i nashi zadachi', in 'Kak vooruzhalas' Revolyutsiya' II/2, pp 93–97.

11. Ibid, p. 125. Not quoted in 'Direktivy...'

12. The Gomel speech was published as 'Voyna belogvardeytsev protiv Sovetskoy Rossii', Moscow (1920).

13. J. V. Stalin. 'Tylovoy Raon Udara,' 'Pravda', 26 May 1920.

14. Lenin. 'Sochinenie' XXV, 287. Quoted by Wandycz, 'Soviet-Polish Relations' op. cit. p. 202.

15. 'Pravda' 10 Oct. 1920.

16. Lenin. 'Sochinenie'. XXV. 298. 12 June 1920. Quoted by Wandycz, op. cit. p. 205.

17. Lenin to Unszlicht. Undated Telegram. Ts. G.A.S.A. f 48/104 op. 1 ed. Khr. 8. Correspondence quoted by A. Leinwand, 'P.P.S. wobec wojny polsko-radzieckiej 1919–20'. Warsaw (1964) pp 183–5.

18. Kakurin, op. cit. pp 475–6.

19. 'Pravda' 28 May 1920.

20. E. I. Naumov, 'V.I. Lenin o Mayakovskom' in 'Novoe o Mayakouskom', Volume 65 of the series 'Literaturnoe Nasledstro', Moscow (1958);

21. 'On Artistic Propaganda', 19 May 1920, in 'Novoe o Mayakovskom' op. cit.

22. D. Fedotoff White, 'The Growth of the Red Army', Princeton, (1944), p. 90.

23. Ibid, p. 102.

24. Kakurin, op. cit. p. 450–3.

25. G. A. Airepetyan, 'Legendarnyy Gai'. Moscow, (1965).

26. Text in 'Krasnoarmeets' (Redarmyman), the daily gazette of the XVI Army. Copy in PRO-FO 371 3919/213076.

27. E. N. Sergeev, 'Ot Dviny k Visle' Moscow (1923) p. 52.

28. G. D. Ghai, 'Komsomolets Vasya' in 'Molodaya Gvardiya' Moscow (1935) No. 4. pp 21–109. Resumé in 'Etapy bol'shogo puti' ed. Moscow (1963).

29. G. D. Ghai, 'Na Varshavu' Moscow (1928) p. 76.

30. M. Wasowicz, 'Obrona Grodna' in 'Przegląd Kawalerii i Broni Pancernej' London. VIII Nr. 59. (1970) pp 181–7.

31. Kakurin op. cit. p. 210.

32. St. Alexandrowicz, 'Bój 13 pułku uhlanów pod Janowem, 25 VII 1920' in 'Przegląd Kawalerii i Broni Pancernej' London VIII Nr. 59. (1970) pp 207–18.

33. J. Piłsudski, 'Pisma Zbiorowe' Warsaw (1937–8) VII p. 97.

34. Hatskevich, *op. cit.* p. 116–9.
35. '*Dokumenty i Materiały*...' III, No. 68.
36. J. Marchlewski, 'Rosja proletariacka a Polska burżuazyjna.' '*Pisma Wybrane*' II, Warsaw (1956) quoted in '*Historia Polski*' IV, pt. 1. p. 389.
37. '*Dokumenty i Materiały*...' III. No. 126.
38. *Ibid*. III. No. 127.
39. Ts. T.A.O.R. f 130, op 4, d 206, 1 161; quoted by Hatskevich, *op. cit*, p. 127. Wandycz. '*Soviet-Polish Relations*' *op. cit.* says a billion roubles.
40. Hatskevich, *op. cit.* pp 134–5.
41. Trotsky Archive (Harvard), T 546; quoted by Wandycz, '*Soviet-Polish Relations*', p. 230.
42. Ts. P.A.I.M.L. f 76, op 1, d 1316, L 1, quoted by Hatskyevich, *op. cit.* p. 139.
43. Ts. P.A. I.M.L. f. 76. op. 1. d. 1290 1 1. *Ibid.* p. 142.
44. V. I. Lenin, '*Sochineniya*'. LI p. 266. *Ibid.* p. 143.
45. F. E. Dzierżyński, '*Izbrannie Proizvedeniya*' I, p. 297. *Ibid.* p. 144.
46. 20 Aug. 1920 '*Dokumenty i Materiały*...' III, 190.
47. '*Historia Polski*' IV. pt. 1. p. 360.
48. '*Dokumenty i Materiały*...' III, pp 186–7.
49. T. Jędruszczak, in '*Historia Polski*', IV pt 1. p. 373.
50. '*Dokumenty i Materiały*...' No. 122.
51. AAN-PRM21431/20. 15978, 15188, 8855, 14998.
52. Quoted by E. H. Carr, '*The Bolshevik Revolution.*' III. (Penguin Edition). London (1966) p. 192.
53. Lloyd George in the House of Commons, 16 April 1919. *Commons Debates.* Series V. Vol. 114 p. 2938.
54. *Documents on British Foreign Policy* (*1st Series*) VIII pp 502–6.
55. Conversation at Villa Fraineuse, Spa. 10 July 1920. Text in VII Session of R.O.P. AAN-PRM Microfilm 20189.
56. PRO-FO 371 4058/209045.
57. Witold Sworakowski, 'An error concerning East Galicia in Curzon's Note...of 11 July 1920.' in '*Journal of Central European Affairs* (1944)'. Vol. IV. No. 1.
58. Lloyd George Papers. F 201/1.
59. Russian text, '*Dokumenty i Materiały*...' III. No. 93; English text, PRO-FO 371 4058/207846.
60. Telegram, V. I. Lenin to J. V. Stalin, 12 or 13 July 1920; quoted in '*Historia Polski*' IV. pt. 1. p. 369. '*Direktivy*...' No. 600.
61. '*Direktivy*...' No. 605.
62. PRO-FO 371 3919/213244.
63. Hankey to Lloyd George, Lloyd George Papers F/57/6/5—.
64. *Ibid.* F/57/6/8.
65. Full MSS text in Lloyd George Papers, F/57/6/13; condensed version in PRO-Cab

24/110 CP 1724, also *Documents on British Foreign Policy* (*1st Series*) Vol. XI. No. 381.

66. *Ibid.*

67. Russo-Polish Situation, Cabinet Office Registered File. PRO-Cab 21/179.

68. PRO-Cab 23/20 C 46. (1920) App. II.

69. *Documents on British Foreign Policy* (*1st Series*). Vol. XI. No. 345.

70. *Ibid.* Nos. 411, 418.

71. '*Dokumenty i Materialy...*' III, Nos. 139, 140, 141, 144, 149, 150, 156, 163, 164, 168, 174, 179, 184.

72. '*Dokumenty i Materialy...*' III, 30 18 May 1920.

73. PRO-FO 371 3913/187247.

74. Francis Williams, '*Ernest Bevin—Portrait of a Great Englishman.*' London. (1952) pp. 83 ff.

75. Lloyd George Papers F/24/3/6.

76. *Commons Debates* (1920) Vol. 133. pp 258–74.

77. *Ibid.*

78. PRO-Cab 21/179 CP 143 22 Aug 1920.

79. At the Scarborough Conference. '*Daily Herald*'. 24 June 1920.

80. See M. K. Dziewanowski, 'Piłsudski's Federal Policy, 1919–21' in '*Journal of Central European Affairs*'. *1950*.

81. Věra Olivová—'Polityka Czechosłowacji wobec Polski podczas wojny polsko-radzieckiej'. in '*Studia z dziejów ZSRR i Europy Środkowej*' Warsaw—Wrocław. Nr. 1. (1967).

82. The evidence derives from a statement by Jan Mazaryk in 1946, discussed by Wandycz, '*Soviet-Polish Relations*'. *op. cit.*

83. V. I. Lenin. Speech 22 ix 1920, '*Dokumenty i Materialy ...*' III, No. 220.

84. F. von Rabenau, '*Seeckt: Aus seinen Leben, 1918–36*' (1940) p. 252. Quoted by E. H. Carr. *op. cit.* III p. 310.

85. '*Dokumenty i Materialy ...*' III p. 200. See E. H. Carr *op. cit.* III, p. 323, Note 4.

86. '*Dokumenty i Materialy ...*' III, No. 131.

87. *Ibid.* No. 143.

88. See S. Wambaugh, '*Plebiscites since the War*', Washington, 1933. Vol. I, Chapter 6.

89. *Documents on British Foreign Policy* (*First Series*), X, 619; XI, 393.

90. *Ibid*, XI nòs. 401, 403

91. Kakurin, *op. cit.*, p. 219.

CHAPTER FIVE

1. Lord D'Abernon. '*The Eighteenth Decisive Battle of World History*' London (1931) passim.

2. '*Dokumenty i Materialy ...*' III, No. 183. 17 Aug. 1920.

3. *Ibid.* III. No. 67.

4. C. E. Calwell, '*Sir Henry Wilson, Life and Diaries*' London (1927). Vol. II p. 253.

5. '*Dokumenty i Materialy ...*' III No. 82, 9 July 1920.

6. Memorandum on Supplies for Poland, 22 July 1920, *Ibid* III No. 105.

7. *Ibid.* III No. 116.

8. *Ibid.* III. No. 102.

9. *Ibid.* III No. 207.

10. Churchill to C.I.G.S. 20 July 1920. Churchill Papers 16/52.

11. Rumbold Papers. Private Correspondence. 18 July 1920.

12. Hankey to Lloyd George, Lloyd George Papers F/57/6/5, 6.

13. *'Dokumenty i Materiały...'* III No. 161.

14. W. Pobóg—Malinowski, *'Najnowsza Historia Polityczna Polski'* II, London (1957), pp 450–1.

15. 24 July 1920. *'Dokumenty i Materiały...'* III. No. 112.

16. These and preceding statistics are from W. Sikorski, *'Nad Wisłą i Wkrą'* Lwów (1928) Annex. II.

17. See Tukhachevsky's conversation with Kamenev, 13 Aug. 1920 in Kakurin, *op. cit.* pp 504–5.

18. J. Piłsudski, *'Rok 1920'* 5th Edn. London (1941) p. 166.

19. Text in W. Sikorski. *op. cit. 'La Campagne Polono-Russe de 1920'* Paris (1928), pp. 53–6.

20. J. Piłsudski, *op. cit.* p. 168.

21. *Ibid.* p. 117 ff.

22. Kakurin *op. cit.* p. 485.

23. W. Sikorski, *op. cit.* p. 88.

24. J. Piłsudski, *op. cit.* p. 127.

25. G. D. Ghai, *'V. Germanskom Lagere'* Moscow (1932) p. 12.

26. G. V. Kuz'min *'Grazhdanskaya Voyna i voennaya interventsiya v SSSR'* Moscow (1958) p. 321.

27. J. Piłsudski, *op. cit.* p. 138.

28. M. Tukhachevsky, 'Pokhod za Vislu' in *'Izbrannie Proizvedeniya'*, Moscow (1964). Vol. I. p. 167.

29. Quoted by Komarnicki, *op. cit.* p. 624.

30. L. B. Trotsky, *'Stalin'* London (1947), pp. 328–32.

31. Kakurin, *op. cit.* p. 229.

32. *'Direktivy Glavonov Komandovaniya Krasnoy Armii (1917–20)*, Moscow (1969), No. 644.

33. Stalin to Trotsky, 31 May 1920; Stalin to Sklyansky, 1 June 1920; text in Kakurin, *op. cit.* p. 458.

34. Budyonny, *op. cit.* Vol. II p. 308.

35. *Ibid*, Vol. II p. 304.

36. *Ibid*, Vol. II. p. 306.

37. *Ibid*, Vol. II, p. 300. note 3.

38. *'Direktivy...'* No. 705 11 Aug. 1920.

39. *Ibid.* No. 707, 12 Aug. 1920.

40. Text of the conversation, 13 Aug. 1920, quoted by Kakurin, *op. cit.* p. 504–5; also in *'Direktivy...'* No. 645.

41. Order 4774/1052. *'Direktivy...'* No. 709.

42. Budyonny, *op. cit.* pp 309–10.

43. Ts. G.A.S.A. f 102 op 3 d 189 1 233. Quoted by Budyonny, *op. cit.* Vol. II pp 310–11.

44. Budyonny, *op. cit.* Vol. II pp 318 ff; also *'Direktivy...'* note 119, p. 807.

45. *Ibid.* Vol. II, p. 304.

46. Order of SW Command, 12 Aug. 1920. Ts. G.A.S.A. f 245, op. 4 d 68 l5, Quoted by Budyonny, *op. cit.* Vol. II. p. 294.

47. Order of SW Command, 13 Aug 1920. Ts. G.A.S.A. f 5/6, op 1, d 260, l 193 ob. Quoted by Budyonny, *op. cit.* Vol. II, p. 303.

48. *Ibid.* Vol. II p. 328–9.

49. *'Leninsky Sbornik XXXVI'* pp 115–6; Ts. P.A.I.M.L. f 3, op 1, d 1928 l 1–4. Quoted by Budyonny, *Ibid.* Vol. II pp 304–5.

50. L. Nikulin. *'Tukhachevskiy'* Moscow (1964) pp 114–130. P. A. Yermolin, 'Ispytaniya' in *'Marshal Tukhachevskiy— Vospominaniya druzey i soratnikov'* Moscow (1965) pp 119–29.

51. Trotsky, *op. cit.* p. 329.

52. Lenin to Sklyansky, not earlier than 14 Aug 1920. *'Direktivy...'* No. 646.

53. Clausewitz *'On War'* Book I, Chapter 7.

54. Rumbold to Lady Rumbold, 5 Aug. 1920. Rumbold Papers.

55. *Documents on British Foreign Policy,* (*1st Series*) Vol. XI No. 411.

56. Rumbold to Lady Rumbold, 17 Aug. 1920. Rumbold Papers.

57. D'Abernon to Curzon, 4 Aug. 1920, D'Abernon to Lloyd George 6 Aug. 1920. *Documents on British Foreign Policy* (*1st Series*) Vol. XI Nos. 383, 394.

58. Maxime Weygand, *'Memoires'* II Paris. (1957). p. 166.

59. Piotr Wandycz, 'General Weygand and the Battle of Warsaw.' in *'Journal of Central European Affairs. 1960'*.

60. Lucerne Communiqué and conversations, PRO-Cab 21/179 CP 143.

CHAPTER SIX

1. PRO Cab 21/179 CP 143.

2. Kornel Krzeczunowicz, *'Na 50 lecie bojów kawalerii i artylerii konnej w 1920 r'* London (1970) p. 11.

3. Przybylski, *op. cit.* p. 154.

4. Budyonny, *op. cit.* Vol. II p. 366.

5. See articles and discussion by General Pragłowski, Rtm. Godyń, Col. Krzeczunowicz, General Bór-Komorowski, Major Bielicki etc., in *'Przegląd Kawalerii i Broni*

Pancernej.' Vol. VIII Nr. 59. London (1970).

6. From Babel's story, *'Zamosts'*.

7. Budyonny *op. cit.* Vol. II. pp. 377–90.

8. *Ibid.* Vol. II. p. 378.

9. *'Direktivy...'* No. 798. note 128. 'Pogrom' is the word used by the Soviet editors, *Ibid.* p. 808.

10. Kakurin, *op. cit.* p. 511.

11. *'Direktivy...'* Nos. 657, 659.

12. Kakurin. *op. cit.* p. 514.

13. J. Piłsudski, *'Pisma'* Warsaw (1937–8) Vol. V. pp. 174–5.

14. 'Vo imya Demokratii', *'Pravda'*, 7 May 1920.

15. Sikorski Institute, London. Photographic Collection (1914 –21) No. 10116.

16. From Babel's story, *'Beresteczko'*.

17. 21 Aug 1920. *'Dokumenty i Materiały...'* III, No. 191.

18. *'Czerwona Gwiazda'* No. 1. 5 Sept. 1920.

19. AAN — PRM 21431/20 14998.

20. AAN — PRM 21431/20 16547.

21. PRO—FO 417/9/60, 69. 30 Sept., 7 Oct. 1920.

22. PRO — WO (Intelligence) 106/973; FO 371 5398/572.

23. 7 Dec. 1920. PRO—FO 417/9/145.

24. I. Cohen. *'Vilna'* Philadelphia, (1943) pp. 358–88.

25. Documents on British Foreign Policy' (*1st series*) Vol XI No. 566.

26. PRO—FO 371 5396/4138.

27. Documents on British Foreign Policy (*1st Series*) Vol. XI. No. 566.

28. See P. Wandycz, 'French diplomats in Poland, 1919– 24' in *'Journal of Central European Affairs, 1964'*.

29. *'Dokumenty i Materiały...'* Nos. 211, 214, 215.

30. Documents on British Foreign Policy (*1st Series*) Vol. XI, Nos. 554, 564.

31. *Ibid.* No. 579.

32. *Ibid.* No. 587.

33. *Ibid.* No. 42.

34. *Ibid.* No. 64.

35. *Ibid.* No. 94.

36. *'Dokumenty i Materiały...'* III, No. 212. pp. 401–3.

37. AAN—AIJP 645.; PRO— FO 371 5398/4688.

38. Budyonny, *op. cit.* Vol. II, p. 341. 21 Aug. 1920.

39. Smolensk Archives, WKP 6 Protocol 32. 7 Aug. 1920.

40. *Ibid.* WKP 6 Protocol 35.

41. *Ibid.* WKP 6. See M. Fainsod. *'Smolensk Under Soviet Rule'* London. (1959). p. 41 ff.

42. *Ibid.* WKP 271.

43. *'Dokumenty i Materiały...'* III, No. 289.

44. S. Grabski, *'The Polish-Soviet Frontier'* London (1943). pp. 24–5.

45. *'Dokumenty i Materiały..,'* III p. 339.

46. *Ibid,* III, p. 350.

47. *Ibid,* III, No. 193.

48. *Ibid,* III, No. 193. note 4.

49. See Chapter 5 note 52.

50. *'Dokumenty i Materiały...'* III, No. 204.

51. *Ibid.* III No. 213.

52. L. B. Trotsky, *'Kak vooruzhalas' revolyutsiya'* II/2, pp. 170–7.

53. *'Leninsky Sbornik'* XXXVI, p. 123.; *'Dokumenty i Materiały...'* III, No. 221.

54. J. Dąbski, *'Pokój Ryski'* Warsaw (1931), p. 119; *'Dokumenty i Materiały...'* III, No. 231.

55. *'Dokumenty i Materiały...'* III, No. 234. Sapieha to Dąbski, 10 Oct. 1920.

56. *'Dokumenty i Materiały...'* III, No. 236. Polish text.

57. *Ibid.* III, p. 468.
58. *Ibid,* III, p. 472–5.
59. *Ibid,* III, No. 237. Russian text.
60. *Ibid* III, Nos. 234, 238.
61. Wandycz, *op. cit.* p. 278.
62. '*Dokumenty i Materiały...*' III, No. 233.
63. *Ibid,* III, No. 229.

64. *Ibid,* III, No. 251.
65. *Ibid,* III, No. 252.
66. *Ibid,* III, No. 267.
67. *Ibid,* III, No. 275.
68. '*Leninsky Sbornik*' XXXVI 130.
69. '*Historia Polski*' Vol. IV. pt. 1 pp. 461–2.

CHAPTER SEVEN

1. J. Piłsudski, '*Rok 1920*', 5th. Impression. London (1941) p. 165.
2. Lord D'Abernon, '*The Eighteenth Decisive Battle of World History*' London (1931), pp. 8–9, 11, 172.
3. *Ibid.* pp. 172–3.
4. Clara Zetkin, '*Reminiscences of Lenin*' London (1929), pp. 19–22.
5. The evidence derives from the Chinese leader Dr. Sun Yat Sen who was in Moscow at the end of 1920. See Wandycz '*Soviet-Polish Relations*' op. cit. p. 257.
6. General Radcliffe's Report. PRO—Cab 21/180.
7. Lord D'Abernon, *op. cit.* p. 117.

8. Weygand, '*Memoires*' II, passim.
9. E.g. Mjr. E. Farman 'The Polish-Bolshevik Cavalry Campaigns' in '*Cavalry Journal*' (*1921*) Nr. 24; Ruby, 'Operations de la cavalerie de Boudienny' in '*Revue de Cavalerie, (1926)*'.
10. In '*Voenno-istoricheskiy zhurnal*' (Moscow) 1962 Nr. 2. Text in M. Tukhachevsky, '*Izbrannie Proizvedeniya*' Vol. II. Moscow (1964) pp. 180 ff.
11. L. Kochan, 'The Russian Road to Rapallo'. in '*Soviet Studies*' (Glasgow) Vol. II, Nr. 2 1950.
12 From, Babel's story '*Ivany*' 22 Aug. 1920.